The Encyclopedia of Religious Debates

Volume 1

(A-B)

Thomas N. Thrasher, Ed.D., Ph.D., Th.D.

Copyright © 2020 Thomas N. Thrasher

All rights reserved.

ISBN: 9781708391423

DEDICATION

To **Lynn & Mary Faye Headrick**,
As A Small Tribute To Their Godly Influence
And Dedication To The Lord They Served
On Earth ... And Now Continue To Serve In A Better Place

INTRODUCTION

Oral and written debates have contributed to the development and refinement of important ideas throughout human history. In the realm of politics and government, debates continue to provide a means of presenting and contrasting conflicting views. Although debating religious issues is far less common than it was a century ago, interest in religious debates seems to have increased somewhat in recent years despite the aversion of most denominational preachers to participation in them. An extensive discussion of the history of religious debating will be provided in Volume 6 of this series.

This writer has collected the data in volumes 1-6 of *The Encyclopedia of Religious Debates* over a period of more than 50 years from countless books, periodicals, letters, announcements, websites, emails, and personal conversations. Since incorporating a reference citation for every piece of data in these volumes would have been impracticable and at least doubled the size of this publication, detailed citations have been omitted. Although such citations might have proved useful to a few researchers, their inclusion would have served little purpose for the vast majority of individuals who peruse these volumes. However, I have deemed it worthwhile to incorporate a detailed list of references in Volume 6. Furthermore, hundreds of references to biographical material on the debaters and debated-related publications can be found throughout the listings.

The basic format for each entry in these listings is as follows:

Debater's Name [Church or Group]

Date of birth (Location)
Date of death (Location)
Related publications and/or comments
Name of opponent (Church or Group); location; date; subject discussed;
number of sessions; attendance; w/ co-participant, if any; remarks.
Propositions. Publication data. [Research data]

In many cases, much of this information on particular debates is not currently available or has not yet been located. The "Group" cited is a term which is often used or which most clearly specifies the group that the person represented. It is not necessarily an official or exclusive designation.

Debates that were not strictly "religious" debates have been included in the listings if they involved topics that were related to Bible teaching. For example, debates on creation/evolution are included even if they were "scientific" rather than "religious" debates.

Your contributions are welcomed! If you have participated in a formal oral or written debate/discussion/exchange, check your listing for accuracy and completeness. I need your biographical data (full name, birth date, birthplace, and photograph) and data concerning each of your formal debates. If you have knowledge about other debates or debaters, check to see if the data is included. Please e-mail me any information you have that would add to or correct what is already listed. If you have any photographs of debaters or photographs that are debate-related, I would appreciate your sharing them with me for possible inclusion. Please send any data, photos, suggestions, or comments you may have to **thomas.thrasher@att.net**. My intention is to provide future updated/expanded editions at appropriate intervals.

ACKNOWLEDGEMENTS

Since I have collected the debate data included in volumes 1-6 of *The Encyclopedia of Religious Debates* over a period of more than 50 years, it would be impossible for me to acknowledge, or even recall, every instance in which different people have provided information. However, special acknowledgement is made of the following individuals who have made substantial or frequent contributions:

Kyle Frank for supplying data on many old debates and access to old periodicals.

Bobby O'Dell for submitting data on many published debates.

Terry J. Gardner for frequent submissions of data for the debate listings.

James L. McMillan for submitting debate and biographical data.

Tom Childers for supplying biographical data and photographs of debaters.

Derald Boman for supplying data on many old published debates.

Willie Ramsey for supplying debate data and photographs of debaters.

Scott Norwood for supplying data on debates by representatives of the Reorganized Church of Jesus Christ of Latter Day Saints.

Tom Olbricht for supplying data on the life and debates of Joe Warlick and others.

Roland Jarrell, Jr. for supplying data on U. W. Jarrell and W. A. Jarrell.

Ancil Jenkins for supplying data on the debates of A. G. Freed.

Gordon Wilson for supplying data for the debate listings.

Jon Gary Williams for making available approximately 1000 Debate Reports at http://www.thelordsway.com/jongarywilliams/framedindex.asp?Group=Home#.W1YjxPZFwic

Granville W. Tyler, **Irvin Himmel**, **Irven Lee**, and **John A. Welch** for providing access to books and/or periodicals for research work.

Patrick T. Donahue for the generous use of his website (www.bibledebates.info) to host the online edition of *The Encyclopedia of Religious Debates*.

Several institutions have also provided significant assistance in my research by allowing me to access their library resources, including **Florida College, David Lipscomb University, Butler University, Heritage Christian University, Disciples of Christ Historical Society**, and **Athens Bible School**.

In addition to these individuals and institutions, many others have shared information about debates, biographical data, or photographs. I want to express my gratitude to all who have generously shared with me in this project. As I continue enlarging and improving *The Encyclopedia of Religious Debates*, I request your help in making this work as accurate and complete as humanly possible. Communications may be directed to me via email (thomas.thrasher@att.net).

The Encyclopedia of Religious Debates
Volume 1 (A - B)

Albert Abbey [Oneness Pentecostal Church]
Birth: ?February 23, 1904 (_, _)
Death: ?August 1967 (_, _)
E. H. Miller (Church of Christ)
Raymond G. Hoekstra (Oneness Pentecostal Church); Flint, MI

George Abbott [Baptist Church]
Birth: _ (_, _)
Death: _ (_, _)
Uriah Huffman (Church of Christ); Urbana, IN; September 26-27, 1883. Book publication: *A Report of the Discussion on Baptism*. _: Carlon & Hollenback, 1883.

Mack D. Abbott [Oneness Pentecostal Church]
Birth: ?March 31, 1894 (_, _)
Death: ?March 10, 1967 (_, ?NM)
Mack E. Kercheville (Church of Christ); 1945; godhead, miracles, conversion
W. Curtis Porter (Church of Christ); c 1953
Jesse G. Jenkins (Church of Christ); Tucumcari, NM; June 3-8, 1963; godhead, instrumental music in worship, church, salvation.
Jesse G. Jenkins (Church of Christ); Roswell, NM; September 9-14, 1963.

Lyman Abbott [Congregationalist Church]
Birth: December 18, 1835 (Roxbury, Suffolk County, MA)
Death: October 22, 1922 (New York, NY)
Biographical sketch: http://www.answers.com/topic/lyman-abbott
Eric Waterhouse (?); written; November-December, 1898; human destiny as conditioned by free will. Book publication: *Abbott-Waterhouse Discussion*. c 1898.

Thomas Abbott [Universalist Society]
Birth: 18_ (_, _)
Death: _ (_, _)
_ Love (Methodist Episcopal Church); Savannah, MO; c 1845; 3 days
James M. Mathes (Church of Christ); Petersburg, Pike County, IN; August 18-_, 1862. Proposition 1: "The Scriptures of the Old and New Testaments teach that all unbelievers and ungodly persons, shall be made holy and happy in the resurrection state, *irrespective* of faith, repentance, baptism, or any other

conditions performed by them in the present life." (Abbott affirmed, Mathes denied). Proposition 2: "The Scriptures of the Old and New Testaments teach that all the finally impenitent and ungodly of mankind will suffer endless punishment beyond the resurrection, and the judgment of the great day." (Mathes affirmed, Abbott denied). Proposition 3: "The New Testament teaches that salvation by Jesus Christ is promised on conditions to be complied with in the present life, which conditions are to be complied with in the present life, which conditions are: faith in Christ, repentance towards God, and baptism in the name of Jesus Christ; and that the salvation in the future life depends upon a faithful continuance in well doing till death." (Mathes affirmed, Abbott denied).

J. Woods (Methodist Church); Jackson, MO
G. W. Hughey (Methodist Episcopal Church); c 1865
W. B. F. Treat (Church of Christ); Olney, IL; 1866
John S. Sweeney (Church of Christ); Golconda, IL; c March 1870. [*Christian Standard* (April 2, 1870)]
John S. Sweeney (Church of Christ); Dawson, KY; June 27-30, 1882
John S. Sweeney (Church of Christ); Dawson Springs, KY; c May 1884. [*Gospel Advocate*, Vol. 26, No. 24 (June 11, 1884), 371]
W. L. Caskey (Cumberland Presbyterian Church); c 1884

Osama Abdallah [Muslim]
Birth: 19_ (_, ?Palestine)
Death: _ (_, _)
Nabeel Qureshi (?). Topic: Did Jesus Rise from the Dead?
Nabeel Qureshi (?); May 9, 2009. Topic: Is the Qur'an Miraculous?
Nabeel Qureshi (?); August 27, 2010. Topic: Scientific Miracles of the Qur'an
James White (Reformed Baptist Church); September 20, 2008. Topic: Was Jesus Crucified or Substituted?
James White (Reformed Baptist Church); September 20, 2008. Topic: Can We Trust the New Testament?
Sam Shamoun (?). Topic: Is Muhammed a True Prophet?
Tony Costa (?). Topic: Is Muhammed a Prophet?
David Wood (?). Topic: Was Muhammed a True Prophet?
Tony Costa (?). Topic: Is the Bible the Word of God?
David Wood (?). Topic: Does Science Show that Islam is True?

George Washington Abell [Church of Christ]
Birth: December 11, 1818 (Albemarle County, VA)
Death: December 27, 1874 (_, ?VA)
Life and Writings of George W. Abell by Peter Ainslie. Richmond, VA: Clemmitt & Jones, 1875.
_ Gilbert (Methodist Episcopal Church); Newport, Giles County, VA; 1869

Cecil Edward Abercrombie, Sr. [Church of Christ]
Birth: May 23, 1918 (Union City, Fulton County, GA)
Death: July 22, 1976 (Jefferson County, AL)
John T. Lewis (Church of Christ); written. Book publication:
John T. Lewis (Church of Christ); c 1944; classes & women teachers
W. C. Phillips (Church of Christ); Morgan City, AL; c 1946; classes & women teachers; tent; 4 sessions
Leroy Garrett (Church of Christ); Montgomery, AL; classes
Leroy Garrett (Church of Christ); Carville, AL; 4 sessions
Rex Turner (Church of Christ); Ashland, AL; classes; 1 session
_ (Church of Christ); Dallas, TX; c 1950; classes
John Staley (Church of Christ); Waco, TX; c 1952; drinking vessels in Lord's supper; 2 sessions
E. H. Miller (Church of Christ); Columbus, GA; drinking vessels in Lord's supper; 4 sessions
Gus Nichols (Church of Christ); Ball Play, AL; classes & women teachers
W. Curtis Porter (Church of Christ); Taft, TN; May 1-6, 1950; classes & women teachers; 6 sessions
W. Curtis Porter (Church of Christ); East Point, GA; December 4-7, 1951; classes & women teachers; 4 sessions. Proposition 1: "The Scriptures teach that when people come together to be taught by the church they should remain in one group, and the teaching should be done by men only, one speaking at a time to the assembly." (Abercrombie affirmed, Porter denied). Proposition 2: "The practice of arranging into groups the people who come together to be taught by the church using both men and women to teach these groups is authorized by the Scriptures." (Porter affirmed, Abercrombie denied). Book publication: *Abercrombie-Porter Debate*. Adamsville, AL: Action Printing Company, 1980. Book publication: *Porter-Abercrombie Debate*. Bowling Green, KY: Guardian of Truth Foundation.
W. W. McMickin (Church of God (7th Day)); Fort Payne, AL; May 3-15, 1953; Sabbath, first day, premillennialism
Charles B. Thomas (Church of Christ); Alabama City, AL; amenability; w/ J. A. Dennis (Church of Christ)
_ (Sabbatarian) & _ (Sabbatarian); Alexander City, AL; c 1958; 1 session
P. C. Key (Church of Christ); written; second serving of Lord's supper. Book publication: *The Second Supper*. Birmingham, AL: Cecil Abercrombie, 1954.

W. N. Abernathy [?]
Birth: _ (_, _)
Death: _ (_, _)
C. F. Parker (Primitive Baptist Church); salvation out of the church. Book publication:

_ Abernathy [Church of Christ]
　Birth: 18_ (_, _)
　Death: _ (_, _)
　John T. Nichols (Methodist Church); July 9-13, 1883

Jalal Abualrub [Muslim]
　Birth: 19_ (_, _)
　Death: _ (_, _)
　James White (Reformed Baptist Church); April 12, 2008. Topic: Does the New Testament Teach that Jesus is God?
　David Wood (?). Topic: Is Muhammed a Prophet?
　Craig Winn (?); November 14, 2005; radio debate on The Mike Gallagher Radio Show.

B. Acworth [?]
　Birth: _ (_, _)
　Death: _ (_, _)

Connie W. Adams [Church of Christ]
　Birth: September 22, 1930 (Hopewell, VA)
　Death: _ (_, _)
　Biographical sketch: *Biblical Authority: Its Meaning and Application* (Florida College Annual Lectures, 1974). Marion, IN: Cogdill Foundation, 1974, page 160.
　Biographical sketch: *They Being Dead Yet Speak* (Florida College Annual Lectures, 1981). Temple Terrace, FL: Florida College Bookstore, 1981, page 119.
　J. T. Payne (Pentecostal Church); 1955; Holy Spirit baptism; Adams' 1st public debate
　A. D. Norris (Christadelphian); Bergen, Norway; January 1958; premillennialism
　O. G. Lodge (Church of God); Orlando, FL; September 16, 1963
　Perriman Dennison (Church of Christ); Zephyrhills, FL; 1964; sponsoring church
　Leonard Lacy (Pentecostal Church); Hillsboro, OH; June 5-6, 8-9, 1972; Holy Spirit baptism & gifts
　Clifton Inman (Church of Christ); Middlebourne, WV; May 29-30, June 1-2, 1978; sponsoring church, church benevolence
　_ (Church of Christ), _ (Church of Christ), _ (Church of Christ), _ (Church of Christ) & _ (Church of Christ); New Albany, IN; February 1989; premillennialism; 2 sessions; w/ Gene Frost (Church of Christ), Paul Earnhart (Church of Christ), Guy Roberson (Church of Christ) & John Humphries (Church of Christ)

Edward Adams [Oneness Pentecostal Church]
　Birth: 19_ (_, _)
　Death: c 1996 (_, _)

Thomas N. Thrasher (Church of Christ); Decatur &
  Moulton, AL; January 17-18, 20-21, 1977; instrumental
  music in worship; 4 sessions
Tom Moody (Church of Christ); Moulton, AL; 1978; 60- 65
Michael J. White (Church of Christ); Moulton, AL; August 2-
  3, 1979; godhead; 2 sessions

Gary Beverly Adams [Church of Christ]
  Birth: January 15, 1926 (Point, Rains County, TX)
  Death: September 9, 2000 (Abilene, Taylor Co., TX)
  Biographical sketch: *Preachers of Today* (Batsell Barrett
    Baxter & M. Norvel Young, eds.). Nashville, TN: The
    Christian Press, 1952, p. 10.
  Biographical sketch: *Preachers of Today, Volume Two*
    (Batsell Barrett Baxter & M. Norvel Young, eds.).
    Nashville, TN: The Gospel Advocate Company, 1959, p.
    2.

  Biographical sketch: *Preachers of Today, Volume Three*
    (Batsell Barrett Baxter & M. Norvel Young, eds.). Nashville, TN: The
    Gospel Advocate Company, 1964, pp. 1-2.
  Biographical sketch: *Preachers of Today, Volume Four* (Batsell Barrett Baxter
    & M. Norvel Young, eds.). Nashville, TN: The Gospel Advocate
    Company, 1970, p. 1.
  _ (Church of Jesus Christ of Latter Day Saints) & _ (Church of Jesus Christ of
    Latter Day Saints); Utrecht, Holland; 1957; w/ Frank Worgan (Church of
    Christ)

George F. Adams [Church of Christ]
  Birth: 18_ (Elizaville, KY)
  Death: 1884 (Blandinsville, IL)
  Biographical sketch:
    http://www.mun.ca/rels/restmov/texts/nhaynes/hdcib/ADAMSGF.HTM
  William McNutt (Baptist Church); Blandinsville, IL; 1883; baptism, church
  D. D. Swindle (Baptist Church); Cuba, IL; 1883; church

James Adams [Primitive Baptist Church]
  Birth: 18_ (_, _)
  Death: _ (_, _)
  William Halliday Trice (Church of Christ); Trinity, TN; September 1903

James Wallace Adams [Church of Christ]
  Birth: August 27, 1914 (Brawley, CA)
  Death: January 21, 2013 (?Lufkin, TX)
  Biographical sketch: *Preachers of Today, Volume Two*
    (Batsell Barrett Baxter & M. Norvel Young, eds.).
    Nashville, TN: The Gospel Advocate Company, 1959, p. 2.
  Biographical sketch: *They Being Dead Yet Speak* (Florida

College Annual Lectures, 1981). Temple Terrace, FL: Florida College Bookstore, 1981, page 183.
Biographical sketch: *They Being Dead Yet Speak* (Florida College Annual Lectures, 1981). Temple Terrace, FL: Florida College Bookstore, 1981, page 171.
Obituary: https://www.carrowayfuneralhome.com/obituary/2033950
A. J. Wall (Baptist Church); Longview, TX; June 19-22, 1951; salvation; 1st debate for each man

Jesse Adams [Cumberland Presbyterian Church]
Birth: March 22, 1816 (Utica, Vennango County, PA)
Death: October 26, 1891 (Waynesburg, PA)
Biographical sketch: http://www.cumberland.org/hfcpc/minister/AdamsJesse.htm
Solomon Deboir (Christian Church); Clarksville, Greene County, PA; January 10-_, 1854; 4 propositions. Book publication: *Debate Between Rev. Solomon Devoir of the Christian or Disciples' Church and Rev. Jesse Adams of the Cumberland Presbyterian Church Upon Four Propositions, Embracing Various Subjects, in the Village of Clarksville, Greene Co., Pa.* Pittsburgh, PA: W. S. Haven, 1854.

Nehemiah Adams [Congregational Church]
Birth: February 19, 1806 (Salem, MA)
Death: October 6, 1878 (?Boston, MA)
Biographical sketch: http://en.wikipedia.org/wiki/Nehemiah_Adams
Obituary: http://virtualology.com/nehemiahadams
Sylvanus Cobb (?Universalist Society); c 1859; future endless punishment. Book publication: *Discussion of the Scripturalness of Future Endless Punishment*. Boston, MA: Samuel T. Cobb, 1860.

James Roland Adams [Church of Christ]
Birth: September 3, 1921 (Obion, TN)
Death: April 9, 2000 (Cordova, Shelby Co., TN)
Biographical sketch: *Preachers of Today, Volume Two* (Batsell Barrett Baxter & M. Norvel Young, eds.). Nashville, TN: The Gospel Advocate Company, 1959, pp. 2-3.
Biographical sketch: *Preachers of Today, Volume Three* (Batsell Barrett Baxter & M. Norvel Young, eds.). Nashville, TN: The Gospel Advocate Company, 1964, p. 2.
Biographical sketch: *Preachers of Today, Volume Four* (Batsell Barrett Baxter & M. Norvel Young, eds.). Nashville, TN: The Gospel Advocate Company, 1970, p. 1.

Obituary: https://www.findagrave.com/memorial/42464621/james-roland-adams
_ (Baptist Church); Fagus, MO; August 1956
_ (?); Lumberton, NC; 1966; WAGR radio

_ Adams [?Baptist Church]
Birth: _ (_, _)
Death: _ (_, _)
Ellis G. Grubb (Church of Christ); 1936; baptism, apostasy

_ Adams [Baptist Church]
Birth: _ (_, _)
Death: _ (_, _)
Fenter Dee Northern (Church of Christ)

William Adamson [Scottish Political Leader]
Birth: April 2, 1863 (Dunfermline, Scotland)
Death: February 23, 1936 (_, _)
Biographical sketch:
   http://en.wikipedia.org/wiki/William_Adamson
Biographical sketch: http://www.spartacus.schoolnet.co.uk/
   TUadamsonW.htm

R. M. Adcock [Baptist Church]
Birth: _ (_, _)
Death: _ (_, _)
Clarence E. McCamie (Church of Christ); 1958; baptism

Isidore "Izzy" Adler [Evolutionist]
Birth: December 25, 1916 (Brooklyn, NY)
Death: March 26, 1990 (Silver Spring, MD)
Duane Gish (Creationist); University of Maryland,_, MD; October 14, 1976;
   1200; w/ Geerat J. Vermeij (Evolutionist)

Romulo B. Agduma [Church of Christ]
Birth: September 5, 1928 (Luzon, Philippines)
Death: November 25, 1979 (Kidapawan, Philippines)
Biographical sketch: *Truth Magazine,* 16(45) (September 21, 1972), 10-11.
Obituary: *Truth Magazine,* 24(6) (February 7, 1980), 108.

C. C. Agee [Primitive Baptist Church]
Birth: 18_ (_, _)
Death: 19_ (_, _)
J. D. Tant (Church of Christ); Centralia, OK; November 9-11, 1920; conditional
   or unconditional salvation

_ Agee [?]
Birth: _ (_, _)
Death: _ (_, _)

Rue Porter (Church of Christ); 1928; apostasy, baptism, Holy Spirit

Johannes Agricola [Protestant Reformer]
Birth: April 20, 1494 (Eisleben, Germany)
Death: September 22, 1566 (Berlin, Germany)
Biographical sketch:
https://en.wikipedia.org/wiki/Johannes_Agricola
Philip Melanchthon (Protestant Reformer). Related
publication: *Law and Gospel: Philip Melanchthon's debate with John Agricola of Eisleben over poenitentia* by Timothy J. Wengert. Grand Rapids, MI: Baker Books, c 1997.

Nadir Ahmed [Muslim]
Birth: 19_ (_, _)
Death: _ (_, _)
David A. Beck (Church of Christ); Peoria, IL; December 3-5, 1998; the Bible is not the inspired word of God, the Koran is not the inspired word of God, plan of salvation; 3 sessions
Denis Giron (Atheist); September 9, 2003; science in the Qur'an. Web publication: http://www.examinethetruth.com/ahmed-giron.htm
Keith Thompson (?). Subject: Is Paul a true apostle? Internet publication: http://www.youtube.com/watch?v=9Gzjy2909ZU
James White (Reformed Baptist Church); Old Dominion University; March 21, 2008. Internet publication:
http://www.youtube.com/watch?v=hcDPtHMCXEU&feature=related
David Wood (?). Topic: God: Trinity or Tauheed
Sam Shamoun (?). Topic: Is Islam a Religion of Peace?

Paul Aiello [Evolutionist]
Birth: 19_ (_, _)
Death: _ (_, _)
Duane Gish (Creationist) & Henry M. Morris (Creationist); Ventura, CA; October 5, 1976; 1000; w/ Thomas O'Neill (Evolutionist)

W(illiam?) A(ngus?) Aiken [Presbyterian Church]
Birth: ?July 16, 1894 (_, _)
Death: ?April 8, 1958 (_, _)
G. C. Wade (Church of Christ); Los Angeles, CA; 1932

Donald Ray Akers [Oneness Pentecostal Church]
Birth: 19_ (_, _)
Death: _ (_, _)
Thomas N. Thrasher (Church of Christ); Ada, OK; June 17, 1994; godhead; 1 session
Patrick T. Donahue (Church of Christ); Ada, OK; June 18, 1994; 1 session; baptismal formula; 60

Robert Akers [Oneness Pentecostal Church]
  Birth: 19_ (_, _)
  Death: _ (_, _)
  J. Bert "Robert" Robertson (Church of Christ); Ada, OK;
    1988; baptismal formula
  Grover Jones (Church of Christ); Ada, OK; c 1989.
  Dale Tollet (Church of Christ); Ada, OK; c 1990

James "Jimmy" Akin [Roman Catholic Church]
  Birth: 19_ (_, TX)
  Death: _ (_, _)
  James White (Reformed Baptist Church); perseverance
  James White (Reformed Baptist Church)

Lorenzo Albacete [Roman Catholic Church]
  Birth: January 7, 1941 (_, Puerto Rico)
  Death: October 24, 2014 (Dobbs Ferry, NY)
  Christopher Hitchens (Atheist); 2008; science & religion

John Godfred Alber [Christian Church]
  Birth: c 1887 (_, IA)
  Death: _ (_, _)
  William Herbert Hanna (Christian Church); written; c 1936; tithing. Periodical
    publication: *The Christian Standard*, 1936. Book publication: Reporter
    Publishing Co., 1936.

Jerry D. Albert [Evolutionist]
  Birth: 19_ (_, _)
  Death: _ (_, _)
  Duane Gish (Creationist); Pasadena, CA; May 17, 1977; 400
  Duane Gish (Creationist); San Diego, CA; September 28, 1981

W. D. Albin [?]
  Birth: _ (_, _)
  Death: _ (_, _)
  J. L. Hines (Church of Christ); Dallas, TX; 1944

William "Wild Bill" Albrecht [Roman Catholic Church]
  Birth: 19_ (_, _)
  Death: _ (_, _)
  Francis Turretin (Reformed Protestant); c 2009; the distinction between latria
    and dulia

Eugene Webster Alderson [Methodist Church]
  Birth: October 15, 1854 (Hart County, KY)
  Death: March 9, 1939 (Dallas County, TX)
  Biographical sketch:
    http://www.tsha.utexas.edu/handbook/online/articles/AA/fal86.html

Obituary: http://boards.ancestry.com/localities.northam.usa.states.texas.
counties.hunt /541/mb.ashx?pnt=1
T. W. Caskey (Church of Christ)
John Woodson Denton, Jr. (Church of Christ)
B. A. Carr (Church of Christ)
Jake Hodges (?); Sulphur Springs, TX; 1887
Jake Hodges (?); Honey Grove, TX; 1887
James A. Harding (Church of Christ)
R. C. Horn (Church of Christ)
J. N. Hall (Missionary Baptist Church)
J. D. Tant (Church of Christ); Troupe, TX; October 1897
Joe S. Warlick (Church of Christ); Celeste, TX; 1903
Joe S. Warlick (Church of Christ); Cumby, TX; 1903

_ Aldridge [Church of God]
Birth: _ (_, _)
Death:_ (_, _)
W. Gaddys Roy (Church of Christ); 1943
Bennie Lee Fudge (Church of Christ); 1947; baptism

Jesse Raymond Alexander [Missionary Baptist Church]
Birth: March 6, 1927 (_, _)
Death: August 13, 2001 (?Henderson, ?TX)
R. Lawrence Crawford (Baptist Church); Hayward, CA; November 19-22, 1980. Proposition 1: "The Scriptures teach that some men are unconditionally elected to salvation and eternal glory." (Crawford affirmed, Alexander denied). Proposition 2: "The Scriptures teach that the sacrificial substitutionary death of Jesus Christ was on behalf of all men." (Alexander affirmed, Crawford denied). Proposition 3: "The Scriptures teach that the grace of God that saves men cannot be successfully resisted by men to whom it is extended." (Crawford affirmed, Alexander denied). Proposition 4: "The Scriptures teach that men can resist the grace of God that brings salvation to men." (Alexander affirmed, Crawford denied). Proposition 5: "The Scriptures teach that there is an effectual call to salvation which is extended only to the elect, and that they cannot successfully reject it." (Crawford affirmed, Alexander denied). Proposition 6: "The Scriptures teach that God, in His sovereign purpose, has decreed all things that happen." (Crawford affirmed, Alexander denied). Book publication: *Alexander vs Crawford Debate*. Yazoo City, MS: Norris-Causey Christian Publications, 1980.
Eugene Britnell (Church of Christ); Camden, AR; April 4-8, 1983; baptism
Thomas N. Thrasher (Church of Christ); Hillsboro, AL; April 2-3, 5-6, 1984; apostasy; 4 sessions
Thomas N. Thrasher (Church of Christ); written; 1984-_; premillennialism

L. K. Alexander [?]
Birth: _ (_, _)
Death: _ (_, _)
E. H. Miller (Church of Christ); 1958. Book publication: *Miller-Alexander Debate*.

Lucius Hodge Alexander, Sr. [Church of Christ]
Birth: March 30, 1912 (Murfreesboro, TN)
Death: May 12, 1994 (Midland, TX)
Biographical sketch: *Preachers of Today* (Batsell Barrett Baxter & M. Norvel Young, eds.). Nashville, TN: The Christian Press, 1952, p. 12.
Biographical sketch: *Preachers of Today, Volume Two* (Batsell Barrett Baxter & M. Norvel Young, eds.). Nashville, TN: The Gospel Advocate Company, 1959, p. 6.
Biographical sketch: *Preachers of Today, Volume Three* (Batsell Barrett Baxter & M. Norvel Young, eds.). Nashville, TN: The Gospel Advocate Company, 1964, p. 5.
_ (Baptist Church); 1937; baptism, apostasy
_ (Pentecostal Church); 1938; godhead
_ (Holiness Church); 1939; baptism, Holy Spirit
_ (Holiness Church); 1956

Robert M. Alexander [Church of Christ]
Birth: March 5, 1894 (near Owensboro, Daviess County, KY)
Death: March 10, 1969 (_, ?OK)
Biographical sketch: *Preachers of Today* (Batsell Barrett Baxter & M. Norvel Young, eds.). Nashville, TN: The Christian Press, 1952, p. 12.
Biographical sketch: *Preachers of Today, Volume Two* (Batsell Barrett Baxter & M. Norvel Young, eds.). Nashville, TN: The Gospel Advocate Company, 1959, p. 6.
Biographical sketch: *The Trail Blazers: Heroes of the Faith* by J. Porter Wilhite. Oklahoma City, OK: Telegram Book Company, 1965, pp. 121-124.
_ Davidson (Christian Church); 1928; instrumental music in worship
_ (Baptist Church); Wewoka, OK; 1938
_ (Holiness Church)

Matthew Alfs [Jehovah's Witnesses]
Birth: _ (_, _)
Death: _ (_, _)
Ray Hawk (Church of Christ); written; c 1977; was "The Word" created or has "He" always existed. Periodical publication: "Alfs-Hawk Debate," *The Beacon*, 1977.

Habib Ali [Muslim]
Birth: 19_ (_, _)
Death: _ (_, _)
Tony Costa (?). Topic: Tawheed vs Trinity

C. B. Allen [Holiness Church]
Birth: _ (_, _)
Death: _ (_, _)
L. Freeman Crowder (Church of Christ); Athens, TN; 1932

C. L. Allen [Foursquare Gospel Church]
Birth: _ (_, _)
Death: _ (_, _)
John W. Wilson (Church of Christ); San Bernardino & Redlands, CA; July 28-31, 1958

Carl A. Allen [Church of Christ]
Birth: 19_ (_, _)
Death:_ (_, _)
L. Chester Guinn (Missionary Baptist Church); Crockett, TX; April - May 1962
_ (?Baptist Church); Jasper, TX; May 17-18, 1979; essentiality of water baptism
C. W. Shew (Oneness Pentecostal Church); 1979; baptismal formula
Tim E. Landry (United Pentecostal Church); Lufkin, TX; August 1-5, 1983; godhead, Holy Spirit baptism; 4 sessions
Bo Norris (Missionary Baptist Church); Crockett, TX; August 30-31, September 2-3, 2004; salvation at the point of faith; necessity of water baptism

Frank Gibbs Allen [Church of Christ]
Birth: March 7, 1836 (_, _)
Death: January 6, 1887 (_, ?KY)
Biography: *Autobiography of Frank G. Allen* by Robert Graham. Cincinnati. OH: Guide Printing and Publishing Company, 1887.
Biographical sketch: *Faith and Facts Quarterly*, Volume 3, Number 1 (January 1975), 17.
J. W. Fitch (Methodist Church); 1871; Allen's 1st debate
Robert Hiner (?); Mt. Byrd, KY; infant baptism
_ (?); Burksville, KY; 1875; 12 nights

George W. Allen [Church of Christ]
Birth: December 14, 1875 (Cherokee Nation, near Fort Smith, AR)
Death: _ (_, _)
Biographical sketch: *Gospel Preachers Who Blazed The Trail* by

C. R. Nichol. Austin, TX: Firm Foundation Publishing House, n.d.
Several debates

James A. Allen [Church of Christ]
Birth: June 21, 1884 (Nashville, TN)
Death: August 3, 1967 (?Nashville, TN)
Biographical sketch: *Preachers of Today* (Batsell Barrett Baxter & M. Norvel Young, eds.). Nashville, TN: The Christian Press, 1952, p. 13.
Biographical sketch: *Preachers of Today, Volume Two* (Batsell Barrett Baxter & M. Norvel Young, eds.). Nashville, TN: The Gospel Advocate Company, 1959, p. 7.
Biographical sketch: *Faith and Facts Quarterly*, Volume 5, Number 4 (October 1977), 11.
Biographical sketch: http://www.therestorationmovement.com/allen,ja.htm

Cyril Wyche (Unitarian Church); Nashville, TN; February 26, 1924; 1200. Proposition 1: "Jesus Christ is the divine Son of God." (Allen affirmed, Wyche denied), Proposition 2: "Liberal religion which denies the virgin birth of Christ, his divinity, his resurrection from the dead, and the divine inspiration of the Bible, is the true religion." (Wyche affirmed, Allen denied).
J. H. Grime (Baptist Church); written; 1927. Periodical publication: "Grime-Allen Discussion." Nashville, TN: *Gospel Advocate* (November 24 - December 29, 1927). Periodical publication: Little Rock, AR: *Baptist and Commoner*, 1927. Book publication: *A Discussion*.
R. H. Pigue (Methodist Church); c November 1928

Jimmy R. Allen [Church of Christ]
Birth: April 16, 1930 (Little Rock, AR)
Death: _ (_, _)
Autobiography: *Fire in My Bones: An Autobiography of Jimmy Allen* by Jimmy Allen. Searcy, AR: author, c 2005. [*The Christian Chronicle*, 62, 5 (May 2005), 32]
Biographical sketch: *Preachers of Today, Volume Two* (Batsell Barrett Baxter & M. Norvel Young, eds.). Nashville, TN: The Gospel Advocate Company, 1959, p. 8.

Biographical sketch: *Preachers of Today, Volume Three* (Batsell Barrett Baxter & M. Norvel Young, eds.). Nashville, TN: The Gospel Advocate Company, 1964, p. 7.
Biographical sketch: *Preachers of Today, Volume Four* (Batsell Barrett Baxter & M. Norvel Young, eds.). Nashville, TN: The Gospel Advocate Company, 1970, p. 4.
Biographical sketch: "Passion, intensity and urgency" by Joy McMillon. The Christian Chronicle, 67(2), February/March 2010, p. 27.
Lester Hathaway (Church of Christ); Prescott, AR; 1954; classes
_ Morrow (Baptist Church); Prescott, AR; 1955; salvation

David Kingdon (Baptist Church) & James Bjornstad (Baptist Church); Chattanooga, TN; July 1982; TV debate on *The John Ankerberg Show*; w/ Jerry Jones (Church of Christ). Internet publication: http://www.youtube.com/watch?v=ImwN3fTq6qg&feature=relmfu

Lindsay Anderson Allen, Jr. [Church of Christ]
Birth: September 5, 1907 (Lynn, AL)
Death: July 11, 1999 (_, _)
Biographical sketch: *Preachers of Today* (Batsell Barrett Baxter & M. Norvel Young, eds.). Nashville, TN: The Christian Press, 1952, p. 14.
Biographical sketch: *Preachers of Today, Volume Two* (Batsell Barrett Baxter & M. Norvel Young, eds.). Nashville, TN: The Gospel Advocate Company, 1959, p. 8.
Albert H. Batts (Church of God); Decatur, AL; February 1-2, 1940; water baptism, Holy Spirit baptism

N. M. Allen [Missionary Baptist Church]
Birth: _ (_, _)
Death: _ (_, _)
R. M. Elvin (Reorganized Church of Jesus Christ of Latter Day Saints); _, NE; January 22, 1883
W. E. Peak (Reorganized Church of Jesus Christ of Latter Day Saints); Council Bluffs, IA; August 21-23, 1888

Tom W. Allen [Baptist Church]
Birth: _ (_, _)
Death: _ (_, _)
C. D. Moore (Church of Christ); _, FL; 1932

W. M. Allen [Second Adventist Church, Church of Christ]
Birth: c 1858 (_, _)
Death: 19_ (_, _)
Had 65 debates representing Adventists. Converted on October 24, 1909 and began preaching with churches of Christ.
J. W. Chism (Church of Christ)
J. W. Chism (Church of Christ); their 2nd debate

_ Allen [Baptist Church]
Birth: _ (_, _)
Death: _ (_, _)
J. Porter Wilhite (Church of Christ); Roundflat community, ?TX; 1933

_ Allen [Methodist Church]
Birth: _ (_, _)
Death: _ (_, _)
Harold Hazelip (Church of Christ); 1955

Frederick William Allendorf [Evolutionist]
Birth: April 29, 1947 (Philadelphia, PA)
Death: _ (_, _)
Duane T. Gish (Creationist); Missoula, MT; October 11, 1983; creation & evolution; 1600

John Allister [Believer]
Birth: _ (_, _)
Death: _ (_, _)
Justin Schieber (Atheist); the slaughter of the Amalekites

Coleman Kurfees Allmond [Church of Christ]
Birth: September 26, 1929 (Lyon, Coahoma County, MS)
Death: May 15, 2009 (Natchez, Adams County, MS)
Biographical sketch: *Preachers of Today* (Batsell Barrett Baxter & M. Norvel Young, eds.). Nashville, TN: The Christian Press, 1952, p. 15.
Biographical sketch: *Preachers of Today, Volume Two* (Batsell Barrett Baxter & M. Norvel Young, eds.). Nashville, TN: The Gospel Advocate Company, 1959, p. 10.
Biographical sketch: *Preachers of Today, Volume Three* (Batsell Barrett Baxter & M. Norvel Young, eds.). Nashville, TN: The Gospel Advocate Company, 1964, p. 9.
_ Scott (Baptist Church); Garden City, MI; May 1959; salvation, apostasy

Hugo Allmond [Church of Christ]
Birth: March 18, 1903 (Obion County, TN)
Death: September 1, 1957 (near Aberdeen, MS)
Biographical sketch: *Preachers of Today* (Batsell Barrett Baxter & M. Norvel Young, eds.). Nashville, TN: The Christian Press, 1952, p. 15.
_ Cobb (Baptist Church); _, AR; 1931; church
Sam Edwards (Missionary Baptist Church); Dodson's Branch, TN; September 20-23, 1932; church
W. S. Miller (Baptist Church); Shiloh, AR; 1932
C. R. Reeves (Baptist Church); Lebanon, TN; 1933
John R. Clark (Baptist Church); 1934; church

Shabir Ally [Muslim]
Birth: 19_ (_, _)
Death: _ (_, _)
Sometimes debated using the name Abul Abu Saffiyah
Bill Musk (Believer); London, England; October 14, 1999.
    Subject: Why I am a Christian? Why I am a Muslim?
    Internet publication: http://www.youtube.com/watch?v=hAT8NrpeMWo&feature=related

Mark Pickering (?); Birmingham, ?England; March 8, 2000
Dave Hunt (?). Topic: Violence in the Bible vs Violence in the Qur'an
Bob Benjamin (?) & Glen Shentke (?); June 22, 2009. Topic: Jesus in the Bible and Quran-- which account is accurate?
Dominee Hans Visser (?). Topic: Who is Jesus Prophet or God?
James White (Reformed Baptist Church); May 7, 2006. Subject: "Is the New Testament as it exists today the inspired word of God?"
Sam Ahamoun (?). Topic: The Bible or the Qura'n Which Is God's Word?
John Gilchrist (?). Topic: Biblical and Quranic Approach to Peace
John Gilchrist (?). Topic: The Divine Origins, of the Bible and the Quran
John Gilchrist (?). Topic: The Crucifixion and Resurrection of Jesus Christ-Fact or Fiction?
David Seccombe (?)
Bob Benjamin (?) & Glen Schenkte (?)
Jay Smith (?); Birmingham, ?England; February 1998. Topic: Historical Sources for the Qur'an and the Bible
Jay Smith (?); Leicester, _; May 8, 1998 Topic: Is the Qur'an the Word of God?
Jay Smith (?); Atlanta, GA; TV debate. Topic: Who Is the Real Jesus?
Jay Smith (?). Topic: Peace and Violence in Christianity and Islam
Jay Smith (?); June 28, 2008. Internet publication: http://www.youtube.com/watch?v=pr4zGSiR4as
Mike Licona (Believer); Regent University; March 2004. Topic: Did Jesus Rise from the Dead?
Mike Licona (Believer); TV debate; November 2004. Topic: Who was Jesus: Divine or Prophet? Web publication: http://www.youtube.com/watch?v= grDPJmb3gAs&safety_mode=true&persist_safety_mode=1
William Lane Craig (Evangelical); 2002. Topic: Who is the Real Jesus?
William Lane Craig (Evangelical); 2002. Topic: Did Jesus Rise From the Dead?
William Lane Craig (Evangelical); 2002. Topic: The Concept of God In Islam and Christianity
William Lane Craig (Evangelical). Topic: What Must I do to be Saved?
James White (Reformed Baptist Church). Topic: Did Jesus Die as a Willing Sacrifice?
James White (Reformed Baptist Church); November 17, 2008. Topics: Is Jesus in the Old Testament? Is Muhammed In the Bible?"
William Lane Craig (Evangelical); 2009. Topic: Did Jesus Rise from the Dead?
_ (?); _, South Africa; June 2009; 3000
_ Shenk (?). Topic: Revelation of God in the Scriptures
_ Shenk (?). Topic: Muslim and Christian Perception of God
_ Shenk (?). Topic: Cross Resurrection and Salvation
_ Shenk (?). Topic: Abraham, Isaac and Ishmael
_ Shenk (?). Topic: Being a Muslim or a Christian--how we see each other
George Shilington (?). Topic: Was Paul the Founder of Christianity
Anthony Buzzard (?). Topic: Who is God and Jesus in the Bible?
Anthony Buzzard (?). Topic: What is the Gospel Jesus Preached?

Robert Morey (?). Topic: Is the Allah of the Qur'an the one true and universal God?
Robert Morey (?). Topic: Is the Qur'an the word of God?
Anis Shorrosh (?). Topic: Allah Vs Trinity
Anis Shorrosh (?). Topic: Is Muhamed in the Bible?
Anis Shorrosh (?). Topic: Crucifiction or Cruci-Fixion
Anis Shorrosh (?). Topic: The Bible or the Qur'an
Tony Costa (?). Topic: Jesus in Christianity, Jesus in Islam, Which account is historically correct?
Tony Costa (?). Topic: The Jesus "Conflict": Who Was Jesus?
Tony Costa (?). Topic: Who is God
Tony Costa (?). Topic: Did Jesus rise from the dead?

Thomas Jonathan Jackson Altizer [Atheist]
Birth: September 28, 1927 (Charleston, WV)
Death: November 28, 2018 (Stroudsburg, PA)
Biographical sketch: http://people.bu.edu/wwildman/ WeirdWildWeb/courses/mwt/dictionary/mwt_themes_ 899_altizer.htm
Biographical sketch: http://en.wikipedia.org/wiki/Thomas_J._J._Altizer
John Warwick Montgomery (Lutheran Church); Chicago, IL; February 24, 1967; situation ethics; 1600. Book publication: *The Altizer-Montgomery Dialogue*. Chicago, IL: Inter-Varsity Press, 1967. Book publication: *Situation Ethics*. Minneapolis, MN: Bethany Fellowship, 1972.
Walter R. Martin (Protestant)

Robert Eugene Amerson, Sr. [Church of Christ]
Birth: c 1942 (_, _)
Death: May 22, 2012 (?Prospect, TN)
Leon Lambert (Oneness Pentecostal Church); Tanner, AL; January 1976; godhead

Fred Ashton Amick [Church of Christ]
Birth: August 23, 1908 (Boonesboro, MO)
Death: September 15, 1994 (Woodburn, OR)
Biographical sketch: *Preachers of Today* (Batsell Barrett Baxter & M. Norvel Young, eds.). Nashville, TN: The Christian Press, 1952, p. 16.
Biographical sketch: *Preachers of Today, Volume Two* (Batsell Barrett Baxter & M. Norvel Young, eds.). Nashville, TN: The Gospel Advocate Company, 1959, p. 10.
_ (Jehovah's Witness); 1948; immortality of soul
_ Ellis (Church of Christ); 1952; carnal warfare

Wilburn Clifton Amos [Church of Christ]
Birth: September 30, 1880 (Columbia, TN)

Death: November 1970 (_, _)
Biographical sketch: *Preachers of Today* (Batsell Barrett Baxter & M. Norvel Young, eds.). Nashville, TN: The Christian Press, 1952, p. 16.
Biographical sketch: *Preachers of Today, Volume Two* (Batsell Barrett Baxter & M. Norvel Young, eds.). Nashville, TN: The Gospel Advocate Company, 1959, p. 11.
_ (Church of God in Christ); instrumental music in worship; before 1952

Abdullah Al Andalusi [Muslim]
Birth: _ (_, _)
Death: _ (_, _)
David Wood (?). Topic: The Concept of God in Islam and Christianity
David Wood (?). Topic: Is Christianity a Religion of Peace?
David Wood (?) & Nabeel Qureshi (?); w/ Seymour Hader Yahya (Muslim). Topic: Is Islam a Religion of Peace?
James White (Reformed Baptist Church). Topic: Is Belief in the Trinity Mandated by God?
James White (Reformed Baptist Church). Topic: The Big Trinity Debate.
Jay Smith (?)/ Topic: Which Is the True Religion of Peace For Today?
Jay Smith (?). Topic: The FITNA of Geert Wilders

Barry Lee Anderson [Church of Christ]
Birth: October 29, 1923 (Gallatin, Sumner County, TN)
Death: May 29, 2014 (Florence, AL)
Biographical sketch: *Preachers of Today* (Batsell Barrett Baxter & M. Norvel Young, eds.). Nashville, TN: The Christian Press, 1952, pp. 16-17.
Biographical sketch: *Preachers of Today, Volume Two* (Batsell Barrett Baxter & M. Norvel Young, eds.). Nashville, TN: The Gospel Advocate Company, 1959, p. 11.
Biographical sketch: *Preachers of Today, Volume Three* (Batsell Barrett Baxter & M. Norvel Young, eds.). Nashville, TN: The Gospel Advocate Company, 1964, p. 10.
Biographical sketch: *Preachers of Today, Volume Four* (Batsell Barrett Baxter & M. Norvel Young, eds.). Nashville, TN: The Gospel Advocate Company, 1970, p. 7.
Obituary: https://www.dignitymemorial.com/fr-ca/obituaries/dothan-al/barry-anderson-5988129
Six debates by 1969
W. T. Cook (Primitive Baptist Church); 1949; unconditional salvation
W. T. Cook (Primitive Baptist Church); 1950; identity of church
W. T. Cook (Primitive Baptist Church)
W. T. Cook (Primitive Baptist Church)

_ Harthern (?); 1951; Holy Spirit baptism

James N. Anderson [Oneness Pentecostal Church]
Birth: 19_ (_, _)
Death: _ (_, _)
Thomas N. Thrasher (Church of Christ); Mount Vernon, TX; July 19-20, 2012; Godhead; 2 sessions

James Anderson [?]
Birth: _ (_, _)
Death: _ (_, _)
Thomas Nisbet (?); 1905; kingdom during the days of John the Baptist. Book publication:

Joe Lee Anderson [Church of Christ]
Birth: 1937 (Hobbs, NM)
Death: _ (_, _)
Biographical sketch: *Preachers of Today, Volume Three* (Batsell Barrett Baxter & M. Norvel Young, eds.). Nashville, TN: The Gospel Advocate Company, 1964, p. 11.
Biographical sketch: *Preachers of Today, Volume Four* (Batsell Barrett Baxter & M. Norvel Young, eds.). Nashville, TN: The Gospel Advocate Company, 1970, p. 8.
_ Hobbs (?); before 1970; miraculous gifts

John Anderson [Preterist]
Birth: 19_ (_, _)
Death: _ (_, _)
Thomas Ice (Premillennialist) & Mark Hitchcock (Premillennialist); Tampa, FL; October 17-18, 2003; 2 sessions; w/ Don Preston (Preterist). Proposition 1: "Resolved: The Parousia, or 2nd coming of Christ, occurred in A.D. 70 with the Fall of Jerusalem." (Preston & Anderson affirmed, Ice & Hitchcock denied). Proposition 2: "Resolved: The Millennial, or Davidic Kingdom is in the future." (Ice & Hitchcock affirmed, Preston & Anderson denied).

L. O. Anderson [Sabbatarian]
Birth: _ (_, _)
Death: _ (_, _)
Rudolph Berry (Church of Christ); Chicago, IL; 1971

Stanley E. Anderson [Baptist Church]
Birth: _ (_, _)
Death: _ (_, _)
Marshall Norman (Church of Christ); written; establishment of church of Christ

Wyatt Wheaton Anderson [Evolutionist]
Birth: March 27, 1939 (_, _)

Death _ (_, _)
Biographical sketch:
   https://en.wikipedia.org/wiki/Wyatt_Anderson
Lane Lester (Creationist) & John N. Moore (Creationist);
   December 11, 1975; teaching of creation in public
   schools; panel format; 100; w/ Ron Simpson (Evolutionist)

Charles Andrews [Church of Christ]
Birth: 19_ (_, _)
Death: _ (_, _)
Robert Morey (Watchman Fellowship); Bessemer, AL; September 18, 1991;
   Church of Christ as a cult; necessity of water baptism; 1 session
Jon B. Smith (Presbyterian Church); Bessemer, AL; June 23-26, 1992;
   Calvinism

D. Lee Andrews [Christian Church]
Birth: _ (_, _)
Death: _ (_, _)
W. L. Totty (Church of Christ); Indianapolis, IN; 1937; premillennialism
Emmett G. Creacy (Church of Christ); Indianapolis, IN; 1938

E. H. Andrews [Creationist]
Birth: 19_ (_, _)
Death: _ (_, _)
Richard Dawkins (Evolutionist), J. Maynard Smith (Evolutionist), Emma Jenks
   (Evolutionist) & Daniella Sieff (Evolutionist); Oxford, England; February
   14, 1986; creation/evolution; w/ A. E. Wilder-Smith (Creationist), Theodore
   Wilson (Creationist) & Peter Ross (Creationist)

John Andrews [Presbyterian Church]
Birth:_ (_, _)
Death: _ (_, _)
L. F. W. Andrews (Universalist Society); c 1830. Book publication:
   *Presbyterianism vs. Universalism; or a Theological Correspondence
   between Rev. John Andrews (Presbyterian) and Dr. L. F. W. Andrews
   (Universalist)*. Cincinnati, OH, 1831.

J. J. Andrews [?]
Birth: _ (_, _)
Death: _ (_, _)
Robert Roberts (Christadelphian)

Lewis Feuilleteau Wilson Andrews [Universalist Society]
Birth: September 7, 1802 (_, _)
Death: March 16, 1875 (Americus, GA)
John Andrews (Presbyterian Church); c 1830. Book publication:
   *Presbyterianism vs. Universalism; or a Theological
   Correspondence between Rev. John Andrews (Presbyterian)*

and Dr. L. F. W. Andrews (Universalist). Cincinnati, OH, 1831.
?John C. Hope (?). Related publication: *A Development of Modern Universalism, Growing Out of a Correspondence in Reference to a Proposed Debate Between Dr. L. F. W. Andrews and Rev. John C. Hope*. Columbia, SC: Morgan's Book and Job Office, 1841.

Tuck Andrews [Church of Christ]
Birth: ?19_ (_, _)
Death: _ (_, _)
William H. Reeves (Church of Christ); Miami, FL; December 1958; institutionalism

_ Andrews [Reorganized Church of Jesus Christ of Latter-day Saints]
Birth: _ (_, _)
Death: _ (_, _)
Robert R. Price (Church of Christ); Modesto, CA; 1943; w/ _ Elliot (Reorganized Latter-day Saint)

A. A. Andrus [?]
Birth: 18_ (_, _)
Death: 19_ (_, _)
A. G. Freed (Church of Christ); Palestine, AR; 1901

Jerry Angelo [Church of Christ]
Birth: July 12, 1939 (_, _)
Death: June 20, 1999 (_, _)
Jim Turner (Baptist Church); Klamath Falls, OR; 1979; limited atonement, apostasy; 4 sessions

_ Angelo [?]
Birth: _ (_, _)
Death: _ (_, _)
Homer Putnam Reeves (Church of Christ); 1938

Robert Jefferson Anthony [Reorganized Church of Jesus Christ of Latter Day Saints]
Birth: November 12, 1831 (Warren, Jackson County, OH)
Death: May 26, 1899 (_, _)
_ Thurman (Church of Jesus Christ of Latter Day Saints) & _ Evans (Church of Jesus Christ of Latter Day Saints); Lehi, UT; January 29-30, 1881; w/ W. W. Blair (Reorganized Church of Jesus Christ of Latter Day Saints)
Andrew Jensen (Church of Jesus Christ of Latter Day Saints); Pleasant Grove, UT; July 20, 1885; *Doctrine and Covenants* and the history of the church up to the death of Joseph Smith

Thabiti M. Anyabwile [Baptist Church]
Birth: 19_ (_, _)

Death: _ (_, _)
Bassam Zawadi (Muslim); Dubai, United Arab Emirates; March 2, 2009. Topic: Who is God and how are we saved?
Ahmed Hameed (Muslim); University of Wollongong, Dubai. Topic: Who is Jesus Christ?

John Early Arceneaux [Church of Christ]
Birth: October 23, 1883 (Dennison, TX)
Death: January 3, 1970 (Waco, TX)
Biographical sketch: *Gospel Preachers Who Blazed The Trail* by C. R. Nichol. Austin, TX: Firm Foundation Publishing House, n.d.
Biographical sketch: *Preachers of Today* (Batsell Barrett Baxter & M. Norvel Young, eds.). Nashville, TN: The Christian Press, 1952, p. 18-19.
Biographical sketch: http://www.therestorationmovement.com/arceneaux.htm
J. A. Curry (Russellite); Leakey, TX; c 1903
_ (Church of Jesus Christ of Latter Day Saints); San Antonio, TX; c 1905
_ (Church of Jesus Christ of Latter Day Saints); Salt Lake City, UT; c 1911
Tom J. Beckham (Methodist Church); Thornton, TX; 1912
_ Poindexter (?); 1917; salvation
A. M. Baker (Church of Jesus Christ of Latter Day Saints); Wetumka (Wewoka?), OK; November 13-_, 1919
J. F. Curtis (Reorganized Church of Jesus Christ of Latter Day Saints); Flint, MI; March 7-18, 1921; 600-1000
J. N. Cowan (Church of Christ); Fort Smith, AR; 1928
R. V. Sarrels (Primitive Baptist Church); Anson, TX; November 16-23, 1931; 8 sessions; 1000. Proposition 1: "The scriptures teach that every person who is regenerated, or born of the Spirit of God, and washed in the blood of Jesus Christ will be eternally saved." (Sarrels affirmed, Arceneaux denied). Proposition 2: "The scriptures teach that baptism in water is a necessary condition to be performed by the alien (or dead) sinner in order to inherit spiritual or eternal life." (Arceneaux affirmed, Sarrels denied).
M. L. Welch (Primitive Baptist Church); Manitou, OK; 1938

George R. Archer [Methodist Church]
Birth: January 2, 1867 (Noble County, OH)
Death: May 15, 1947 (Portland, OR)
Claude Adrian Guild (Church of Christ); La Grande, OR; February 18-19, 1942; immersion

Mrs. Sibyl Mae Archer [Foursquare Gospel Church]
Birth: _ (_, _)
Death: _ (_, _)
William Floyd Thompson (Church of Christ)

_ Archer [Evolutionist]
Birth: 19_ (_, _)
Death: _ (_, _)
Duane Gish (Creationist); Sidney, New South Wales, Australia; January 1986; TV debate

W. E. Archibald [Presbyterian Church]
Birth: _ (_, _)
Death: _ (_, _)
T. H. Blenus (Church of Christ); 1878. Book publication: *A Debate on the Action of Baptism*. 1878.

_ Archibald [Church of Christ]
Birth: 18_ (_, _)
Death: _ (_, _)
E. L. Kelley (Reorganized Church of Jesus Christ of Latter Day Saints); Richey County, WV; August 7-_, 1888. Proposition: "Is the *Book of Mormon* of divine origin and worthy of the belief of all men?"

Charles Richard Arehart [Metropolitan Community Church]
Birth: October 7, 1937 (Seneca, Newton Co., MO)
Death: August 24, 2012 (Neosho, Newton Co., MO)
Obituary: https://www.findagrave.com/memorial/ 148458873/charles-richard-arehart
Jeff Asher (Church of Christ); TV debate; before 1994; homosexuality; their first debate
Jeff Asher (Church of Christ); Denver, CO; April 4-7, 1994; homosexuality
Jeff Asher (Church of Christ); Amarillo, TX; May 9-10, 12-13, 1994; homosexuality
Patrick T. Donahue (Church of Christ); Washington, DC; March 21, 2009; 1 session. Proposition: "Homosexuality is not consistent with Biblical Christianity." (Donahue affirmed, Arehart denied).

Dave Armstrong [Creationist]
Birth: _ (_, _)
Death: _ (_, _)
Yom Schreurs (Evolutionist); methodology of citing evolutionists with regard to the fossil record as a potential disproof of evolution
Steven J. Conifer (Evolutionist); the evolution of the eye, irreducible complexity, & intelligent design

John Nelson Armstrong [Church of Christ]
Birth: January 6, 1870 (near Gadsden, Crockett County, TN)
Death: August 12, 1944 (Searcy, AR)
Biographical sketch: *Gospel Preachers Who Blazed The Trail* by C. R. Nichol. Austin, TX: Firm Foundation

Publishing House, n.d.
Biographical sketch: *In Memoriam* by Gussie Lambert.
Shreveport, LA: Gussie Lambert, 1988, pp. 13-16.
Biographical sketch: http://www.therestorationmovement
.com/armstrong.htm
Daniel Sommer (Church of Christ); written; 1908; establishment of religio-secular schools. Book publication: *A Written Discussion on the Bible School*. No publication data.
D. Austen Sommer (Church of Christ); written; colleges; w/ J. C. McQuiddy (Church of Christ). Book publication: *The College Question Discussed*. Indianapolis, IN: Apostolic Review, n.d.

Richard Lee "Dick" Armstrong [Evolutionist]
Birth: August 4, 1937 (Seattle, WA)
Death: August 9, 1991 (Vancouver, British Columbia, Canada)
Duane Gish (Creationist); Vancouver, British Columbia, Canada; June 30, 1983; radio debate over CJOR

R. A. Armstrong [?]
Birth: _ (_, _)
Death: _ (_, _)
Charles Bradlaugh (Atheist); 2 nights. Book publication: *Is it Reasonable to Worship God? Verbatim report of two nights' debate at Nottingham between the Rev. R. A. Armstrong and Charles Bradlaugh*. 1878.

Charlie Franklin Arnett [Church of Christ]
Birth: September 14, 1913 (Lynn Grove, KY)
Death: July 29, 2009 (_, ?TN)
Biographical sketch: *Preachers of Today, Volume Three* (Batsell Barrett Baxter & M. Norvel Young, eds.). Nashville, TN: The Gospel Advocate Company, 1964, p. 13.
2 debates by 1964

_ Arnold [Seventh-day Adventist Church]
Birth: _ (_, _)
Death: _ (_, _)
John Shields (Reorganized Church of Jesus Christ of Latter Day Saints); Orton, Ontario, Canada; December 19, 1890; the seventh day of the week is the Sabbath of the Christian dispensation

Robert Wilson Arrington [Church of Christ]
Birth: August 8, 1867 (near Stephens, AR)
Death: September 17, 1922 (near Stephens, AR)
Obituary: *Gospel Advocate* (October 19, 1922)
Biographical sketch: *Arkansas Angels* by Boyd E. Morgan. Paragould, AR: College Bookstore & Press, 1967 (Second

Printing), pp. 44-45.

Ben M. Bogard (Missionary Baptist Church); near Bearden, AR; December 18-21, 1906; general church; 4 days

C. C. Winters (Missionary Baptist Church); Troy (near Stephens), AR; January 23-26, 1917. Proposition 1: "The Scriptures teach that the church or kingdom of Christ was set up (established) on the first Pentecost after the resurrection of Christ from the dead." (Arrington affirmed, Winters denied). Proposition 2: "The Scriptures teach that through repentance and faith, justification, remission of sins, and like spiritual blessings are obtained independent of baptism." (Winters affirmed, Arrington denied). Proposition 3: "The Scriptures teach that a child of God (one born of God) can and may so far apostatize as to be finally lost." (Arrington affirmed, Winters denied). [*Gospel Advocate*, vol. 59, no. 7 (February 15, 1917), 162]

L. W. Evans (Holiness Church); Winnsboro, LA; November 12-_, 1917

_ Arterburn [Baptist Church]
Birth: _ (_, _)
Death: _ (_, _)
J. Stanley Jones (Church of Christ); establishment of church, Lord's supper.

Hobart Edwin Ashby [Church of Christ]
Birth: September 17, 1917 (Knobel, AR)
Death: June 1982 (_, _)
Biographical sketch: *Preachers of Today* (Batsell Barrett Baxter & M. Norvel Young, eds.). Nashville, TN: The Christian Press, 1952, p. 20.

Biographical sketch: *Preachers of Today, Volume Two* (Batsell Barrett Baxter & M. Norvel Young, eds.). Nashville, TN: The Gospel Advocate Company, 1959, p. 16.
Biographical sketch: *Preachers of Today, Volume Three* (Batsell Barrett Baxter & M. Norvel Young, eds.). Nashville, TN: The Gospel Advocate Company, 1964, p. 15.
Biographical sketch: *Preachers of Today, Volume Four* (Batsell Barrett Baxter & M. Norvel Young, eds.). Nashville, TN: The Gospel Advocate Company, 1970, p. 12.
A. M. Patterson (?); Portageville, MO; 1942

Lloyd Ashenfelter [Baptist Church]
Birth: _ (_, _)
Death: _ (_, _)
J. T. Smith (Church of Christ); Lookeba, OK; March 7-10, 1966; baptism, apostasy

Jeffrey Stephen Asher [Church of Christ]
Birth: March 27, 1958 (Pine Bluff, AR)
Death: _ (_, _)

Biographical sketch: *Faith and Facts Quarterly*, Volume 31, Number 2 (April 2003), 80.

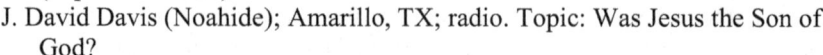

George Battey (Church of Christ); Amarillo, TX; April 3-4, 6-7, 1990; drinking vessels in Lord's supper, classes & women teachers; 1st debate for both

Dudley Ross Spears (Church of Christ); written; c 1986; 1 John 1:1-10. Periodical publication: *Gospel Anchor* (September 1986).

J. David Davis (Noahide); Amarillo, TX; radio. Topic: Was Jesus the Son of God?

Robert Williams (Episcopalian); Amarillo, TX; January 20, 1990; radio debate; homosexuality

Glen Stocker (Pauline Dispensationalist); Amarillo, TX; April 4-5, 1992; baptism, faith alone; 120

Charles Richard Arehart (Metropolitan Community Church); TV debate; before 1994; homosexuality; their first debate

Charles Richard Arehart (Metropolitan Community Church); Denver, CO; April 4-7, 1994; homosexuality

Charles Richard Arehart (Metropolitan Community Church); Amarillo, TX; May 9-10, 12-13, 1994; homosexuality

Jerry Healen (Yahweh New Covenant Assembly); Amarillo, TX; November 1994; Sabbath; radio debate

Mac Deaver (Church of Christ); Amarillo & Wellington, TX; April 4-8, 1996; church cooperation

Bob Berard (Church of Christ); Huntsville, TX; February 1-5, 1998; church-sponsored social meals

Jorge Ramon (Sabbatarian); Corozal, Belize; February 10-13, 1998; Sabbath

David D. Bonner (Church of Christ); Amarillo, TX; August 2-3, 5-6, 1999; deity & humanity of Jesus; 80-200; 4 sessions

David D. Bonner (Church of Christ); Lufkin, TX; August 23-24, 26-27, 1999; deity & humanity of Jesus; 150-250; 4 sessions

David Proctor (Missionary Baptist Church); Carthage, TX; August 8-9, 11-12, 2005; 4 sessions. Proposition 1: "The Scriptures teach that one is saved at the point of faith before and without water baptism." (Proctor affirmed, Asher denied). Proposition 2: "The Scriptures teach that water baptism is for (in order to obtain) the remission of past sins." (Asher affirmed, Proctor denied).

_ Ashley [?]
Birth: _ (_, _)
Death: _ (_, _)
Elvis H. Huffard (Church of Christ); 1949; instrumental music in worship

C. A. Ashlock [Church of Christ]
Birth: _ (_, _)
Death: _ (_, _)
?W. P. Jordan (Baptist Church); Plum Springs, KY; 1932

Hiram Hunter Ashmore [Cumberland Presbyterian Church]
Birth: 1829 (_, _)
Death: 1908 (_, _)
Harmon Gregg (Church of Christ); Westfield, IL; 1868

William Casey "Billy" Ashworth [Church of Christ]
Birth: October 8, 1919 (_, _)
Death: March 7, 2000 (_, _)
Obituary: "Billy Ashworth Passes" by Steve Wolfgang. *Truth Magazine* (XLIV:13, July 6, 2000, pp. 8-10).
William Sullivan (?); Franklin, TN; June 1963; Holy Spirit; 2 sessions
P. D. Ballard (Baptist Church)
P. D. Ballard (Baptist Church); Fairview, TN; October 3-4, 6-7, 1966
Ray Hadley (?); Nashville, TN; April 1966
Jack Rudd (Church of Christ); New Hope, TN; February 26-27, March 1-2, 1979; benevolence, cooperation

Aminah Assilmi [Muslim]
Birth: 19_ (_, _)
Death: _ (_, _)
She died at age 65.
Deborah Scroggins (?). Topic: Women's rights and roles in Islam

Julius Sidney Astin [Church of Christ]
Birth: August 31, 1915 (Macon, GA)
Death: _ (_, _)
Biographical sketch: *Preachers of Today* (Batsell Barrett Baxter & M. Norvel Young, eds.). Nashville, TN: The Christian Press, 1952, p. 20-21.
Biographical sketch: *Preachers of Today, Volume Two* (Batsell Barrett Baxter & M. Norvel Young, eds.). Nashville, TN: The Gospel Advocate Company, 1959, p. 16.
_ (Church of Jesus Christ of Latter Day Saints); 1947
_ (Adventist); 1949

Ali Atarie [Muslim]
Birth: 19_ (_, _)
Death: _ (_, _)
Mike Licona (Believer); Davis, CA; November 2006. Topic: What was the First Century Fate of Jesus?
David Wood (?). Topic: Who was Muhammed?

Peter William Atkins [Atheist]
Birth: August 10, 1940 (Amersham, Buckinghamshire, England)
Death: _ (_, _)

Alister McGrath (Theist)
Stephen C. Meyer (Theist)
William Lane Craig (Evangelical)
Shmuley Boteach (Jew)
Richard Swinburne (Theist)

B. H. Atkinson [Church of Christ]
Birth: _ (_, _)
Death: _ (_, _)
Raymond Bosworth (Jehovah's Witnesses); Sunbury, PA; 1947
_ (Baptist Church); ?Danville, PA; November 6-8, 1947
Arthur Stabile (Roman Catholic Church); Sunbury, PA; c August 1950. Proposition: "The Roman Catholic (sometimes called the Holy Apostolic Catholic) Church is the church of the New Testament." (Stabile affirmed, Atkinson denied).
Arthur Stabile (Roman Catholic Church); Staten Island, NY; August 28-30, 1950. Proposition: "The Church of Christ of which I am a member is of divine origin and is the church of the New Testament." (Atkinson affirmed, Stabile denied).

Scott Atran [?]
Birth: 19_ (_, _)
Death: _ (_, _)
Sam Harris (Atheist); Beyond Belief '06; November 6, 2006. Web video: http://www.freethoughtpedia.com/wiki/Scott_Atran_vs._Sam_Harris

J. A. C. F. Auev [Humanist]
Birth: _ (_, _)
Death: _ (_, _)
Julian Hartt (?); Yellow Springs, OH; April 20, 1950; can faith rest on scientific knowledge alone, is it religion if it lacks God, what can a reasonable man believe. Book publication: *Auev-Hartt Debate*. N.p.: Antioch Press, 1951.

Augustine of Hippo [Catholic Church]
Birth: November 13, 354 (Tagaste, Algeria, Africa)
Death: 430 (Hippo Regius, ?Algeria, Africa)
_ (Arian)
_ (Manichaean)
_ (Pelagian)
_ (Donatist); Carthage, _, Africa; June 1-3, 411
Julian (?); c 430

_ Ausdenmoore [Catholic Church]
Birth: _ (_, _)
Death: _ (_, _)
John Fairs Nichols (Church of Christ); Dayton, OH; 1934

Charles Smith Austin [Church of Christ]
Birth: November 24, 1881 (Scotts Hill, Decatur Co., TN)
Death: June 19, 1964 (Mt. Pleasant, Maury Co., TN)
Biographical sketch: *Preachers of Today* (Batsell Barrett Baxter & M. Norvel Young, eds.). Nashville, TN: The Christian Press, 1952, p. 21.
Biographical sketch: *Preachers of Today, Volume Two* (Batsell Barrett Baxter & M. Norvel Young, eds.). Nashville, TN: The Gospel Advocate Company, 1959, p. 17.
Obituary by Larimore Austin. *Gospel Advocate*, July 16, 1964, p. 463.
_ Hayes (?); 1912; instrumental music in worship
J. S. Dean (?Christian Church); Fulton, KY; January 27-30, 1914. Proposition: "The scriptures teach that the use of instrumental music in the worship of the Church of Jesus Christ is sin." (Austin affirmed, Dean denied).
_ Moore (?Baptist Church); 1913; apostasy

George William Austin [Church of Christ]
Birth: June 25, 1872 (near Henderson, TN)
Death: 19_ (_, _)
Biographical sketch: *Preachers of Today* (Batsell Barrett Baxter & M. Norvel Young, eds.). Nashville, TN: The Christian Press, 1952, p. 21.
Biographical sketch: *Preachers of Today, Volume Two* (Batsell Barrett Baxter & M. Norvel Young, eds.). Nashville, TN: The Gospel Advocate Company, 1959, p. 18.
Biographical sketch: *Preachers of Today, Volume Three* (Batsell Barrett Baxter & M. Norvel Young, eds.). Nashville, TN: The Gospel Advocate Company, 1964, p. 16.
_ (Baptist Church); Austin's first debate
A. S. Bradley (Materialist); 1910

John Mather Austin [Universalist Society]
Birth: September 26, 1805 (Redfield, Oswego County, NY)
Death: December 20, 1880 (Rochester, NY)
David Holmes (?);Cayuga County, NY; December 28, 1847 – January 5. 1848. Book publication: *A Debate on the Doctrines of Atonement, Universal Salvation, and Endless Punishment.* Auburn, NY: Alden & Markham, 1848.
Related publication: *End of the Argument for Free Believing ; a Review of Mr. Austin's Nineteen Arguments, in a Debate with Rev. Mr. Holmes* by Silas Comfort. Auburn, NY: Wm. J. Moses, 1853.

Paul Austin [Oneness Pentecostal Church]
Birth: 19_ (_, _)
Death: _ (_, _)

Howard See (Church of Christ); Nashville, TN; May 15, 18, 22, 25, 1978. Proposition 1: "The Scriptures teach that there are three separate and distinct persons in the Godhead." (See affirmed, Austin denied). Proposition 2: "The Scriptures teach that there is only one person of the Godhead." (Austin affirmed, See denied). Proposition 3: "Resolved that the Scriptures teach that those who have been taught the Gospel of Christ are to be baptized into the name of the Father, the Son, and the Holy Spirit for the remission of sins and that this may be done without saying a formula of words over those being baptized.' (See affirmed, Austin denied). Proposition 4: "The Scriptures teach that the proper name Jesus must be vocally invoked during the rite of baptizing a person in water in order for that person's sins to be remitted." (Austin affirmed, See denied).

W. C. Austin [Freewill Baptist Church]
Birth: 18_ (_, _)
Death: _ (_, _)
Will Thompson (Church of Christ); Centrahoma, OK; October 17-22, 1919
L. R. Wilson (Church of Christ); Townley, AL; 1928
Charley Nichols (Church of Christ); Mount Harmony, AL; c 1928
Rue Porter (Church of Christ)

Allen Hill Autry [Baptist Church]
Birth: March 16, 1865 (Denton County, TX)
Death: February 1, 1932 (Little Rock, AR)
James W. Zachary (Church of Christ); Huntsville, AR; c 1896
Francis O. Howell (Church of Christ)
G. W. Wolf (Church of Christ); Board Camp, AR; December 7-12, 1908. Proposition 1: "The Missionary Baptist church is scriptural in origin, doctrine and practice." (Autry affirmed, Wolf denied). Proposition 2: "The church of God (or Christ) is scriptural in origin, doctrine and practice." (Wolf affirmed, Autry denied). [*Firm Foundation*, Vol. 25, No. 3 (January 19, 1909), 7]
C. H. Cayce (Primitive Baptist Church); near Board Camp, AR; July 16-19, 1912; 4 days

Edward Bibbens Aveling [Atheist]
Birth: November 29, 1849 (Stoke Newington, London, England)
Death: August 2, 1898 (Battersea, _)
Biographical sketch: "Edward Bibbens Aveling" by Paul Henderson. In A. Thomas Lane (Ed.), *Biographical Dictionary of European Labor Leaders*. [Two Volumes]. Westport, CT: Greenwood Press, 1995.
Biographical sketch: http://www.spartacus.schoolnet.co.uk/TUaveling.htm

Ahmed Mohammed Awal [Muslim]
Birth: 19_ (_, _)
Death: _ (_, _)
Tony Costa (?). Topic: Crucifixion or Crucifiction?
James White (Reformed Baptist Church); June 20, 2010. Topic: Is the Bible We Have Today the Word of God?

Frank Thomas Awbrey [Evolutionist]
Birth: October 16, 1932 (_, _)
Death: May 31, 1998 (_, _)
Duane Gish (Creationist) & Henry M. Morris (Creationist); San Diego, CA; April 26, 1977; 1500; w/ William Thwaites (Evolutionist)
Duane T. Gish (Creationist); San Diego, CA; October 22, 1984; 400; w/ William Thwaites (Evolutionist)
Duane T. Gish (Creationist) & Henry M. Morris (Creationist); Long Beach, CA; September 28, 1985; 1400; w/ William Thwaites (Evolutionist)

William Murray Aylor [Reorganized Church of Jesus Christ of Latter-day Saints]
Birth: January 9, 1864 (Oneida, IL)
Death: March 28, 1928 (_, _)

Samuele R. Bacchiocchi [Seventh-day Adventist Church]
Birth: January 29, 1938 (Rome, Italy)
Death: December 20, 2008 (_, _)
John T. Lewis (Church of Christ); written; 1997; Sabbath day. Publication: Lone Grove, OK: John T. Lewis, 1997. Web publication: http://www.bible.ca/7-Bacchiocchi-lewis-debate.htm

Origen Bacheler [?]
Birth: November 6, 1799 (Sutton, MA)
Death: 18_ (_, _)
Robert Dale Owen (Skeptic); written; 1831. Periodical publication: *New-York Free Enquirer*. Book publication: *Discussion on the Existence of God*. London, England: J. Watson, 1840. Book publication: *Discussion on the Authenticity of the Bible*. Philadelphia, PA: E. Haskell, 1854. Book publication: *Discussion on the Existence of God and the Authenticity of the Bible*. London: James Watson, 1853. Web publication: http://books.google.com/books?id=hIQm1JttIL4C&dq=origen+bacheler&printsec=frontcover&source=web&ots=0KiO1z7KkJ&sig=GH10JuihEhoodAW8o35pZQr2KAU#PPP1,M1

_ Bachus [Church of God]
Birth:_ (_, _)
Death: _ (_, _)
Walter E. Bankes (Church of Christ); 1943. Proposition: "Baptism of the Holy Spirit is not in force today." (Bankes affirmed, Bachus denied).

Jamal A. Badawi [Muslim]
Birth: November 10, 1939 (_, Egypt)
Death: _ (_, _)

D. Woodberry (Believer), H. Voglarr (Believer), Paul Martison (Believer), & _ Chastain (Believer); 1991; the Concept of God in Islam and Christianity, Was Jesus Divine Or was He a Prophet of God?, Is Muhammed a Prophet of God?, Is the Bible the Word of God?, Is the Qur'an the Word of God?, The Way to Salvation; w/ Hussein Morsi (Muslim), Sayed El Sayed (Muslim), Jeffery Lang (Muslim)
Robert Douglas (Believer) & Gleason Archer (Believer); 1992; God as Viewed in the Bible and the Qur'an, The Authenticity of the Bible, The Authenticity of the Qur'an, The Cross and Salvation; w/ Hussein Morsi (Muslim)
D. Bishop (Believer), Lois Livezey (Believer), Jean Hughes (Believer), J. J Pawlikowski (Believer), & J Sherer (Believer); 1993; Basic Human Rights as Viewed by Christianity and Islam, Treatment of Women in Morsi (Muslim)
Mark David Roberts (Church of Christ); Beaumont, TX; November 3, 1994; deity of Christ; 1 session; 500-600
Jack Evans (Church of Christ); Washington, D.C.; May 4, 1996; Christianity & Islam; 1500
James Burns, Jr. (Presbyterian Church)
William Lane Craig (Evangelical); Texas A&M University; February 1997
William Lane Craig (Evangelical); Texas A&M University; February 17, 2004
Jay Smith (?); Trinity College, University of Cambridge; August 9, 1995. Topic: Is the Qur'an the word of God?" Christianity and Islam, Treatment of Minorities in Christianity and Islam; w/ Sayed El Sayed (Muslim), Aysha Bey (Muslim), & Yvonne Haddad (Muslim)
Anis Shorrosh (Believer) & Gleason Archer (Believer);series of TV debates on the John Ankerberg TV Show; The Concept of God in Christianity and Islam, Is Jesus God or a Prophet?, Is Muhammed a Prophet of God?, The Crucifiction of Jesus: Muslim and Christian perspectives, Is the Bible the Word of God?, Is the Qur'an the Word of God?, The Way to Salvation in Christianity and Islam; w/ Hussein
Anis Shorrosh (?). Topic: The Qura'n word of God or word of Muhammed?
Anis Shorrosh (?). Topic: Is Jesus God?
Robert Morey (?); Columbia University, SC; November 9, 1996. Topic: Is the Allah of the Qur'an the one true and universal God?

Robert Morey (?). Topic: Is the Qur'an the word of God?
John Rittenhouse (?). Topic: Is Jesus God?

James T(homas?) Bagby [Methodist Church]
Birth: 18_ (_, _)
Death: 19_ (_, _)
W. H. Trice (Church of Christ); written. Proposition 1: "The Bible teaches that baptism in water is a condition of salvation." (Trice affirmed, Bagby denied). Proposition 2: "The Bible teaches that the sprinkling of water upon a proper subject is baptism." (Bagby affirmed, Trice denied). Book publication: *Bagby-Trice Discussion on the Design and Action of Baptism*. Nashville, TN: McQuiddy Printing Co., 1914.
J. W. Ballard (Church of Christ); October 15-__, 1919

_ Bagby [Baptist Church]
Birth: _ (_, _)
Death: _ (_, _)
Fenter Dee Northern (Church of Christ)

Vardimon David Baggerly [Reorganized Church of Jesus Christ of Latter Day Saints]
Birth: April 14, 1846 (Clark County, IN)
Death: January 15, 1898 (Derby, Perry County. IN)
_ Terry (Church of Christ); ?West Fork, IN; April _-7, 1889

Greg L. Bahnsen [Orthodox Presbyterian Church]
Birth: September 17, 1948 (Auburn, WA)
Death: December 11, 1995 (_, _)
_ Feinberg (?); Toronto, Canada; 1981; held during the annual meeting of the Evangelical Theological Society
George H. Smith (Atheist)
Gordon Stein (Atheist)
Edward Tabash (Atheist)

Allen Bailey [Church of Christ]
Birth: c 1955 (_, _)
Death: _ (_, _)
_ Norton (Pentecostal Church); October 30, 1976; godhead
Thomas N. Thrasher (Church of Christ); Athens, AL; August 7, 1993; 2 sessions. Proposition 1: "The Scriptures teach that an assembly of the church of Christ in the communion must use one cup (drinking vessel) for the distribution of the fruit of the vine." (Bailey affirmed, Thrasher denied). Proposition 2: "The Scriptures teach that an assembly of the church of Christ may use individual cups (drinking vessels) for the distribution of the fruit of the vine." (Thrasher affirmed, Bailey denied).
Patrick T. Donahue (Church of Christ); West Monroe, LA; April 13-14, 1995; drinking vessels in Lord's supper; 80; 2 sessions

B. (?Byron) C. (?Charles) Bailey [Baptist Church]
Birth: ?June 29, 1919 (_, _)
Death: October 19, 2008 (Birmingham, Jefferson County, AL)
Edward O. Bragwell (Church of Christ); Gardendale, AL; May 22-23, 25-26, 1972; baptism; 4 sessions

George Willis Bailey [Church of Christ]
Birth: April 3, 1922 (Kaufman, Kaufman Co., TX)
Death: November 11, 2017 (_, TX)
Biographical sketch: *Preachers of Today* (Batsell Barrett Baxter & M. Norval Young, eds.). Nashville, TN: The Christian Press, 1952, p. 23.
Biographical sketch: *Preachers of Today, Volume Two* (Batsell Barrett Baxter & M. Norval Young, eds.). Nashville, TN: The Gospel Advocate Company, 1959, p. 19.
Biographical sketch: *Preachers of Today, Volume Three* (Batsell Barrett Baxter & M. Norval Young, eds.). Nashville, TN: The Gospel Advocate Company, 1964, p. 17.
Biographical sketch: *Preachers of Today, Volume Four* (Batsell Barrett Baxter & M. Norval Young, eds.). Nashville, TN: The Gospel Advocate Company, 1970, p. 14.
Obituary: https://www.findagrave.com/memorial/185132504/george-willis-bailey
_ Chapman (?); 1949; instrumental music in worship

John Carlos Bailey [Church of Christ]
Birth: September 13, 1903 (Meaford, Ontario, Canada)
Death: July 2, 2001 (_, Saskatchewan, Canada)
Autobiography: *Forty Years A Canadian Preacher* by John Carlos Bailey. Privately published, 1962.
Biographical sketch: *Preachers of Today* (Batsell Barrett Baxter & M. Norval Young, eds.). Nashville, TN: The Christian Press, 1952, pp. 23-24.
Biographical sketch: *Preachers of Today, Volume Two* (Batsell Barrett Baxter & M. Norval Young, eds.). Nashville, TN: The Gospel Advocate Company, 1959, p. 20.
Biographical sketch: *Preachers of Today, Volume Three* (Batsell Barrett Baxter & M. Norval Young, eds.). Nashville, TN: The Gospel Advocate Company, 1964, p. 17.
_ Snowden (Anglican Church); Bengough, Saskatchewan, Canada; 1931; infant baptism; 1 session; 400
_ Rice (United Church of Canada); Bengough, Saskatchewan, Canada; 1932; the nature of the church; 400
_ (Lutheran); Bengough, Saskatchewan, Canada; 1933; the nature of the church; 400

_ (Jehovah's Witnesses); c February 1933
A. R. Scherling (Independent); Bengough, Saskatchewan, Canada; 1935; the supremacy of conscience
L. L. McGill (Church of Christ); Bromhead, Saskatchewan, Canada; 1936; Bible classes
A. R. Scherling (Independent); Regina, Saskatchewan, Canada; 1937; the supremacy of conscience. Book publication: *Bailey-Scherling Debate*.
_ Brost (Church of God); Estevan, Saskatchewan, Canada; c 1950; spiritual gifts
A. R. Scherling (Independent); Vancouver, WA; July 20-23, 1953; the supremacy of conscience; their 3rd debate. Book publication: *Scherling-Bailey Debate*. Longview, WA: Telegram Book Co., 1954.
James B. Reesor (Church of God); Wawota, Saskatchewan, Canada; 1953; work of the Holy Spirit
James B. Reesor (Church of God); Saskatoon, Saskatchewan, Canada; 1953; work of the Holy Spirit
_ Wright (Church of Christ); Longview, WA; c 1954; amenability
W. Carl Ketcherside (Church of Christ); Regina, Saskatchewan, Canada; c 1955; located preachers
_ (Church of Jesus Christ of Latter Day Saints); Dauphin, Manitoba, Canada; summer 1958; Mormonism; JCB's last debate

Jesse R. Bailey, Sr. [Church of Christ]
Birth: July 28, 1902 (McMinnville, TN)
Death: April 1976 (?McMinnville, ?TN)
Biographical sketch: *Preachers of Today, Volume Two* (Batsell Barrett Baxter & M. Norval Young, eds.). Nashville, TN: The Gospel Advocate Company, 1959, p. 20.
_ (Church of Jesus Christ of Latter Day Saints)
_ (Adventist Church)
_ (Holiness Church)

Paul Bailey [Church of Christ]
Birth: 19_ (_, _)
Death: _ (_, _)
Paul O. Nichols (Church of Christ); Red Bluff & Redding, CA; October 29-30, 1976; drinking vessels in Lord's supper

W. H. Bailey [Presbyterian Church]
Birth: 18_ (_, _)
Death: c 1882 (_, _)
E. A. Land (Church of Christ); Mount Carmel, TN; July 1880; 800; Bailey quit on the third day of a scheduled 8-day debate

Walter Bailey [Church of Christ]
Birth: _ (_, _)
Death: _ (_, _)

Jimmy Thomas (Church of Christ); Newport, KY; 1970
Thomas G. O'Neal (Church of Christ); Belfast, VA; October 16-17, 1980; located preachers

Wilford S. Bailey [Evolutionist]
Birth: March 2, 1921 (_, _)
Death: October 7, 2000 (Opelika, AL)
Obituary: https://www.legacy.com/obituaries/name/wilford-bailey-obituary?pid=144502157
Harold Slusher (Creationist), Jody Dillow (Creationist), Tom Newberger (Creationist) & Richard Bliss (Creationist); Dallas, TX; February 24, 1977; 300; broadcast on TV; w/ Ken Gjemere (Evolutionist), Virginia Currey (Evolutionist), _ Jagger (Evolutionist) & _ (Evolutionist)

William Mark Bailey [Church of Christ]
Birth: c 1960 (_, _)
Death: _ (_, _)
Patrick T. Donahue (Church of Christ); written; 1992; head coverings. Book publication: *The Bailey-Donahue Debate on 1 Corinthians 11:2-16.* 1992. Privately published, 1992.
Patrick T. Donahue (Church of Christ); Athens, AL; August 5-6, 1993; head coverings of 1 Corinthians 11; 125; 2 sessions

Ermon Benjamin Bain [Church of Christ]
Birth: December 16, 1915 (Town Creek, AL)
Death: March 1, 1995 (?Decatur, AL)
Biographical sketch: *Preachers of Today, Volume Three* (Batsell Barrett Baxter & M. Norval Young, eds.). Nashville, TN: The Gospel Advocate Company, 1964, p. 17.
1 debate by 1964

_ Bain [Baptist Church]
Birth: _ (_, _)
Death: _ (_, _)
George A. Maddox (Church of Christ); 1942; establishment of church, apostasy; 4 nights

Oval P. Baird [Church of Christ]
Birth: June 1, 1912 (Alexandria, TN)
Death: July 8, 1999 (_, _)
Biographical sketch: *Preachers of Today* (Batsell Barrett Baxter & M. Norval Young, eds.). Nashville, TN: The Christian Press, 1952, pp. 24-25.

Biographical sketch: *Preachers of Today, Volume Two* (Batsell Barrett Baxter & M. Norval Young, eds.). Nashville, TN: The Gospel Advocate Company, 1959, p. 21.

Biographical sketch: *Preachers of Today, Volume Three* (Batsell Barrett Baxter & M. Norval Young, eds.). Nashville, TN: The Gospel Advocate Company, 1964, p. 18.

Biographical sketch: *Preachers of Today, Volume Four* (Batsell Barrett Baxter & M. Norval Young, eds.). Nashville, TN: The Gospel Advocate Company, 1970, p. 15.

_ Lee (?); 1940. Proposition 1: "The soul and the body are one, and when the soul is dead the body is dead." (Lee affirmed, Baird denied). Proposition 2: "The finally unsaved ones shall suffer eternal conscious punishment." (Baird affirmed, Lee denied).

A. M. Baker [Reorganized Church of Jesus Christ of Latter Day Saints]
Birth: 18_ (_, _)
Death: 19_ (_, _)
Bynum Black (Church of Christ); Bell, AR; c March 1917; 8 nights; general church propositions

W. G. Roberts (Church of Christ); Lebo, IL; December 1918; general church

Early Arceneaux (Church of Christ); Wetumka (Wewoka?), OK; November 13-_, 1919

A. Y. Baker [Church of Jesus Christ of Latter Day Saints]
Birth: _ (_, _)
Death: _ (_, _)
J. D. Tant (Church of Christ); DeQueen, AR; 1932

Bert Abram Baker, Sr. [Berean Bible Church]
Birth: _ (_, _)
Death: _ (_, _)
Bill L. Rogers (Church of Christ); Rogers Springs, TN; August 31 - September 5, 1953; 6 nights; 500. Proposition 1: "The Scriptures teach that the present dispensation began after the conversion of Saul of Tarsus, and since that time alien sinners are justified by faith alone." (Baker affirmed, Rogers denied). Proposition 2: "The Scriptures teach that the present dispensation began on the first Pentecost after the resurrection of Christ, and that water baptism to the penitent believer is for (to obtain) the remission of alien sins." (Rogers affirmed, Baker denied). Proposition 3: "The Scriptures teach that the Kingdom of Christ was established (or set up) on the first Pentecost after our Lord's resurrection, and that Christ now reigns on David's throne." (Rogers affirmed, Baker denied). Proposition 4: "The Scriptures teach that the Kingdom of Christ will be established (or set up) after the second Coming of Christ, and that He will reign for one thousand years on David's throne in Jerusalem." (Baker affirmed, Rogers denied). Book publication: *The Rogers-Baker Debate on Dispensationalism*. Tupelo, MS: L. D. Willis,

1954.

Ira Baker [Church of Christ]
Birth: _ (_, _)
Death: _ (_, _)
Ellis Lindsey (Church of Christ); Hoyte (near Cameron), TX; 1968; divorce & remarriage

Joe Baker [Church of Christ]
Birth: _ (_, _)
Death: _ (_, _)
_ Kostura (?); written. Question: "Was Darwin right?"

Laberton Haywood "Bud" Baker [Baptist Church]
Birth: October 9, 1855 (Berry, Fayette County, AL)
Death: July 29, 1916 (Fayette County, AL)
G. C. Brewer (Church of Christ); Liberty Hill, AL; 1906; establishment of church; Brewer's first debate

Robert Baker [Evolutionist]
Birth: 19_ (_, _)
Death: _ (_, _)
Duane T. Gish (Creationist) & Henry Morris (Creationist); Lubbock, TX; February 9, 1975; 2700; w/ Rae Harris (Evolutionist)

S. W. Baker [Church of Christ]
Birth: _ (_, _)
Death: _ (_, _)
L. H. Brown (Baptist Church); c 1940; immortality of soul; eternal punishment

Tom Baker [Church of Christ]
Birth: _ (_, _)
Death: _ (_, _)
Bill Hunt (Church of Christ); Phoenix, AZ; January 16-17, 19-20, 1961; church benevolence

William H. Baker, Jr. [Church of Christ]
Birth: May 30, 1915 (_, _)
Death: November 13, 2001 (_, _)
_ Smith (Church of Christ); near Coalgate, OK; c 1953; the "cup" in the Lord's supper

_ Balbin [Church of Christ]
Birth: 19_ (_, _)
Death: _ (_, _)
Cyrus Gesulga (Church of Christ); _, Philippines; October 1981; premillennialism.

Jim Balch [Baptist Church]
Birth: _ (_, _)
Death: _ (_, _)
H. F. Sharp, Sr. (Church of Christ); January 16-19, 1951
H. F. Sharp, Sr. (Church of Christ); Dyess, AR; May 15-18, 1951
H. F. Sharp, Sr. (Church of Christ); Damascus, AR; December 13-14, 1951
H. F. Sharp, Sr. (Church of Christ); Egypt, AR; c 1953
H. F. Sharp, Sr. (Church of Christ); Humphrey, AR

Benjamin Ulice Baldwin [Church of Christ]
Birth: September 21, 1890 (Granbury, TX)
Death: August 1974 (Sacramento, ?CA)
Biographical sketch: *Preachers of Today, Volume Two* (Batsell Barrett Baxter & M. Norval Young, eds.). Nashville, TN: The Gospel Advocate Company, 1959, p. 22.
Biographical sketch: *Preachers of Today, Volume Three* (Batsell Barrett Baxter & M. Norval Young, eds.). Nashville, TN: The Gospel Advocate Company, 1964, p. 19.
_ (Baptist Church); _, AR; 1933

Elizabeth Baldwin [Evolutionist]
Birth: _ (_, _)
Death: _ (_, _)
Duane T. Gish (Creationist); Kalamazoo. MI; October 29, 1975; 1500

William H. "Judge" Baldwin [Restoration Universalist]
Birth: c 1802 (_, _)
Death: November 19, 1852 (Blanchester, OH)
Biographical sketch: http://www25.uua.org/uuhs/duub/register/1864.html
Charles H. Parker (Baptist Church); c 1850. Subject: Do the Scriptures of the Old and New Testament teach the final forgiveness and salvation of all men, irrespective of their character during this life? Book publication: *A Debate between Rev. Charles H. Parker, Baptist, and Mr. William Baldwin, Restoration Universalist.*

_ Baldwin [?]
Birth: 18_ (_, _)
Death: 19_ (_, _)
Frank Strickland (Church of Christ); Center, AR; 1908

James David Bales [Church of Christ]
Birth: November 5, 1915 (Tacoma, WA)
Death: August 16, 1995 (Searcy, AR)
Autobiography: *Forty Two Years on the Firing Line* by James D. Bales. Shreveport, LA: Lambert Book House, Inc., n.d.

Biographical sketch: *Preachers of Today* (Batsell Barrett Baxter & M. Norval Young, eds.). Nashville, TN: The Christian Press, 1952, pp. 25-26.

Biographical sketch: *Preachers of Today, Volume Two* (Batsell Barrett Baxter & M. Norval Young, eds.). Nashville, TN: The Gospel Advocate Company, 1959, p. 22.

Biographical sketch: *Preachers of Today, Volume Three* (Batsell Barrett Baxter & M. Norval Young, eds.). Nashville, TN: The Gospel Advocate Company, 1964, p. 19.

Biographical sketch: http://www.encyclopediaofarkansas.net/encyclopedia/entry-detail.aspx?search=1&entryID=4724

Christian, Contend For Thy Cause by James D. Bales. Searcy, AR: Bales' Book Club, ?1949. A book about religious debating.

At least 8 written debates; about 20 debates by 1964

_ (?); Reno, NV; 1944

G. R. West (Sabbatarian); San Francisco, CA; 1944; Sabbath, Lord's day

_ Ballard (Baptist Church); 1947; faith, baptism, apostasy

P. W. Stonestreet (Church of Christ); written; c 1947; carnal warfare. Book publication: *Bales-Stonestreet Discussion on the Christian and Carnal Warfare: A Written Debate*. Searcy, AR: J. D. Bales, 1947.

F. P. Wortman (Atheist); inspiration of Bible

Kenneth Farnsworth (Church of Jesus Christ of Latter Day Saints);

T. B. Sharp (Church of Jesus Christ of Latter Day Saints); March 1948. Proposition; "Resolved: The Book of Mormon is of Divine Origin" (Sharp affirmed, Bales denied). Book publication: *The Bales-Sharp Debate*. _: _, 1949.

Woolsey Teller (Atheist); Searcy, AR; October 6-9, 1947. Book publication: *The Existence of God: A Debate*. ?Dallas, TX: Eugene S. Smith, ?1948.

Woolsey Teller (Atheist); Memphis, TN; May 23-27, 1949

Woolsey Teller (Atheist); c 1950

Burton W. Barber (Christian Church); written; 1950-1954. Proposition 1: "Resolved: That there is authority for the instrument in worship services, when it is used to aid singers." (Barber affirmed, Bales denied). Proposition 2; "Resolved: That the authority allowing song books, tuning forks, pitch pipes, communion cups and trays, and collection baskets in worship services, when used as aids, does not permit the instrument in worship services when it is used as an aid." (Bales affirmed, Barber denied). Book publication: *The Bales-Barber Debate*. _: Bales Bookstore, 1964.

F. P. Wortman (Atheist); Albany, GA; June 6-8, 1952; naturalism

Woolsey Teller (Atheist); Charleston, WV; June 18-21, 1952; atheistic naturalism, Bible; their 4th debate

William V. Ischie, Jr. (?); Philadelphia, PA; 1956

Bhikkhu Upaya (Buddhist); written; 1958. Proposition: "The teachings of Gautama Buddah are more noble than the teachings of Jesus of Nazareth." (Upaya affirmed, Bales denied). Book publication: *The Upaya-Bales Debate*. 1958.

William S. Thurman (?); Dallas, TX; December 20-22, 1958; premillennialism
William S. Thurman (?); written; 1959-1972. Book publication: *Thurman-Bales Debate on Instrumental Music*. _: Bales Bookstore, _.
H. Brent Davis (Atheist); Little Rock, AR; June 28-30, 1966; creation, evolution, Bible
Carl Sagan & Ernan McMullin (1st night), R. C. Lewontin & Thomas K. Shotwell (2nd night); Little Rock, AR; June 28-29, 1966; creation & evolution; w/ Jack Wood Sears
O. Boyd Mathias (?); Stockton, CA; May 22-23, 1969; evolution
H. B. Dodd (?); Orange, TX; 1969
Arvin Schmid (?); 1949; contribution of Christianity to society. Book publication:
Jerry Moffitt (Church of Christ); written; c 1982. Proposition: "Resolved: The Bible teaches that 'if the unbelieving departeth' the believer is released from the marriage bondage and is free to remarry." (Bales affirmed, Moffitt denied). Periodical publication: Bales-Moffitt Debate. *Thrust,* III: 3 (Austin, TX: Southwest Church of Christ, 1982).
_ Jackson (?); written; c 1986; divorce & remarriage. Book publication:
Roy Deaver (Church of Christ); written; c 1988; amenability. Book publication: *Bales-Deaver Debate.*
E. H. Miller (Church of Christ)

Calvert Lafayette Ballard [Methodist Church]

Birth: September 7, 1854 (Marshall Co., MS)
Death: November 28, 1910 (Sherman, Grayson Co., TX)
J. D. Tant (Church of Christ); Copper, TX; January 1896
Joe S. Warlick (Church of Christ)
C. R. Nichol (Church of Christ)
C. R. Nichol (Church of Christ); Dunn, TX
C. R. Nichol (Church of Christ); Fargo, TX
C. R. Nichol (Church of Christ); Lometa, TX; 1907
C. R. Nichol (Church of Christ); infant baptism. Book publication: *Debate on Infant Baptism.* Clifton, TX: Mrs. C. R. Nichol, _.
C. R. Nichol (Church of Christ)
Allen Booker Barret (Church of Christ); Barret's first debate

James W. Ballard [Church of Christ]

Birth: October 24, 1875 (near Athens, Henderson Co., TX)
Death: May 30, 1959 (_, _)
Biographical sketch: *Gospel Preachers Who Blazed The Trail* by C. R. Nichol. Austin, TX: Firm Foundation Publishing House, n.d.
Many debates
_ McTues (Methodist Church); Sulphur, OK; July 6-11, 1914; sprinkling or pouring water upon a proper subject was the

apostolic mode of baptism; an alien sinner is saved by faith alone; immersion is apostolic mode of baptism.
James T. Bagby (Methodist Church); October 15-__, 1919

Louis Samuel "L.S. or Sam" Ballard [Missionary Baptist Church]
Birth: October 23, 1881 (Cabool, Texas Co., MO)
Death: January 12, 1962 (Hot Springs, AR)
Obituary: https://www.findagrave.com/memorial/ 5380433/louis-samuel-ballard
W. P. Clark (Methodist Church), Traskwood, _; before   1914
E. M. Borden (Church of Christ); Salem, AR; 1913
E. M. Borden (Church of Christ); Little Rock, AR; March 3- 8, 1914; 6 sessions. Proposition 1: "The Scriptures teach that faith in Christ procures salvation without further acts of obedience." (Ballard affirmed, Borden denied). Proposition 2: "The Scriptures teach that water baptism is for (in order to) remission of past sins." (Borden affirmed, Ballard denied). Book publication: *The Ballard-Borden Debate*.
C. R. Nichol (Church of Christ); Nancy, TX; 1927
C. R. Nichol (Church of Christ); Summerfield, TX; 1928
J. W. Chism (Church of Christ); Dallas, TX; 1933
Flavil L. Colley (Church of Christ); 1933
Flavil L. Colley (Church of Christ); Dallas, TX; 1934
Logan Buchanan (Church of Christ); 1935; baptism, apostasy
W. R. Yowell (Church of Christ); Blue Ridge, TX; 1938
John W. Hedge (Church of Christ); Greggton, TX; 1938
John W. Hedge (Church of Christ); White Oak, TX; 1938
Joe H. Blue (Church of Christ); Harmony, AR
Carl S. Stephens (Church of Christ). Proposition: "That tithing, paying one tenth of the income, was a part of the Mosaic Law, and was done away when the Law was done away." (Stephens affirmed, Ballard denied). Book publication: *Great Discussion on Tithing*.
Eugene S. Smith (Church of Christ); Dallas, TX; November 24-27, 1942. Proposition 1: "The Scriptures teach that faith in Christ procures salvation without further acts of obedience." (Ballard affirmed, Smith denied). Proposition 2: "The Scriptures teach that water is for, in order to obtain, the remission of past sins." (Smith affirmed, Ballard denied). Book publication: *Smith-Ballard Debate*. Dallas, TX: Gospel Broadcast, n.d.
James D. Bales (Missionary Baptist Church); 1947; faith, baptism, apostasy
E. C. Fuqua (Church of Christ); written; Baptist Church. Periodical publication: *The Vindicator*. Book publication: *Fuqua-Ballard Debate*
J. L. Hines (Church of Christ); Dallas, TX; February 26-29, 1952; apostasy, salvation
Thomas B. Warren (Church of Christ); Ft. Worth, TX; July 23-26, 1952. Proposition 1: "The Scriptures teach that faith in Christ procures salvation

without further acts of obedience." (Ballard affirmed, Warren denied). Proposition 2: "The Scriptures teach that water baptism is for (in order to obtain) the remission of past sins." (Warren affirmed, Ballard denied). Book publication: *Warren-Ballard Debate*. Longview, WA: Telegram Book Company, 1953.

W. Curtis Porter (Church of Christ); Lufkin, TX; December 10-_, 1957; baptism, apostasy; 4 sessions

Paul Dempsey Ballard [Baptist Church]

Birth: May 5, 1926 (Sycamore community, _)
Death: ?December 26, 1998 (Sallisaw, Sequoyah County, OK)

W. Curtis Porter (Church of Christ); Portales, NM; July 7-10, 1959; baptism, apostasy; 4 sessions

G. E. Jones (Baptist Church); written. Proposition 1: "The Bible teaches us one future judgment of all men, saved & unsaved, for all will he judge in the judgment." (Ballard affirmed, Jones denied). Proposition 2: "I affirm that the Bible teaches that there will be two distinct events in the 2nd advent of Christ first when he comes in the air to raise the dead in Christ, those sleeping in their graves at that time, and to translate the living saints, and second He shall come all the way back to this earth for the purpose of reigning on this earth 1000 years with His glorified saints, at which time Israel will be re-established in Canaan land." (Jones affirmed, Ballard denied). Book publication: *A Written Scriptural Discussion*. No publication data.

James P. Lusby (Church of Christ)

Jimmy Thomas (Church of Christ); Columbia, TN; September 1964

John W. Wilson (Church of Christ); Oroville, CA; October 1965

Thomas G. O'Neal (Church of Christ); Murfreesboro, TN; June 13-14, 16-17, 1966; 4 sessions; tent debate. Proposition 1: "The Scriptures teach that baptism in water is for (in order to obtain) remission of sins." (O'Neal affirmed, Ballard denied). Proposition 2: "The Scriptures teach that a child of God (one washed in the blood of Christ) cannot so sin as to be finally lost in hell." (Ballard affirmed, O'Neal denied).

Billy Ashworth (Church of Christ);

Billy Ashworth (Church of Christ); Fairview, TN; October 1966

Thomas G. O'Neal (Church of Christ); Murfreesboro, TN; May 15-16, 18-19, 1967; depravity, operation of Spirit, establishment of church

Thomas G. O'Neal (Church of Christ); Lindsey, OK; July 17-18, 20-21, 1967; baptism, apostasy

Jesse Whitlock (Church of Christ); Blanchard, OK; April 29-30, 1985. Proposition: "The Scriptures teach that a born again child of God, one redeemed by the blood of Christ, cannot sin and be lost in hell." (Ballard affirmed, Whitlock denied).

Reginald Rogers (church of Christ); _, OK. Proposition: "Water baptism is for, in order to obtain, remission of sins." (Rogers affirmed, Ballard denied). Book publication: *Ballard-Rogers Debate on Water Baptism*. _, _: _, 1996.

T. E. Ballard [Universalist Society]
Birth: 18_ (_, _)
Death: _ (_, _)
John R. Daily (Primitive Baptist Church); Carroll County, IN; May 31-June 3, 1898. Book publication.

Voyd N. Ballard [Church of Christ]
Birth: December 1, 1919 (_, _)
Death: August 1, 2003 (_, _)
M. J. Duncan (Baptist Church); Woodville, CA; November 30-December 3, 1953
Don Rudd (Church of Christ); Ventura, CA; March 11-14, 1957; Herald of Truth, orphan homes
Lyle McCollum (Church of Christ); Shafter, CA; March 23-26, 1959; Herald of Truth, orphan homes
A. A. Harris (Baptist Church); Atwater, CA; August 18-21, 1969
Lee Wright (Baptist Church); Atwater, CA; 1970
J. T. Smith (Church of Christ); Grants Pass, OR; May 17-20, 1982; classes & women teachers, drinking vessels in Lord's supper
Bob Strom (?); written. Proposition 1: "The Scriptures teach that water baptism to a believing penitent is for the remission of his sins." (Ballard affirmed, Strom denied). Proposition 2: "The Scriptures teach that obedience is from the inside out. We are first changed in the inner man via the new birth and then the outward 'good fruit' of obedience including Baptism results. Thus we are born-again/saved/forgiven at the moment we confess our sins and accept Christ as our savior – believing in Him as our Savior is the moment of salvation." (Strom affirmed, Ballard denied). Web publication.

Wesley Dair Ballard [Church of Christ]
Birth: March 18, 1918 (_, _)
Death: October 31, 1998 (_, ?TX)
Thomas B. Warren (Church of Christ); Dallas, TX; November 9-12, 1953; classes & women teachers

_ Ballard [?]
Birth: _ (_, _)
Death: _ (_, _)
Harold C. Thurman (Church of Christ); 1953

_ Ballard [?]
Birth: 19_ (_, _)
Death: _ (_, _)
_ Clayton (?); November 18-19, 1991

_ Ballard [?]
Birth: _ (_, _)
Death: _ (_, _)

_ Stephens (?)

Eli Ballou [Universalist Society]
Birth: December 1, 1808 (Leroy, NY)
Death: March 12, 1883 (_, ?VT)
Luther Lee (?); c 1857. Subject: Do the Scriptures teach that any part or portion of Mankind will be Endlessly Punished for Sins committed in this life? Book publication: *A Discussion on the doctrine of Endless Punishment*. Montpelier, _. 1857.

Hosea Ballou [?Universalist]
Birth: 18_ (_, _)
Death: _ (_, _)
Edward Turner (?Universalist); 1817-1818; newspaper debate; *Boston Kaleidoscope*.

Richard Bambach [Evolutionist]
Birth: 19_ (_, _)
Death: _ (_, _)
Henry M. Morris (Creationist); Blacksburg, VA; November 8, 1975; 1100

James Madison Bandy [Baptist Church]
Birth: April 26, 1864 (Carrol County, AR)
Death: February 25, 1949 (Sarcoxie, MO)
Claud F. Witty (Church of Christ); Nebo, IL; 1904
H. E. Moler (Reorganized Church of Jesus Christ of Latter Day Saints); Twelve Corners, MO; July 1918; general church; 4 days
Joe S. Warlick (Church of Christ)

John Hugh Banister [Church of Christ]
Birth: April 20, 1910 (Thalia, TX)
Death: April 29, 1995 (_, _)
Biographical sketch: *Preachers of Today* (Batsell Barrett Baxter & M. Norval Young, eds.). Nashville, TN: The Christian Press, 1952, p. 26.
Biographical sketch: *Preachers of Today, Volume Four* (Batsell Barrett Baxter & M. Norval Young, eds.). Nashville, TN: The Gospel Advocate Company, 1970, p. 16.
_ (Adventist Church); 1939
_ (Adventist Church); 1940
_ (Jehovah's Witnesses); 1941

Walter Elston Bankes [Church of Christ]
Birth: May 19, 1901 (Malta, OH)
Death: September 1986 (_, _)
Biographical sketch: *Preachers of Today* (Batsell Barrett Baxter

& M. Norval Young, eds.). Nashville, TN: The Christian Press, 1952, pp. 27-28.
Biographical sketch: *Preachers of Today, Volume Two* (Batsell Barrett Baxter & M. Norval Young, eds.). Nashville, TN: The Gospel Advocate Company, 1959, p. 24.
Biographical sketch: *Preachers of Today, Volume Three* (Batsell Barrett Baxter & M. Norval Young, eds.). Nashville, TN: The Gospel Advocate Company, 1964, p. 21.
_ (Catholic Church); 1940. Proposition: "The Catholic Church is not the church of the New Testament." (Bankes affirmed, _ denied).
_ (Jehovah's Witnesses); before 1959
_ Bachus (Church of God); 1943. Proposition: "Baptism of the Holy Spirit is not in force today." (Bankes affirmed, Bachus denied).

Thomas Raymond Bankhead [Church of Christ]
Birth: April 16, 1904 (Oglesby, TX)
Death: May 16, 1995 (_, TX)
Biographical sketch: *Preachers of Today, Volume Two* (Batsell Barrett Baxter & M. Norval Young, eds.). Nashville, TN: The Gospel Advocate Company, 1959, p. 24.
2 debates

Joe Lawrence Banks [Church of Christ]
Birth: September 1, 1920 (Casville, MO)
Death: March 1986 (_, _)
Biographical sketch: *Preachers of Today* (Batsell Barrett Baxter & M. Norval Young, eds.). Nashville, TN: The Christian Press, 1952, p. 28.
Biographical sketch: *Preachers of Today, Volume Two* (Batsell Barrett Baxter & M. Norval Young, eds.). Nashville, TN: The Gospel Advocate Company, 1959, p. 25.
_ Hartenberger (Lutheran Church); 1950; baptism
Kermit Lynch (Church of Christ); classes; before 1959
Ralph Gage (Church of Christ) & Kermit Lynch (Church of Christ); Fayetteville, AR; December 5-9, 1955; classes & women teachers; w/ F. I. Stanley (Church of Christ)

John Milton Banks [Church of Christ]
Birth: October 4, 1922 (Altus, OK)
Death: September 7, 2007 (_, _)
Biographical sketch: *Preachers of Today, Volume Two* (Batsell Barrett Baxter & M. Norval Young, eds.). Nashville, TN: The Gospel Advocate Company, 1959, p. 25.
Biographical sketch: *Preachers of Today, Volume Four* (Batsell Barrett Baxter & M. Norval Young, eds.).

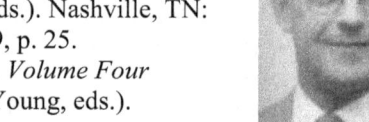

Nashville, TN: The Gospel Advocate Company, 1970, pp. 16-17.
J. I. Easterly (Seventh Day Baptist Church); 1952
_ (?); evolution; before 1970
_ (?); race; before 1970

John Thomas Banks [Methodist Church]
Birth: March 16, 1875 (Clay, Webster County, KY)
Death: October 25, 1947 (near Chic, _)
A. G. Freed (Church of Christ)
A. G. Freed (Church of Christ); Old Harmony, TN; 1923

R. T. Banks [Baptist Church]
Birth: _ (_, _)
Death: _ (_, _)
H. T. Wilson (Church of Christ); Pickensville, AL

_ Banks [?]
Birth: _ (_, _)
Death: _ (_, _)
J. D. Tant (Church of Christ)

William Slater Banowsky [Church of Christ]
Birth: March 4, 1936 (Abilene, TX)
Death: April 28, 2019 (_, _)
Biographical sketch: *Preachers of Today, Volume Two* (Batsell Barrett Baxter & M. Norval Young, eds.). Nashville, TN: The Gospel Advocate Company, 1959, p. 25.
Biographical sketch: *Preachers of Today, Volume Three* (Batsell Barrett Baxter & M. Norval Young, eds.). Nashville, TN: The Gospel Advocate Company, 1964, pp. 21-22.
Biographical sketch: *Preachers of Today, Volume Four* (Batsell Barrett Baxter & M. Norval Young, eds.). Nashville, TN: The Gospel Advocate Company, 1970, p. 17.
Obituary: https://www.dignitymemorial.com/obituaries/colleyville-tx/william-banowsky-8268246
Anson Mount (?);1967; televised debate
James A. Pike (Episcopal Church); Santa Barbara, CA; January 3, 1969; morality. Periodical publication: "Sex and Morality: A Confrontation." Nashville, TN: 20th Century Christian, n.d.
Joseph Fletcher (?Episcopal Church); Ball State University, IN; April 21, 1969; situation ethics; 1 session; 2000. Periodical publication: "The Fletcher-Banowsky Debate." *20th Century Christian*, volume 31, number 10 (July 1969).

Benjamin (?H.) Banta [Evolutionist]
Birth: ?January 2, 1927 (_, _)

Death: ?June 26, 1999 (_, _)
Duane T. Gish (Creationist) & Henry M. Morris (Creationist); San Diego, CA; April 7, 1976; 1400; w/ Hale Wedberg (Evolutionist)

_ Banta [Christadelphian]
Birth: 18_ (_, _)
Death: _ (_, _)
J. A. Currie, Jr. (Reorganized Church of Jesus Christ of Latter Day Saints); Bandera County, TX; January 18-_, 1889; the breath of man is the spirit and the only spirit of man, and the breath and body are soul; 10 sessions

H. D. Banteau [Church of Christ]
Birth: 18_ (_, _)
Death: _ (_, _)
W. A. Jarrel (Baptist Church); Millsap, TX; January, 1883; 6 days

David Bantz [Evolutionist]
Birth: 19_ (_, _)
Death: _ (_, _)
Duane T. Gish (Creationist); Racine, WI; June 18, 1982; 800

N. Barbanell [Spiritualist National Union]
Birth: _ (_, _)
Death: _ (_, _)

Al "Pee Wee" Barber [House of Prayer for All Nations]
Birth: 19_ (_, _)
Death: _ (_, _)
Bob Myhan (Church of Christ); Cleveland, TN; 1978

Burton Willard Barber [Christian Church]
Birth: September 16, 1918 (Sheridan, WY)
Death: January 8, 1996 (Galax, VA)
Robert R. Price (Church of Christ); San Jose, CA; 1944
Robert R. Price (Church of Christ); 1944
Rue Porter (Church of Christ)
Guy N. Woods (Church of Christ)
Will Thompson (Church of Christ)
Ira Rice (Church of Christ)
Carl Ketcherside (Church of Christ)
Roy F. Osborne, Jr. (Church of Christ); Hutchinson, KS; 1948
G. K. Wallace (Church of Christ); Cedar Rapids, IA; November 13-18, 1950; 6 sessions. Proposition 1: "That I can use song books communion sets, tuning fork, and collection plates as aids in Christian worship with authority, and that the same authority excludes the use of instrumental music in said Christian worship." (Wallace affirmed, Barber denied). Proposition 2: "That instrumental music aids the individual to sing, and that he has authority to so use it in Christian worship service." (Barber affirmed, Wallace denied).

Book publication: *Wallace-Barber Debate*. Abilene, TX: Beacon Publications, 1953.

James D. Bales (Church of Christ); written; 1950-1954. Proposition 1: "Resolved: That there is authority for the instrument in worship services, when it is used to aid singers." (Barber affirmed, Bales denied). Proposition 2; "Resolved: That the authority allowing song books, tuning forks, pitch pipes, communion cups and trays, and collection baskets in worship services, when used as aids, does not permit the instrument in worship services when it is used as an aid." (Bales affirmed, Barber denied). Book publication: *The Bales-Barber Debate.* _: Bales Bookstore, 1964.

Guthrie Dean (Church of Christ); 1952; instrumental music in worship

J. W. Barber [?]
Birth: _ (_, _)
Death: _ (_, _)
R. L. Colley (Church of Christ)
R. L. Colley (Church of Christ)

Paul Barber [Church of Christ]
Birth: 19_ (_, _)
Death: _ (_, _)
James White (Reformed Baptist Church); predestination and election

Thomas Barber [?]
Birth: _ (_, _)
Death: _ (_, _)

William C. Barber [Baptist Church]
Birth: _ (_, _)
Death: _ (_, _)
?Orland W. Rury (Church of Christ); Arlington & Grand Prairie, TX; May 16-17, 19-20, 1955; baptism, faith only

James Hughes Barger [Methodist Episcopal Church]
Birth: June 29, 1831 (_, KY)
Death: October 31, 1861 (near Quincy, IL)
Walter P. Bowles (Church of Christ); DeWitt County, IL; 1840's

Daniel Edwin "Dan" Barker [Atheist]
Birth: June 25, 1949 (Santa Monica, CA)
Death: _ (_, _)
Michael Horner (Believer); Cedar Falls, IA; c 1992. Subject: Does God exist?
Michael Horner (Believer); Cedar Falls, IA; April 2, 1996; 1 session; 450. Subject: Did Jesus really rise from the dead? Web publication: http://www.ffrf.org/debates/barker_horner.html
Richard Howe (Theist); Gainesville, FL; 1997. Subject: Does

God exist?
Douglas Wilson (Evangelical); Newark, DE; March 11, 1997; 1 session. Proposition: "Resolved: The triune God of Scripture lives."
Rubel Shelly (Church of Christ); Birmingham, AL; 1998. Subject: Does God exist?
Tom Rode (Theist); Columbus, OH; 1999. Subject: Does God exist?
Phil Fernandes (Theist); Bellevue Community College; 2000. Subject: Does God exist?
Mike Licona (Believer); Madison, WI; April 2003. Topic: Did Jesus Rise from the Dead?
Hassanain Rajabali (?) & Michael Corey (?); Dearborn, MI; May 2004; w/ Richard Carrier (Atheist). Subject: Does God not exist.
James White (Reformed Baptist Church); Phoenix, AZ; radio debate
Jason Gastrich (Believer). Web audio: http://www.freethoughtpedia.com/wiki/Dan_Barker_vs._Jason_Gastrich
Peter Payne (?); Madison, WI; 2005. Subject: Does ethics require God?
Janet Parshall (?); February 25, 2005
_ (?); Stevens Point, WI; March 2005. Subject: Does ethics require God?
_ (?); Moscow, ID; October 18, 2005; 800
Todd Friel (Believer); University of Minnesota; 2006; radio. Subject: Does God exist?
John Rankin (?); Plymouth, MA; 2006. Subject: Evolution and Intelligent Design—What are the issues?
_ (?); _, MN; 2006
_ (?); _, AR; 2006
_ (?); _, CT; 2006
_ (?); _, WI; 2006
_ (?); _, OH; 2006
_ (?); 2006
_ (?); 2006
_ (?); 2006
_ (?); 2006
_ (?); 2006
_ (Roman Catholic Church); _, OH; 2007
Richard Swinburne (Theist); Dublin, Ireland; 2007
Dinesh D'Souza (Theist); Harvard University; 2008
_ (?); Tufts University; 2008
_ (?); 2008
_ (?); 2008
Kyle Butt (Church of Christ); Columbia, SC; February 12, 2009; 1 session; existence of God; 550. Book publication:
Mark Chavalas (?); LaCrosse, WI; 2009. Subject: The Bible: Fact or fiction?
Dan Waugh (?); Indiana University; 2009. Subject: Can we be good without God?
Dinesh D'Souza (Theist); _, TX; 2009. Subject: Good without God

_ (?); 2009
_ (?); 2009
_ (?); 2009
_ (?); 2009
_ (?); 2009
_ (?); 2009
_ (?); 2009
_ (?); 2009
_ (?); 2009
George Pell (Roman Catholic Church); Sydney, Australia; 2010
Dinesh D'Souza (Theist); 2010
Mat Staver (Theist); 2010
_ (?); 2010
_ (?); 2010
_ (?); 2010
_ (Muslim); 2011
_ (Muslim); 2011
_ (?); 2011
_ (?); 2011
_ (?); 2011
_ (?); 2011
_ (?); 2011
_ (?); 2011
_ (?); 2011
_ (?); 2011
_ (?); 2011
_ (?); 2012
_ (?); 2012
_ (?); 2012
Peter Kitchens (Theist); Oxford, England, November 8, 2012
Jay Richards (Roman Catholic Church); Tempe, AZ; March 26, 2015. Topic: "Resolved: Religion is Bad for America"

J. D. Barker [?]
Birth: _ (_, _)
Death: _ (_, _)
N. L. Clark (Church of Christ); 1929; eternal punishment. Periodical publication:

James Barker [?]
Birth: 19_ (_, _)
Death: _ (_, _)
James White (Reformed Baptist Church). Subjects: the will of man, limited atonement

Joseph Barker [Freethinker, Methodist Church]
Birth: May 11, 1806 (Bramley, Yorkshire, England)
Death: September 15, 1875 (Omaha, NE)
Autobiography: Barker, Joseph. (1880). *Life of Joseph Barker*. London:_.
Biographical sketch: "Joseph Barker," *Biographies of Ancient and Modern Celebrated Freethinkers* by "Iconoclast," Collins, & Watts. New York: Peter Eckler, pp. 369-387.
Biographical sketch: http://en.wikipedia.org/wiki/Joseph_Barker_(minister)
William Cooke (Methodist Church); Newcastle, England; August 19-22, 26-28, September 2-4, 1845; atonement, Trinity, natural depravity, eternal torments, what is a Christian. Book publication: *Barker-Cooke Debate*. London, England: J. Chapman, 1845.
Jonas Hartzel (Church of Christ); July 1853. Book publication: *A Defense of the Bible Against the Charges of Modern Infidelity*. Cincinnati, OH: Columbian Printing Co. (printer), 1854.
_ McCalla (Presbyterian Church); Philadelphia, PA; December 1853; 5 nights.
J. F. Berg (?Presbyterian Church); ?Philadelphia, PA; January 9-10, 12-13, 16-19, 1854; 8 sessions; 2000-2500. Book publication: *Great Discussion on the Origin, Authority and Tendency of the Bible, between Rev. J. F. Berg, D.D. of Philadelphia and Joseph Barker of Ohio (Debate of 8 nights duration)*. Boston, MA: J. B. Yerrinton & Son, Printers, 1854.
Brewin Grant (?); Halifax, _; 1855; 10 nights. Book publication: *Report of a Public Discussion between Joseph Barker, Esq., and the Rev. Brewin Grant, B. A.* Glasgow, _: Robert Stark, 1855. [Book includes *Mormonism Unveiled, being a Narrative of a Residence in Illinois in 1844, 1845 and 1846* by Ralph Liddle]

Ted C. Barker [Baptist Church]
Birth: 19_ (_, _)
Death: _ (_, _)
David West (Church of Christ); ?Orlando, FL; August 1-2, 8-9, 1975

W. Barker [?]
Birth: _ (_, _)
Death: _ (_, _)
Charles Bradlaugh (Atheist) Book publication: *Modern Atheism and the Bible: Report of the Discussion between the Rev. W. Barker ... and Iconoclast ...* 1862.

_ Barker [?]
Birth: _ (_, _)
Death: _ (_, _)
_ Clark (?)

Darryl L. Barksdale [?Church of Jesus Christ of Latter Day Saints]
Birth: 19_ (_, _)
Death: _ (_, _)

James White (Reformed Baptist Church)

P. O. Barnard [Christadelphian]
Birth: _ (_, _)
Death: _ (_, _)
Rodney Wald (Church of Christ); Windsor & Parrametta, N.S.W., Australia; March 4-5, 18-19, 1957; immortality of soul, premillennialism

Robert Barnes [Holiness Church]
Birth: _ (_, _)
Death: _ (_, _)
W. L. Totty (Church of Christ); E. Liverpool, OH; June 28-29, _; healing

_ Barnes [Sabbatarian]
Birth: _ (_, _)
Death: _ (_, _)
Ector R. Watson (Church of Christ); 1947; the two covenants, Sabbath, Lord's day

D. N. Barnett [Church of Christ]
Birth: 18_ (_, _)
Death: 19_ (_, _)
J. R. McLain (Church of Jesus Christ of Latter Day Saints); Massac County, IL; 1911

Maurice Barnett [Church of Christ]
Birth: 19_ (_, _)
Death: _ (_, _)
Philip F. Lydic (Church of Christ); written; 1962; divorce and remarriage. Book publication: *Lydic-Barnett: A Debate on Divorce and Remarriage*.
David Harkrider (Church of Christ); written; Lord's supper. Periodical publication: *Gospel Anchor*, starting December 1981
Jeff Smelser (Church of Christ); written; 2003-2004; Mark 10:11-12. Periodical publication: *Gospel Truths*. Web publication.
_ Watts (Church of Christ); written. Proposition: "The Scriptures teach that in the context of a lawful marriage there is only one lawful reason for divorce." (Watts affirmed, Barnett denied). Periodical publication: *Preceptor*.

_ Barnett [?]
Birth: _ (_, _)
Death: _ (_, _)
_ Cheatham (?)

_ Barnett [?]
Birth: _ (_, _)
Death: _ (_, _)
_ Little (?)

Joe E. Barnhart [Philosopher]
Birth; 19_ (_, _)
Death: _ (_, _)
Thomas B. Warren (Church of Christ); Denton, TX; November 3-6, 1980; ethics. Book publication: *The Warren-Barnhart Debate*. Jonesboro, AR: National Christian Press, Inc., 1981.

John Basil Barnhill [?]
Birth: 18_ (_, _)
Death: 19_ (_, _)
Henry M. Tichenor (Socialist); written; early 1900s; socialism. Book publication: *Written Debate on Socialism*.

Roger Baron [Church of Christ]
Birth: 19_ (_, _)
Death: _ (_, _)
Dwayne Dunning (Christian Church) & Kenny Boles (Christian Church); Bland, MO; August 1992; 3 nights; w/ Jerry D. McDonald (Church of Christ).

Edward Dean Barr [Christian Church]
Birth: January 21, 1906 (_, _)
Death: December 1974 (?Beaver, OK)
W. Clay Callaway (Church of Christ); Beaver, OK; February 1950; instrumental music in worship

Vernon Lee Barr [Missionary Baptist Church]
Birth: November 18, 1906 (Jacksonville, Cherokee Co., TX)
Death: December 3, 1982 (Dallas, Dallas Co., TX)
Participated in 56 debates
_ Weathersby (Pentecostal Church); Waco, TX; Barr's first debate
Kermit Upshaw (Church of Christ) & Logan Buchanan (Church of Christ); Healdton, OK; 1938
A. A. Harris (Baptist Church); near Fresno, CA
Gussie Lambert (Church of Christ); 1940; establishment of church, baptism, apostasy
Gussie Lambert (Church of Christ); Rush Springs, OK
Rue Porter (Church of Christ); Antlers, OK
Clyde Sloan (?); Walters, OK
Clyde Sloan (?); western OK
Van Bonneau (Church of Christ); _, OK
John O'Dowd (Church of Christ); written; 1946. Proposition: "Authentic history teaches that the church with which John O'Dowd stands identified, known to him and his brethren as the church of Christ, was organized in the year 1827 by Alexander Campbell." (Barr affirmed, O'Dowd denied). Periodical

publication: *The Rock of Ages* (Vernon L. Barr, Ed.) and *Sound Words* (John O'Dowd, Ed.).
John O'Dowd (Church of Christ); June 1946; Dallas, TX
John O'Dowd (Church of Christ); Dallas, TX
John O'Dowd (Church of Christ); Fort Worth, TX
John O'Dowd (Church of Christ)
John O'Dowd (Church of Christ)
John O'Dowd (Church of Christ)
Logan Buchanan (Church of Christ); Marietta, OK
_ Price (Church of Christ); Antioch, CA
Thomas G. Butler (Church of Christ); Lakeland, FL; May 30 - June 2, 1949; apostasy, baptism
Thomas G. Butler (Church of Christ); 1950; church
W. Curtis Porter (Church of Christ); Center, TX; September 12-_, 1950; 8 sessions
H. C. McCaghren (Church of Christ); Dallas, TX
J. Cullis Smith (Baptist Church); Henderson, TX; c 1952. Proposition: "The Missionary Baptist Association of Texas is scriptural in doctrine and practice." (Barr affirmed, Smith denied). Book publication: *Barr-Smith Debate*. Lufkin, TX: The Celtic Cross, 1992 reprint.
W. Curtis Porter (Church of Christ); Pensacola, FL; February 19-24; 1952; Church of Christ, baptism; 6 sessions
John W. Wilson (Church of Christ);
John W. Wilson (Church of Christ); Long Beach, CA; January 26-29, 1953; their 2nd debate
Wilson M. Coon (Church of Christ); Dallas, TX
Wilson M. Coon (Church of Christ);
W. Curtis Porter (Church of Christ); Boliver, TN; October 1953
W. Curtis Porter (Church of Christ); Amory, MS; October 27-30, 1953
Bill L. Rogers (Church of Christ); Corinth, MS; September 14-17, 1954
Guy N. Woods (Church of Christ); Mountain View, OK
Guy N. Woods (Church of Christ); _, AL
A. C. Grider (Church of Christ); Somerset, KY; May 29 - June 1, 1956; baptism, apostasy
W. Curtis Porter (Church of Christ); McGhee, AR; November 6-9, 1956; apostasy; their last debate
Bill L. Rogers (Church of Christ); Sheffield, AL; September 23-26, 1958. Proposition 1: "The Scriptures teach that alien sinners are saved at the point of faith before and without water baptism." (Barr affirmed, Rogers denied). Proposition 2: "The Scriptures teach that water baptism, to the penitent believer, is for (to obtain) the remission of alien sins." (Rogers affirmed, Barr denied). Book publication: *The Famous Alabama Debate on The Plan of Salvation*. Dallas, TX: Vernon L. Barr, n.d.
Jack L. Holt (Church of Christ); Grand Prairie, TX; March & May 1965
Jack L. Holt (Church of Christ); Lewisville, TX

Elmer Moore (Church of Christ); Center, TX; August 1966
Charles A. Holt (Church of Christ); Mt. Pleasant, TX
Charles A. Holt (Church of Christ); Lufkin, TX; November 28-29, 1966
Charles A. Holt (Church of Christ); Borger, TX
Charles A. Holt (Church of Christ); Columbia, TN
Ward Hogland (Church of Christ); Greenville, TX; March 1968
Thomas N. Thrasher (Church of Christ); written; September 21, 1971 – March 6, 1973. Proposition 1: "The Missionary Baptist Church, of which I am a member, is scriptural in origin, doctrine, and practice." (Barr affirmed, Thrasher denied). Proposition 2: "The church of Christ, of which I am a member, is scriptural in origin, doctrine, and practice." (Thrasher affirmed, Barr denied). Book publication: *Thrasher-Barr Debate*. Decatur, AL: Gospel Defender Publishing Co., 1973. Book publication: *Thrasher-Barr Debate*. Decatur, AL: Thrasher Publications, 2000.
Jack Evans (Church of Christ); Dallas, TX; July 8-9, 11-12, 1974; establishment of church, Missionary Baptist Church, salvation. Book publication: *Evans-Barr Debate*. Terrell, TX: Southwestern Christian College, c 1974.
Jack Evans (Church of Christ); Terrell, TX; November 24-25, 1975; John the Baptist was not a Christian, racial intermarriage. Book publication: *The Curing of Ham*. DeQueen, AR: Harrywell Printers, 1976. Note: Only the second proposition (racial intermarriage) was published in this book.
Keith Sharp (Church of Christ); Piggott, AR; May 31, June 1, 3-4, 1982. Proposition 1: "Resolved: The Scriptures teach that the sinner is saved by repentance and faith before and without water baptism." (Barr affirmed, Sharp denied). Proposition 2: "Resolved: The Scriptures teach that the Kingdom of Christ of Old Testament promise and prophecy is the church of Christ, is spiritual in its nature and was established on the first Pentecost after Jesus' resurrection from the dead." (Sharp affirmed, Barr denied).

_ Barr [?]
Birth: _ (_, _)
Death: _ (_, _)
Possibly E. Dean Barr
L. O. Sanderson (Church of Christ); written; *psallo* & instrumental music in worship

Allen Booker Barret [Church of Christ]
Birth: July 15, 1879 (near Covington, Tipton County, TN)
Death: 1951 (_, ?TN)
Biographical sketch: *Gospel Preachers Who Blazed The Trail* by C. R. Nichol. Austin, TX: Firm Foundation Publishing House, n.d.
Biographical sketch: *The Shattered Chain, or Baptist Theory of Succession of Churches and Doctrines Broken to Shivers* by A. B. Barret. Henderson, TN: n.p., 1942-43.
More than 15 oral debates and several written debates

C. L. Ballard (Methodist Church); Barret's 1st debate
_ Garland (Methodist Church); near Paducah, Livingston Co., KY; c April 1907; sanctification is a second blessing obtained by a baptism of the Holy Spirit in answer to prayer; sanctification is a cleansing from sin received after justification.
J. C. Mason (Christian Church); Mt. Vernon, TX; July 9-11, 1907. Proposition: "The Texas Christian Missionary Society Convention, with its executive committee, is working in harmony with the New Testament." (Mason affirmed, Barret denied).
G. S. Raburn (Missionary Baptist Church);
G. S. Raburn (Missionary Baptist Church); Center Point, MS;
Allen Hill Autry (Baptist Church); Bunger, Young Co., TX; July 31-August 5, 1913; general church propositions
Jesse Neal (Missionary Baptist Church); Almo, KY; October 30-November 2, 1917
C. B. "Cap" Massey (Baptist Church); Bowling Green, KY; 8 nights
J. N. Cowan (Church of Christ);
?J. H. Johnson (?); Sheffield, AL; 1927
G. S. Raburn (Missionary Baptist Church); Centreville, MS; November 5-8, 1935; general church propositions

Lionel Barrett [?]
Birth: _ (_, _)
Death: _ (_, _)
_ (?); _, TN; c 1973
George W. DeHoff, Sr. (Church of Christ); Murfreesboro, TN; October 21, 1975; legalizing marijuana; 400. Book publication: *The Great Marijuana Debate: Shall We Legalize and Decriminalize?* Murfreesboro, TN: DeHoff Publications, 1983.

Cyrille Barrette [Evolutionist]
Birth: 19_ (_, _)
Death: _ (_, _)
Duane T. Gish (Creationist); before February 1999
Laurence Tisdall (Creationist); Laval University, Quebec; February 10, 1999; origin of life; 400

Ron Barrier [Atheist]
Birth: 19_ (_, _)
Death: _ (_, _)
Ray Comfort (?); Orlando, FL; 2001

Shute Barrington [Church of England]
Birth: May 26, 1734 (Beckett Hall, Berkshire, Great Britain)
Death: March 25, 1826 (Soho, Middlesex, United Kingdom)
Biographical sketch:
https://en.wikipedia.org/wiki/Shute_Barrington

John Barron [Believer]
Birth: _ (_, _)
Death: _ (_, _)
Justin Schieber (Atheist). Topic: Is abortion murder?

Charles Bartlett [Church of Christ]
Birth: October 20, 1960 (_, _)
Death: _ (_, _)
Ted Hoogsteen (Canadian Reformed Church); Jordan, Ontario, Canada; February 10, 17, 1995; total depravity; 2 sessions; 140

J. Bartlett [Seventh-day Adventist Church]
Birth: 18_ (_, _)
Death: _ (_, _)
D. H. Bays (Reorganized Church of Jesus Christ of Latter Day Saints); Maple Valley, IA; January 27-_, 1880

C. D. Barton [Baptist Church]
Birth: _ (_, _)
Death: _ (_, _)
?William Edgar Morgan (Church of Christ); Knoxville, TN; 1938

_ Barton [Baptist Church]
Birth: _ (_, _)
Death: _ (_, _)
Glen E. Green (Church of Christ); Marvel, AR; 1932

S. H. Bashor [?]
Birth: 18_ (_, _)
Death: _ (_, _)
William Dillon (United Brethren Church); Louisville, Stark County, OH; March 1-5, 1881. Book publication: *The Louisville Discussion*. Canton, OH: C. C. Thompson.

Hulan F. Bass [Primitive Baptist Church]
Birth: March 21, 1931 (Crosbyton, TX)
Death: _ (_, _)
J. L. Davidson (Church of Christ); written; March 30, 1979 - April 12, 1982; salvation. Book publication: *Wind of Doctrine: Debate on Salvation, Conditional or Unconditional?* Conroe, TX: J. L. Davidson, 1984.

Jesse Bass [Primitive Baptist Church]
Birth: _ (_, _)
Death: _ (_, _)
M. F. Manchester (Church of Christ); Comanche, TX; January 18-21, 1954

W. G. Bass [Church of Christ]
Birth: _ (_, _)
Death: _ (_, _)
Polly A. Durham (Holiness Church); Doucette, TX; November 8-10, 1942

Jerry Bassett [Church of Christ]
Birth: 19_ (_, _)
Death: _ (_, _)
Gayland L. Osburn (?); Cottage Grove, OR; July 1965
Jack Holt (Church of Christ); San Antonio, TX; ?March 1992; divorce & remarriage
Jack Holt (Church of Christ); _, OR; ?March 1992; divorce & remarriage

N. S. Bastian [Church of Christ]
Birth: _ (_, _)
Death: _ (_, _)
J. L. Crane (Methodist Episcopal Church); Paris, IL; c 1858

George F. Battey, Jr. [Church of Christ]
Birth: 19_ (_, _)
Death: _ (_, _)
Jeff Asher (Church of Christ); Amarillo, TX; April 3-4, 6-7, 1990; drinking vessels, classes & women teachers; 1st debate for both
Thomas N. Thrasher (Church of Christ); Mableton, GA; June 23-24, 1994; 2 sessions. Proposition 1: "When the church comes together for the purpose of teaching the Bible, it is scriptural to divide into classes for this teaching, some of which may be taught by women." (Thrasher affirmed, Battey denied). Proposition 2: "The Scriptures teach that when the church comes together for the purpose of teaching the Bible, the people must be taught in an undivided assembly by men only." (Battey affirmed, Thrasher denied).
Patrick T. Donahue (Church of Christ); Jonesboro, GA; June 25, 1994; 30; 2 sessions. Proposition 1: "The Scriptures teach that an assembly of the church of Christ, for the communion, must use one cup (drinking vessel) in the distribution of the fruit of the vine." (Battey affirmed, Donahue denied). Proposition 2: "The Scriptures teach that an assembly of the church of Christ, for the communion, may use individual cups (drinking vessels) in the distribution of the fruit of the vine." (Donahue affirmed, Battey denied).

Albert Holmes Batts [Church of God]
Birth: September 13, 1903 (Henrietta, TN)
Death: June 24, 2001 (Chattanooga, TN)

Obituary: https://www.findagrave.com/memorial/
14404255/albert-holmes-batts
Cecil Dean Williams (Church of Christ)
Lindsay Allen (Church of Christ); Decatur, AL; 1940
Gus Nichols (Church of Christ)
Gus Nichols (Church of Christ)
Gus Nichols (Church of Christ)
Gus Nichols (Church of Christ)

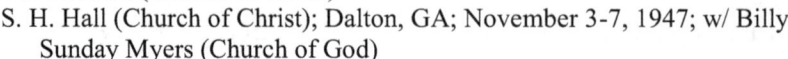

S. H. Hall (Church of Christ); Dalton, GA; November 3-7, 1947; w/ Billy Sunday Myers (Church of God)
A. C. Grider (Church of Christ); Harriman, TN; July 1949; baptism, Holy Spirit baptism
W. Curtis Porter (Church of Christ); Huntsville, AL; May 20-23, 1952; baptism, Holy Spirit baptism, Church of Christ, Church of God
Harold Sain (Church of Christ); Morrison, TN; February 15-18, 1965; necessity of water baptism, Holy Spirit baptism; 1000-1500. Book publication: *Sain-Batts Debate*. McMinnville, TN: Sain's Book, Gift and Novelty Shop, 1965.
Carrol R. Sutton (Church of Christ); Albertville, AL; September 14-17, 1965; water baptism, Holy Spirit baptism; 400-600
Gus Nichols (Church of Christ); Anniston, AL; November 1967; water baptism, Holy Spirit baptism, instrumental music in worship; 5 nights. Book publication: *Albert Batts and Gus Nichols: Debate on Instrumental Music in Worship*. The book contains only the last night (on instrumental music in worship). Web publication (Holy Spirit baptism): http://www.therestorationmovement.com/audio/Holy%20Spirit%20Baptism.rm. Web publication (instrumental music): http://www.therestorationmovement.com/audio/Instrumental%20Music%20Debate.rm
?Guy N. Woods (Church of Christ)

Hardy Ernest Baugh [Church of Christ]
Birth: March 21, 1882 (Wise, TX)
Death: 19_ (_, _)
W. H. Clark (Seventh-day Adventist Church); Randlett, Cotton Co., OK; c June 1928; 10 days

Ernest Belfort Bax [?]
Birth: July 23, 1854 (Royal Leamington Spa, UK)
Death: November 26, 1926 (London, UK)
Biographical sketch:
https://en.wikipedia.org/wiki/Ernest_Belfort_Bax
Charles Bradlaugh (Atheist); written. Book publication: *Will Socialism Benefit the English People? A Written debate between E. Belfort Bax and Charles Bradlaugh*. 1887.

_ Baxley [Church of Christ]
Birth: 18_ (_, _)
Death: 19_ (_, _)
_ Riggins (Baptist Church); Mt. Pleasant, Chilton Co., AL; March 29-30, 1918; baptism

I. L. Baxter, Jr. [Pentecostal Church]
Birth: 19_ (_, _)
Death: _ (_, _)
E. H. Miller (Church of Christ); LaGrange, GA; August 23-26, 1976

_ Baxter [?]
Birth: _ (_, _)
Death: _ (_, _)
Clifton Inman (Church of Christ); before 1959; eternal punishment

_ Baxter [?]
Birth: _ (_, _)
Death: _ (_, _)
David Nichol (Church of Christ)

Otis Bayer [Holiness Church]
Birth: _ (_, _)
Death: _ (_, _)
W. L. Totty (Church of Christ); Indianapolis, IN

Robert E. Bayer [Oneness Pentecostal Church]
Birth: 1935 (_, _)
Death: _ (_, _)
S. C. Kinningham (Church of Christ); Tupelo, MS; March 30-April 1, 1978
Bill Jackson (Church of Christ); Fulton, MS; July 30 – August 3, 1979; 5 nights. Book publication: *The Jackson-Bayer Debate on Pentecostalism*. Fulton, MS: Sowing the Seed Books, 1980.
John A. Welch (Church of Christ); Benton, IL; June 16-17, 19-21, 1980; Holy Spirit baptism & miracles; 400
John A. Welch (Church of Christ); Indianapolis, IN; May 17-_, 1987; baptismal formula; 250

Joseph Baylee [Church of England]
Birth: 1808 (_, _)
Death: July 7, 1883 (_, _)
Biographical sketch: https://en.wikipedia.org/wiki/Joseph_Baylee
Thomas Joseph Brown (Roman Catholic Church); 1852; infallibility of church. Book publication:
Matthew Bridges (Roman Catholic Church); 1856; Protestantism versus Catholicism. Book publication:
Edward Miall (Roman Catholic Church); church establishments. Book publication:

Charles Bradlaugh (Atheist); June 1860; 3 nights. Book publication: *God, Man, and the Bible. Three Nights' Discussion between the Rev. Joseph Baylee ... and Charles Bradlaugh ... June, 1860 ...*

Davis Henry Bays [Reorganized Church of Jesus Christ of Latter Day Saints]
Birth: March 5, 1839 (Corpus Christi, TX)
Death: October 24, 1905 (Persia, Harrison County, IA)
_ (Infidel); c 1871
_ (Church of Christ); c 1871
A. Marquis (Church of Christ); Stockdale, TX; July 1878
_ Stuart (Church of Christ); Oak Island, TX; 1878
J. Bartlett (Seventh Day Adventist Church); Maple Valley, IA; January 27-_, 1880

James Clayton Bays [Church of Christ]
Birth: January 21, 1913 (Chautauqua, KS)
Death: January 9, 1998 (Smyrna, TN)
Biographical sketch: *Preachers of Today* (Batsell Barrett Baxter & M. Norval Young, eds.). Nashville, TN: The Christian Press, 1952, p. 31.
Biographical sketch: *Preachers of Today, Volume Two* (Batsell Barrett Baxter & M. Norval Young, eds.). Nashville, TN: The Gospel Advocate Company, 1959, p. 29.
Biographical sketch: *Preachers of Today, Volume Three* (Batsell Barrett Baxter & M. Norval Young, eds.). Nashville, TN: The Gospel Advocate Company, 1964, p. 26.
Biographical sketch: *Preachers of Today, Volume Four* (Batsell Barrett Baxter & M. Norval Young, eds.). Nashville, TN: The Gospel Advocate Company, 1970, p. 20.
Biographical sketch: https://www.therestorationmovement.com/_states/tennessee/bays.html
William Bilyue (Baptist Church); Crossville, TN; 1941

George F. Beals [Church of Christ]
Birth: September 17, 1944 (Brockton, MA)
Death: _ (_, _)
Biographical sketch: *Do You Understand Expediency?* (Brian R. Kenyon, Ed.). Lakeland, FL: Florida School of Preaching, 2010, p. 40.
Thom Saffold (American Baptist Church) & Fran Mayes (American Baptist Church); Ann Arbor, MI; April 8-9, 1994. Proposition: "All homosexual acts are sinful." (Beals affirmed, Saffold & Mayes denied).

Ernest Beam [Church of Christ]
Birth: _ (_, _)
Death: 1957 (_, _)
_ (Seventh-day Adventist Church); Turlock, CA; 1928
_ (Seventh-day Adventist Church); Dinuba, CA; 1931
F. S. Fries (Seventh-day Adventist Church); Dinuba, CA; 1932
_ (Church of Jesus Christ of Latter Day Saints); Phoenix, AZ; 1932
William Floyd Thompson (Church of Christ)

J. E. Bean [Pentecostal Church]
Birth: _ (_, _)
Death: _ (_, _)
G. K. Wallace (Church of Christ); El Reno, OK; 1937

Culver Beard [Catholic Church]
Birth: _ (_, _)
Death: _ (_, _)
Porter Norris (Church of Christ); Fresno, CA; 1927

Morris M. Beard [Church of Christ]
Birth: 18_ (_, _)
Death: 19_ (_, _)
W. M. Harrison (Methodist Church); Craigfield, TN; July 5-8, 1915. Proposition: The scriptures teach that men are being saved without water baptism." (Harrison affirmed, Beard denied).

_ Bearden [Church of Christ]
Birth: ?18_ (_, _)
Death: _ (_, _)
G. A. Strain (Universalist Society)

Gerald A. Beasley [Church of Christ]
Birth: July 19, 1920 (Sapulpa, OK)
Death: _ (_, _)
Biographical sketch: *Preachers of Today, Volume Three* (Batsell Barrett Baxter & M. Norval Young, eds.). Nashville, TN: The Gospel Advocate Company, 1964, p. 27.
_ (Sabbatarian); written; before 1964. Publication: mimeographed.

W. T. Beasley [Church of Christ]
Birth: 18_ (_, _)
Death: 19_ (_, _)
Isaac Debusk (Missionary Baptist Church); February 3-6, 1908; general church propositions; w/John Forrest (Baptist Church), H. O. Daugherty (Baptist Church). Debusk quit the first day and his moderator (Forrest) took over. Forrest did not show up the second day so Daugherty debates the final three days.

J. F. Williams (Seventh-day Adventist Church); Bell's Branch, Hickman Co., TN; November 25, 1909

James B. Hardy (Primitive Baptist Church); Craigfield, Williamson Co., TN; March 1-4, 1910 Proposition 1: "The scriptures teach that in regeneration the Spirit of God operates upon the alien sinner independent of the word." (Hardy affirmed, Beasley denied). Proposition 2: "The scriptures teach that water baptism to a penitent believer is for, or in order to, the remission of past or alien sins." (Beasley affirmed, Hardy denied).

J. F. Williams (Seventh-day Adventist Church); Morgan's Creek, Hickman Co., TN; c August 1910

J. W. Griffin (Universalist Society); Liberty, TN; November 3-6, 1910. Proposition 1: "The Bible speaks of and teaches that there is an eternal hell or place of endless punishment after natural death and the resurrection that the wicked will spend the endless ages of eternity in." (Beasley affirmed, Griffin denied). Proposition 2: "Universal salvation." (Griffin affirmed, Beasley denied).

C. B. Massey (Missionary Baptist Church); Pleasant Shade, TN; November 6-12, 1911. Proposition 1: "The scriptures teach that the repenting sinner is commanded to pray for the remission of sins and expect to receive it in answer to prayer before water baptism." (Massey affirmed, Beasley denied). Proposition 2: "The scriptures teach that the repenting sinner is not commanded to pray for the remission of sins, but to expect it in water baptism." (Beasley affirmed, Massey denied). Proposition 3: "The Church of which I, C. B. Massey, am a member was set up, or established, during Christ's earthly ministry." (Massey affirmed, Beasley denied). Proposition 4: "The Church of which I, W. T. Beasley, am a member was set up, or established, on the first Pentecost after the resurrection of Christ." (Beasley affirmed, Massey denied).

H. O. Daugherty (Missionary Baptist Church); Bon Aqua, TN; December 4-7, 1911. Proposition: "The church with which I stand identified is apostolic in faith, doctrine, and practice." (Each man affirmed the proposition for two days).

C. B. Massey (Missionary Baptist Church); Willette, Macon Co., TN; December 17-20, 1912; Beasley's 24th debate. Proposition 1: "The scriptures teach that faith, repentance, and baptism are conditions of pardon to the alien sinner, baptism being for (in order to) the remission of past or alien sins; and as Naaman was cleansed from leprosy while buried the seventh dip, so a person is saved from sin while buried with his Lord in baptism." (Beasley affirmed, Massey denied). Proposition 2: "The scriptures teach that the repenting sinner must pray for the remission of sins, and expect to receive it in answer to prayer, through faith, before he is baptized." (Massey affirmed, Beasley denied).

W. M. Harrison (Methodist Church); Craigfont (perhaps Craigfield), TN; September 21-24, 1915. Proposition: "The Church of Christ of which I am a member, is scriptural in origin, faith, doctrine, name and practice." (Beasley

affirmed, Harrison denied).
A. U. Nunnery (Baptist Church)
A. U. Nunnery (Baptist Church); View Point (near Milam), TN; March 21-24, 1922; general church propositions
A. U. Nunnery (Baptist Church); Lake Creek, OK; November 15-22, 1923
F. S. Gibson (Missionary Baptist Church); Yuma, TN; December 7-12, 1925; Beasley's 42nd debate with Baptists
W. C. Davis (Primitive Baptist Church); Burns, ?Dickson Co., TN; October 18-21, 1927. Proposition 1: "The scriptures teach that faith, repentance, confession, and water baptism are conditions of pardon in the alien dead sinner." (Beasley affirmed, Davis denied). Proposition 2: "The scriptures teach that salvation is unconditional to the alien dead sinner." (Davis affirmed, Beasley denied).
W. C. Davis (Primitive Baptist Church); McEwen, TN; 1928
W. C. Davis (Primitive Baptist Church); Lyle, TN; 1929
R. C. Cooper (Northern Methodist Church); Pleasantville (Hickman Co.), TN; November 5-7, 1929

Reginald Woodrow Beaver [Church of Christ]
Birth: April 8, 1918 (Seymour, TX)
Death: December 8, 1973 (Healdton, OK)
Biographical sketch: *Preachers of Today, Volume Two* (Batsell Barrett Baxter & M. Norval Young, eds.). Nashville, TN: The Gospel Advocate Company, 1959, p. 31.
Biographical sketch: *Preachers of Today, Volume Three* (Batsell Barrett Baxter & M. Norval Young, eds.). Nashville, TN: The Gospel Advocate Company, 1964, p. 28.
Obituary: https://www.findagrave.com/memorial/61513688/reginald-woodrow-beaver
_ Brooks (Church of Christ); 1955; classes & women teachers

_ Beaver [Baptist Church]
Birth: 18_ (_, _)
Death: 19_ (_, _)
Mike M. Young (Church of Christ); 1917

George Beavers [Missionary Baptist Church]
Birth: 18_ (_, _)
Death: 19_ (_, _)
Will M. Thompson (Church of Christ); Denison (near Division), TX; November 10-13, 1919
J. Cullis Smith (Baptist Church); written; 1936; millennium. Book publication: *Smith-Beavers Debate.* Kirk, CO: J. Cullis Smith, ?1936.

David A. Beck [Church of Christ]
Birth: August 17, 1946 (_, _)
Death: _ (_, _)

Nadir Ahmed (Muslim); Peoria, IL; December 3-5, 1998; the Bible is not the inspired word of God, the Koran is not the inspired word of God, plan of salvation; 3 sessions

Thomas Jesse Beckham [Methodist Church]
Birth: November 24, 1860 (Limestone County, AL)
Death: April 28, 1942 (Dallas, TX)
Henry E. Warlick (Church of Christ); Greer County, OK; 1901
Early Arceneaux (Church of Christ); Thornton, TX; 1912

Francis J. "Frank" Beckwith [Roman Catholic Church]
Birth: 1960 (New York, NY)
Death: _ (_, _)
Biographical sketch: https://en.wikipedia.org/wiki/Francis_J._Beckwith
Timothy George (?); Wheaton, _; September 3, 2009. Topic: Can you be Catholic and Evangelical?

E. A. Bedicheck [Church of Christ]
Birth: October 28, 1876 (_, ?TX)
Death: 19_ (_, _)
Biographical sketch: *Gospel Preachers Who Blazed The Trail* by C. R. Nichol. Austin, TX: Firm Foundation Publishing House, n.d.
At least 26 debates by 1911
J. T. Blackman (Missionary Baptist Church); May 1908; 8 days
S. A. Paine (Primitive Baptist Church); Orso, TX; May 23-27, 1908; conditional or unconditional life
_ (Free Methodist Church); before 1911
_ (Church of Jesus Christ of Latter Day Saints); Lone Star, CA; 1908
_ (Church of Jesus Christ of Latter Day Saints); Fresno, CA; 1908
_ (Atheist); before 1911

_ Bedinger [Presbyterian Church]
Birth: 18_ (_, _)
Death: _ (_, _)
J. B. Moody (Baptist Church)

John H. Beebe [Church of Christ]
Birth: February 11, 1916 (Sumner County, KS)
Death: _ (_, _)
Biographical sketch: *Preachers of Today* (Batsell Barrett Baxter & M. Norval Young, eds.). Nashville, TN: The Christian Press, 1952, p. 32.
Biographical sketch: *Preachers of Today, Volume Two* (Batsell Barrett Baxter & M. Norval Young, eds.). Nashville, TN:

The Gospel Advocate Company, 1959, p. 32.
Ben Crawford (Baptist Church); 1949; general church propositions
Ben Crawford (Baptist Church); 1950; general church propositions

Jim Beech [Church of Christ]
Birth: 19_ (_, _)
Death: _ (_, _)
_ Simpson (Seventh-day Adventist Church); _, Australia; August 6-7, 1973; Sabbath

Vernon Beeks [Jehovah's Witnesses]
Birth: _ (_, _)
Death: _ (_, _)
Richard P. Duncan (Church of Christ)

Ulrich Rische Beeson [Church of Christ]
Birth: September 7, 1893 (El Reno, OK)
Death: March 10, 1983 (El Dorado, AR)
Biographical sketch: *Preachers of Today* (Batsell Barrett Baxter & M. Norval Young, eds.). Nashville, TN: The Christian Press, 1952, p. 32.
Biographical sketch: *Preachers of Today, Volume Two* (Batsell Barrett Baxter & M. Norval Young, eds.). Nashville, TN: The Gospel Advocate Company, 1959, pp. 32-33.
Biographical sketch: *Preachers of Today, Volume Three* (Batsell Barrett Baxter & M. Norval Young, eds.). Nashville, TN: The Gospel Advocate Company, 1964, p. 29.
Biographical sketch: *In Memoriam* by Gussie Lambert. Shreveport, LA: Gussie Lambert, 1988, pp. 23-24.
_ Morris (Holiness Church); 1918
_ Thorburn (Russellite); 1921
S. C. Swinney (Baptist Church); Millville, AR; c January 1925; 6 days
_ Zangarra (Catholic Church); before 1959

Justus Beetge [Pentecostal Church]
Birth: _ (_, _)
Death: _ (_, _)
Don Gardner (Church of Christ); Pretoria, South Africa; December 12, 1951; Gardner's first debate

Eric Beevers [Roman Catholic Church]
Birth: _ (_, _)
Death: _ (_, _)
Eldred Stevens (Church of Christ); Stillwater, OK; May 13-16, 1952; New Testament authority, Roman Catholic Church; 4000-6000. Book publication: *Stevens-Beevers Debate*. Fort Worth, TX: Eldred Stevens, 1953.

Mike Begon [?Atheist]
Birth: 19_ (_, _)
Death: 20_ (_, _)
William Lane Craig (Evangelical); 2007

Michael J. Behe [Intelligent Design]
Birth: 1952 (Altoona, PA)
Death: _ (_, _)
Barry Lynne (Evolutionist), Eugenie Scott (Evolutionist); Michael Ruse (Evolutionist) & Kenneth Miller (Evolutionist); PBS TV *Firing Line*; December 19, 1997; w/ Philip Johnson (Creationist), William F. Buckley (Creationist) & David Berlinski (Anti-Darwinist). Proposition: "Resolved: Evolution should acknowledge creation."

Ernest Calvin Beisner [Trinitarian]
Birth: December 6, 1955 (_, _)
Death: _ (_, _)
N. A. Urshan (Oneness Pentecostal Church) & Robert Sabin (Oneness Pentecostal Church); 1986; godhead; John Ankerburg Show (TV); w/ Walter Martin (Trinitarian)

James Semple Bell [Church of Christ]
Birth: October 20, 1838 (Antrim, Ireland)
Death: 1910 (_, ?NY)
Ira Turner (Primitive Baptist Church); Macoupin County, IL; 1887; hereditary total depravity

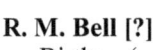

R. M. Bell [?]
Birth: _ (_, _)
Death: _ (_, _)
Jimmy Thomas (Church of Christ); written

Royce P. Bell [Church of Christ]
Birth: August 16, 1948 (_, _)
Death: _ (_, _)
Ben Franklin (Church of Christ); Venice, CA; 1974; Pentecostalism, gifts & baptism of the Holy Spirit
Jack W. Langford (Dispensationalist); Irving & Fort Worth, TX; September 11-12, 14-15, 18-19, 21-22, 1978; water baptism & salvation, Holy Spirit baptism; 8 sessions
Olan Hicks (Church of Christ); Sparks, NV; 1985; divorce & remarriage

_ Bell [Baptist Church]
   Birth: 18_ (_, _)
   Death: _ (_, _)
   Foy E. Wallace, Sr. (Church of Christ); Long Branch, TX; April 1896; apostasy, establishment of church, total depravity, baptism

E. P. Bellche [Church of Christ]
   Birth: 18_ (_, _)
   Death: _ (_, _)
   John Hughes (Universalist Society); Union, IL; 1868

Laureano N. Belo [Church of Christ]
   Birth: July 4, 1912 (Nampicuan, Nueva Ecija, Philippines)
   Death: _ (_, _)
   Biographical sketch: *Preachers of Today, Volume Three* (Batsell Barrett Baxter & M. Norval Young, eds.). Nashville, TN: The Gospel Advocate Company, 1964, p. 30.
   About 60 debates before 1965
   _ (Seventh-day Adventist Church); before 1965
   _ (Methodist Church); before 1965
   _ (Iglesia ni Cristo/Manalo); before 1965
   _ (Christian Alliance); before 1965
   _ (Jehovah's Witnesses); before 1965
   _ (Baptist Church); before 1965
   _ (Catholic Church); before 1965
   _ (UCCP); before 1965
   _ (Pentecostal Church); before 1965
   _ (Union Spiritist); before 1965

Aubrey Curtis Belue, Jr. [Church of Christ]
   Birth: July 23, 1931 (Columbus, MS)
   Death: August 8, 2015 (Columbus, MS)
   Biographical sketch: *Biblical Authority: Its Meaning and Application* (Florida College Annual Lectures, 1974). Marion, IN: Cogdill Foundation, 1974, p. 96.
   Obituary: http://www.gunterandpeel.com/obituary/5697672
   William G. Reese (?Christian Church); Benton, IL; December 1958; instrumental music in worship; 4 sessions; Belue's first debate
   D. L. Welch (Oneness Pentecostal Church); summer 1962
   Sidney French (Church of Christ); Gary, IN & Chicago, IL; December 1965; 4 sessions
   Marvin A. Hicks (Oneness Pentecostal Church); Aurora, IL; March 20-24, 1967; godhead, miracles, instrumental music in worship; 4 sessions
   J. D. Childress (Oneness Pentecostal Church); Griffith & Portage, IN; September 5-8, 1961; Holy Spirit baptism, godhead

Raymond G. Bishop (Oneness Pentecostal Church); 5 sessions
Raymond G. Bishop (Oneness Pentecostal Church); 5 sessions; their 2nd debate
Roy Hall (Church of Christ); near Beckley, WV; c 1982; 4 sessions; marriage & divorce
John Newsome (Baptist Church); Beckley, WV; 2 nights

J. D. Bennett [Reorganized Church of Jesus Christ of Latter Day Saints]
Birth: 18_ (_, _)
Death: _ (_, _)
Cyrus Johnson (Congregationalist); Clay County, KS; March 1-3, 1880; "Resolved, That Joseph Smith, the founder of the Latter Day Saint sect, was not a true Prophet and Saint, but an impostor, polygamist, and thief, and that his immediate followers were no better than himself."

Raymond S. Bennett [Christian Church]
Birth: _ (_, _)
Death: _ (_, _)
James E. Cooper (Church of Christ); Campbellsville, KY; June 4-5, 1959; instrumental music in worship

Weldon Bailey Bennett [Church of Christ]
Birth: February 19, 1916 (Ralls, TX)
Death: _ (_, _)
Biographical sketch: *Preachers of Today* (Batsell Barrett Baxter & M. Norval Young, Eds.). Nashville, TN: The Christian Press, 1952, p. 34.
Biographical sketch: *Preachers of Today, Volume Three* (Batsell Barrett Baxter & M. Norval Young, eds.). Nashville, TN: The Gospel Advocate Company, 1964, p. 31.
_ Duncan (Baptist Church); 1944; kingdom, premillennialism, apostasy, baptism

Eris Bonner Benson [Church of Christ]
Birth: August 3, 1922 (East Tallassee, AL)
Death: March 24, 1997 (_, _)
Biographical sketch: *Preachers of Today* (Batsell Barrett Baxter & M. Norval Young, eds.). Nashville, TN: The Christian Press, 1952, p. 34.
Biographical sketch: *Preachers of Today, Volume Two* (Batsell Barrett Baxter & M. Norval Young, eds.). Nashville, TN: The Gospel Advocate Company, 1959, p. 32-33.
Biographical sketch: *Preachers of Today, Volume Three* (Batsell Barrett Baxter & M. Norval Young, eds.). Nashville, TN: The Gospel Advocate Company, 1964, p. 31.
Biographical sketch: *Preachers of Today, Volume Four* (Batsell Barrett Baxter & M. Norval Young, eds.). Nashville, TN: The Gospel Advocate Company, 1970, p. 22.

Obituary: https://www.findagrave.com/memorial/139857263/eris-bonner-benson
_ Carey (?); 1949; water baptism
Finis J. Dake (Church of God); Columbus, GA; 1951; water baptism, Holy Spirit baptism, miracles

James Thomas Bentley [Church of Christ]
Birth: June 5, 1875 (Greenville, TX)
Death: December 1958 (?Dallas, TX)
_ Gregory (Baptist Church); Eastland County, TX
_ Gregory (Baptist Church); Eastland County, TX

Jerome Kearby Bentley [Church of Christ]
Birth: July 16, 1896 (Georgetown, TX)
Death: June 17, 1986 (Mesquite, TX)
Son of James Thomas Bentley
Biographical sketch: *Preachers of Today, Volume Two* (Batsell Barrett Baxter & M. Norval Young, eds.). Nashville, TN: The Gospel Advocate Company, 1959, p. 34.
Biographical sketch: *The Trail Blazers: Heroes of the Faith* by J. Porter Wilhite. Oklahoma City, OK: Telegram Book Company, 1965, pp. 119-120.
Obituary: https://www.findagrave.com/memorial/93694341/jerome-kearby-bentley
_ (Russellite); Lubbock, TX; 1918

Jerry K. Bentley [?Seventh-day Adventist Church]
Birth: 19_ (_, _)
Death: _ (_, _)
Rick King (Church of Christ); Regina, KY; March 19-20, 22-23, 1984; Sabbath, eternal punishment

William Andrew Bentley [Church of Christ]
Birth: January 11, 1871 (Camden, AR)
Death: May 12, 1954 (Abilene, TX)
Biographical sketch: *Preachers of Today* (Batsell Barrett Baxter & M. Norval Young, eds.). Nashville, TN: The Christian Press, 1952, p. 36.
Biographical sketch: *Gospel Preachers Who Blazed The Trail* by C. R. Nichol. Austin, TX: Firm Foundation Publishing House, c 1911.
Obituary: https://www.findagrave.com/memorial/53975678/william-andrew-bentley
12 debates by 1911
_ Wright (Baptist Church); establishment of church
_ Newman (Baptist Church); church

_ Webb (Baptist Church); church
S. A. Paine (Primitive Baptist Church); before 1911

Obie F. Benton [Seventh Day Church of God]
Birth: 19_ (_, _)
Death: _ (_, _)
Howard See (Church of Christ); Lexington, TN; October 21-25, 1985
Howard See (Church of Christ); Lexington, TN; April 7-8, 10-11, 1986
Howard See (Church of Christ); Lexington, TN; July 7-8, 10-11, 1986; first day of week

Terry Wane Benton [Church of Christ]
Birth: 19_ (_, _)
Death: _ (_, _)
Dan Billingsly (Church of Christ); written. Proposition 1: "The Scriptures teach that the four books of Matthew, Mark, Luke and John are before the cross, and belong to the Old and not the New Testament." (Billingsly affirmed, Benton denied). Proposition 2: "The Scriptures teach that one will be blessed today who obeys Jesus' righteous principles for His kingdom described to some extent in Matthew, Mark, Luke, and John in the parts of their documents that describe what Jesus said before He died on the cross." (Benton affirmed, Billingsly denied). Web publication.

Bob Berard [Church of Christ]
Birth: c 1945 (_, _)
Death: August 3, 2003 (Khampong Cham, Cambodia)
Jeff Asher (Church of Christ); Huntsville, TX; February 1-5, 1998; church-sponsored social meals

_ Berard [?]
Birth: _ (_, _)
Death: _ (_, _)
_ Haley (?)

J. F. Berg [?Presbyterian Church]
Birth: _ (_, _)
Death: _ (_, _)
Joseph Barker (Freethinker). January 9-10, 12-13, 16-19, 1854; 8 sessions; 2000-2500. Book publication: *Great Discussion on the Origin, Authority and Tendency of the Bible, between Rev. J. F. Berg, D.D. of Philadelphia and Joseph Barker of Ohio (Debate of 8 nights duration)*. Boston, MA: J. B. Yerrinton & Son, Printers, 1854.

Scott Bergeson [Church of Jesus Christ of Latter Day Saints]
Birth: _ (_, _)

Death: _ (_, _)
Carrol R. Sutton (Church of Christ); Peoria, IL; March 13, 20, 1960

David Berlinski [Anti-Darwinist] 
Birth: 1942 (New York, NY)
Death: _ (_, _)
The Deniable Darwin by David Berlinski.
Biographical sketch:
  https://en.wikipedia.org/wiki/David_Berlinski
Barry Lynne (Evolutionist), Eugenie Scott (Evolutionist); Michael Ruse (Evolutionist) & Kenneth Miller (Evolutionist); PBS TV *Firing Line*; December 19, 1997; w/ Philip Johnson (Creationist); Michael Behe (Anti-Darwinist) & William F. Buckley (Creationist). Proposition: "Resolved: Evolution should acknowledge creation."

_ Bernard [?Oneness Pentecostal Church]
Birth: 19_ (_, _)
Death: _ (_, _)
_ Cook (?); godhead

Floyd Jefferson Berry [Church of Christ] 
Birth: October 3, 1884 (Italy, TX)
Death: August 17, 1947 (Vanderpool, TX)
Biographical sketch: *Gospel Preachers Who Blazed The Trail* by C. R. Nichol. Austin, TX: Firm Foundation Publishing House, n.d.
Obituary: https://www.findagrave.com/memorial/42257040/floyd-jefferson-berry
J. W. Jackson (Church of Jesus Christ of Latter Day Saints); Apple Springs, TX; 1919

Rudolph Berry [Church of Christ]
Birth: 19_ (_, _)
Death: _ (_, _)
L. O. Anderson (Sabbatarian); Chicago, IL; 1971

W. C. Berry [?]
Birth: 18_ (_, _)
Death: _ (_, _)
A. G. Freed (Church of Christ); Palestine, AR; 1901

_ Berry [Presbyterian Church]
Birth: _ (_, _)
Death: _ (_, _)
C. R. Nichol (Church of Christ)

_ Berry [Jehovah's Witnesses]
  Birth: _ (_, _)
  Death: _ (_, _)
  Joe Gilmore, Jr. (Church of Christ); 1951

_ Berryhill [?]
  Birth: _ (_, _)
  Death: _ (_, _)
  C. L. Overturf (Church of Christ); 1935; church

_ Berryhill [Holiness Church]
  Birth: _ (_, _)
  Death: _ (_, _)
  G. F. Gibbs (Church of Christ); _, TN; 1939

Annie Wood Besant [Secularist, Theosophist]
  Birth: October 1, 1847 (Clapham, London, England)
  Death: September 20, 1933 (Adyar, India)
  Biography: *Annie Besant: A Biography* by Anne Taylor. Oxford University Press, 1991.
  Biographical sketch: http://www.csuchico.edu/phil/sdobra_mat/besantpaper.html
  Biographical sketch: http://www.spartacus.schoolnet.co.uk/Wbesant.htm
  Biographical sketch: http://www.alpheus.org/html/articles/theosophy/bevir3.html
  G. W. Foote (?); 4 nights. Book publication: *Is Socialism Sound? Verbatim report of a four nights' debate between Annie Besant and G. W. Foote ...* 1887.
  A. Hatchard (?). Book publication: *The Besant-Hatchard Debate.* 1880.
  G. F. Handel Rowe (?). Book publication: *Atheism and Its Bearing on Morals. A Debate between Annie Besant and the Rev. G. F. Handel Rowe ...* 1887.
  Charles Bradlaugh (Atheist); written. Book publication: *Socialism; for and against: written debate with Mrs. Besant.* 1887.

Frederick Beversdorf [Lutheran Church]
  Birth: _ (_, _)
  Death: _ (_, _)
  Edward O. Bragwell (Church of Christ); Hanceville, AL; 1960

Bill Bewley [Church of God]
  Birth: 19_ (_, _)
  Death: _ (_, _)
  Jim Deason (Church of Christ); written; conditions of salvation. Periodical publication: "Deason-Bewley Debate." Columbia, TN: *Search*, 2(1), 1984.

Alexander William Bickerton [?]
  Birth: January 7, 1842 (Alton, Hampshire, England)

Death: January 21, 1929 (London, England)
W. W. Collins (Freethinker); Christchurch, New Zealand; January 18, 1892. Proposition: "That man from the mode of his evolution is a worshipping creature." (Bickerton affirmed, Collins denied).

Marion Bickford [Evolutionist]
Birth: 19_ (_, _)
Death: _ (_, _)
Duane T. Gish (Creationist) & Henry M. Morris (Creationist); Lawrence, KS; September 17, 1976; 3500; w/ E. O. Wiley (Evolutionist)

O. E. Billingsley [Church of Christ]
Birth: ?April 29, 1876 (_, _)
Death: ?June 23, 1927 (_, _)
S. C. Swinney (Baptist Church); _, ?AR; December 25-28, 1918

Price Billingsley [Church of Christ]
Birth: April 22, 1877 (Corinth, MS)
Death: January 13, 1959 (Nashville, TN)
Biographical sketch: *Preachers of Today* (Batsell Barrett Baxter & M. Norval Young, eds.). Nashville, TN: The Christian Press, 1952, p. 37.
Biographical sketch: *Gospel Preachers of Yesteryear* by Loyd L. Smith, c 1986.
F. H. Redwine (?); Tussy, ?OK; 1901; Billingsley's 1st debate

_ Billingsley [?Baptist Church]
Birth: 18_ (_, _)
Death: _ (_, _)
Flavil Joseph Hall (Church of Christ); 1915; baptism, apostasy

Dan Billingsly [Church of Christ]
Birth: March 25, 1929 (_, _)
Death: _ (_, _)
Marvin A. Hicks (Oneness Pentecostal Church); Dallas, TX; November 3-5, 1975; tongues
Dave Reagan (?); 1981; premillennialism
Andrew M. Connally, Jr. (Church of Christ); 1982
Ralph Blair (Evangelical); Denton, TX; February 26, 1983; homosexuality. Book publication: *Blair/Billingsly Debate*.
Wayne Joiner (Pentecostal Church); 1983; godhead
Dub McClish (Church of Christ); Denton, TX; June 16-17, 1986; amenability. Book publication: *The McClish-Billingsly Debate*. Denton, TX: Valid Publications, Inc., 1986.

Mac Deaver (Church of Christ); divorce & remarriage

Don W. Tarbet (Church of Christ); Colbert, OK; October 11-12, 1993; marriage, divorce & remarriage. Book publication: Tarbet Pub.

Terry Benton (Church of Christ); written. Proposition 1: "The Scriptures teach that the four books of Matthew, Mark, Luke and John are before the cross, and belong to the Old and not the New Testament." (Billingsly affirmed, Benton denied). Proposition 2: "The Scriptures teach that one will be blessed today who obeys Jesus' righteous principles for His kingdom described to some extent in Matthew, Mark, Luke, and John in the parts of their documents that describe what Jesus said before He died on the cross." (Benton affirmed, Billingsly denied). Web publication.

Ethan R. Longhenry (Church of Christ); written. Proposition 1: "The Scriptures teach that the 'Sermon on the Mount,' Matthew chapters 5 through 7, contains both Old and New Testament doctrine." (Longhenry affirmed, Billingsly denied). Proposition 2: "The Scriptures teach that the 'Sermon on the Mount,' Matthew chapters 5 through 7, is exclusively Old Testament doctrine" (Billingsly affirmed, Longhenry denied). Web publication.

C. Edwin Bills [Church of Christ]

Birth: November 13, 1924 (Granbury, TX)
Death: _ (_, _)
Biographical sketch: *Preachers of Today, Volume Two* (Batsell Barrett Baxter & M. Norval Young, eds.). Nashville, TN: The Gospel Advocate Company, 1959, p. 37.
_ (?); 1957; instrumental music in worship

J. Peter Bilyeu [Baptist Church]

Birth: _ (_, _)
Death: _ (_, _)
Willie Silas Hunter (Church of Christ); Netherland, TN; 1928
Willie Silas Hunter (Church of Christ); Samaria, TN; c 1932; salvation, apostasy

William Bilyue [Baptist Church]

Birth: _ (_, _)
Death: _ (_, _)
James C. Bays (Church of Christ); Crossville, TN; 1941

F. R. "Red" Bingham [Baptist Church]

Birth: _ (_, _)
Death: _ (_, _)
John H. Brinn (Church of Christ); Bandana, KY; 1940
James P. Miller (Church of Christ); Central City, KY; 1946
Raymond Ford (Church of Christ); Toledo, OH; May 4-7, 1955
?Harold Hazelip (Church of Christ); 1956

Wilburn Eural Bingham [Church of Christ]
Birth: July 5, 1928 (_, _)
Death: _ (_, _)
?Albert R. Hill, Jr. (Church of Christ); Rienzi, MS; 1960
Alan E. Highers (Church of Christ); near Corinth, MS;
  November 20-21, 23-24, 1967; church benevolence; 500.
  Book publication: *The Highers-Bingham Debate*. Clinton,
  MS: Pervie Nichols Publications, 1969. Related publication:
  A Statement Regarding The Highers-Bingham Debate by W. Eural Bingham.

Samuel F. "Sam" Binkley, Jr. [Church of Christ]
Birth: September 28, 1919 (Mocksville, Davie County, NC)
Death: November 13, 2019 (Athens, AL)
Obituary: https://www.limestonechapel.com/obituaries/
  Sam-F-Binkley-Jr?obId=8889721
Samuel F. Binkley, Jr. is the full name.
_ Dobles (Seventh-day Adventist Church); Tarcutta, New South
  Wales, Australia; 1970

Samuel Binns [Cumberland Presbyterian Church]
Birth: 1856 (_, _)
Death: _ (_, _)
Clark Braden (Christian Church); Casey, IL; 1870; baptism

Sam Binns [Universalist Society]
Birth: 18_ (_, _)
Death: _ (_, _)
Clark Braden (Christian Church); Reynoldsburg, OH; 1871
_ Holt (Church of Christ); Union Chapel, near Terre Haute, IN; September 26-
  29, 1871. Proposition 1: "Do the Scriptures of the Old and New Testaments
  teach the ultimate holiness and happiness of the entire human race?" (Binns
  affirmed, Holt denied). Proposition 2: "Do the Scriptures of the Old and New
  Testaments teach that any portion of mankind will suffer endless
  punishment?" (Holt affirmed, Binns denied).

W. H. Bird [Church of Christ]
Birth: 18_ (_, _)
Death: 19_ (_, _)
Lon Davis (Baptist Church); Adairsville, GA; December 29, 1918-January 1919
Lon Davis (Baptist Church); Adairsville, GA; March 16-_, 1919

Alvie Bishop [Oneness Pentecostal Church]
Birth: _ (_, _)
Death: 19_ (_, _)
Ules G. Reid, Jr. (Church of Christ); Hartselle & Trinity, AL; May 22-23, 25-26,
  1967; w/ J. L. Pipkin (Oneness Pentecostal Church). Proposition 1: "The

scriptures teach that there are three separate and distinct persons in the one Godhead: God the Father, God the Son, and God the Holy Spirit." (Reid affirmed, Bishop denied). Proposition 2: "The scriptures teach that there is but one person in the Godhead, namely, the Lord Jesus Christ." (Bishop affirmed, Reid denied). Proposition 3: "The scriptures teach that baptism in the Holy Spirit, speaking in tongues, and miracles extend to this present age." (Pipkin affirmed, Reid denied). Proposition 4: "The scriptures teach that baptism in the Holy Spirit, speaking in tongues, and miracles do not extend to this present age." (Reid affirmed, Pipkin denied).

C. C. Bishop [Baptist Church]
Birth: _ (_, _)
Death: _ (_, _)
J. Porter Wilhite (Church of Christ); Minden, LA; 1940

Linwood Ernest Bishop [Church of Christ]
Birth: February 8, 1909 (Brown County, TX)
Death: _ (_, _)
Biographical sketch: *Preachers of Today* (Batsell Barrett Baxter & M. Norval Young, eds.). Nashville, TN: The Christian Press, 1952, pp. 37-38.
Biographical sketch: *Preachers of Today, Volume Two* (Batsell Barrett Baxter & M. Norval Young, eds.). Nashville, TN: The Gospel Advocate Company, 1959, p. 37-38.

M. S. Groom (Baptist Church); Laird Hill, TX; May 6-9, 1941; baptism, operation of Holy Spirit, apostasy
_ Hardin (?Baptist Church); 1943; baptism, depravity, operation of Spirit, apostasy
J. Ervin Waters (Church of Christ); _, CA; 1947; classes & women teachers, drinking vessels in Lord's supper
_ (Seventh-day Adventist Church); before 1959
_ (Pentecostal Church); before 1959

Raymond G. Bishop [Oneness Pentecostal Church]
Birth: August 2, 1935 (_, _)
Death: _ (_, _)
Aubrey C. Belue (Church of Christ); 5 sessions
Aubrey C. Belue (Church of Christ); 5 sessions; their 2nd
David Harkrider (Church of Christ); Ensley, AL; December 4-5, 7-8, 1967; 4 sessions. Proposition 1: "The Scriptures teach that baptism in water is the only baptism necessary to salvation." (Harkrider affirmed, Bishop denied). Proposition 2: "The Scriptures teach that the baptism of the Holy Spirit and fire is necessary to complete the new birth." (Bishop affirmed, Harkrider denied).
David Harkrider (Church of Christ); Myrtle, MS; December 11-12, 14-15, 1967;

Holy Spirit baptism; 4 sessions
Alan Highers (Church of Christ)
Ken Green (Church of Christ); Jeffersontown, KY; May 22-24, 1973; godhead, Holy Spirit baptism. Review: "The Bishop-Green Debate" by Dick Blackford. *The South End Expounder*, 8(34), August 28, 1973, pp. 1-4.
David D. Bonner (Church of Christ)
Thomas N. Thrasher (Church of Christ); New Albany, MS; November 14, 1996; godhead; 1 session; 200
Patrick T. Donahue (Church of Christ); New Albany, MS; November 15, 1996; baptismal formula; 1 session; 150
Patrick T. Donahue (Church of Christ); Tupelo, MS; February 24, 26, 2000; miraculous gifts, baptismal formula; 2 sessions; 100
Thomas N. Thrasher (Church of Christ); Tupelo, MS; February 25, 2000; godhead; 1 session; 100.

Levoy Bivens [Church of Christ]
Birth: November 29, 1912 (Tracy City, TN)
Death: December 18, 1983 (Murfreesboro, TN)
Biographical sketch: *Preachers of Today, Volume Two* (Batsell Barrett Baxter & M. Norval Young, eds.). Nashville, TN: The Gospel Advocate Company, 1959, p. 38.
Biographical sketch: https://www.therestorationmovement.com/states/tennessee/bivens.html
_ (?); before 1959; instrumental music in worship

James Bjornstad [Baptist Church]
Birth: December 23, 1940 (Brooklyn, NY)
Death: _ (_, _)
Jerry Jones (Church of Christ) & Jimmy Allen (Church of Christ); Chattanooga, TN; July 1982; TV debate on *The John Ankerberg Show*; w/ David Kingdon (Baptist Church). Internet publication: http://www.youtube.com/watch?v=ImwN3fTq6qg&feature=relmfu

Bynum Ferrill Black [Church of Christ]
Birth: March 28, 1871 (Williford, Sharp County, AR)
Death: February 2, 1944 (Oklahoma City, OK)
Biographical sketch: *Arkansas Angels* by Boyd E. Morgan. Paragould, AR: College Bookstore & Press, 1967 (Second Printing), pp. 53-55.
E. H. C. Kenner (Missionary Baptist Church); Pander, MO; c November 1905; ?6 days; general church propositions
_ Davis (?); Rose Hill, MO; 1906; 4 days
Ben M. Bogard (Missionary Baptist Church); Plunkett, AR; August 14-17, 1906; general church; 4 days

_ Davis (Church of Jesus Christ of Latter-Day Saints); Woodside, MO; 1906; 6 days
W. C. Austin (?); Economy, AR; 1906; 6 days
H. N. Hanson (?); Council Bluffs, MO; 1906; 6 days
Ben M. Bogard (Missionary Baptist Church); Clay, White County, AR; February 18-23, 1907; general church; 6 days
Ben M. Bogard (Missionary Baptist Church); near Williford, AR; September 24-29, 1907; 6 days
_ (Church of Jesus Christ of Latter Day Saints); Gravelly, AR; 1907
William Murray Aylor (Reorganized Church of Jesus Christ of Latter Day Saints); late 1911
Ben M. Bogard (Missionary Baptist Church); Newark, AR; December 12-15, 1911; general church; 4 days
W. E. Sherrill (Missionary Baptist Church); Dierks, AR; late December 1911; general church; Black's 64th debate
Ben M. Bogard (Missionary Baptist Church); Reese, TX; July 29 - August 1, 1913; 4 days
George H. Cramer (Come Outer); Lyon Co., KY; October 14-18, 1913. Proposition 1: "Water baptism as taught by the holy apostles is for (in order to) remission of past or alien sins, and was given as a commandment to both Jews and Gentiles, and the New Testament so teaches." (Black affirmed, Cramer denied). Proposition 2: "The worship as observed by the Church of Christ on the first day of the week, such as singing and praying and eating the Lord's Supper, is required by the New Testament." (Black affirmed, Cramer denied).
A. M. Baker (Reorganized Church of Jesus Christ of Latter-Day Saints); Bell, AR; c March 1917; 8 nights; general church propositions
J. F. Curtis (Church of Jesus Christ of Latter Day Saints); Utleyville, CO; September 2-12, 1923; 11 nights; Black's 28th debate with Mormons
F. S. Croswell (Adventist Church); Hilltop, OK; c January 1925
_ (Church of Jesus Christ of Latter Day Saints); _, AZ?; 6 days
_ (Methodist Church);
A. U. Nunnery (Baptist Church); Dewar, OK; c November 1927
T. H. Dixon (Freewill Baptist Church); Checotah, OK; August 27-_, 1930
Burt F. Marrs (Adventist Church); Ashland, OK; summer 1931; 11 nights
_ Ward (Church of Jesus Christ of Latter Day Saints); Williford, AR; 9 days

Willet A. Black [Church of Christ]
Birth: January 1, 1904 (_, _)
Death: March 8, 1980 (?Vernon, AL)
R. E. Higdon (?); Millport, AL; 1934
W. H. Hopper (Baptist Church); Berea (near Burnsville), MS; December 1939
G. S. Raburn (Baptist Church); Christian Chapel (Lamar Co.), AL; c January 1940
Finis J. Dake (Church of God); Alabama City, AL; 1941

Black [Baptist Church]
Birth: _ (_, _)
Death: _ (_, _)
J. Porter Wilhite (Church of Christ); Salmon, TX; c 1928

W. B. Blackburn [Methodist Church]
Birth: _ (_, _)
Death: _ (_, _)
T. B. Larimore (Church of Christ); Rock Creek, AL; Summer 1869; one session; differences between the Methodist Church and Church of Christ

Dick Blackford [Church of Christ]
Birth: 19_ (_, _)
Death: _ (_, _)
Robert Daugherty (Pentecostal Church); Central City, KY; May 17-19, 1972; baptismal formula, Holy Spirit baptism, miracles. Review: "The Blackford-Daugherty Debate" by Ken Green. *The Expounder*, 7(21), May 23, 1972, pp. 2-3.
John T. Wallace (?); Central City, KY; April 29-30, May 2-3, 1974; Sabbath, first day
Paul Dabdoub (Baptist Church); Dyersburg, TN; December 8-9, 1977. Proposition 1: "The Scriptures teach that water baptism is essential for the salvation of the alien sinner." (Blackford affirmed, Dabdoub denied). Proposition 2: "The Scriptures teach that the alien sinner is saved solely through penitent faith, before and without water baptism." (Dabdoub affirmed, Blackford denied).
W. C. Nevil (Baptist Church); Cadiz, KY; May 22-25, 1978. Proposition 1: "The Scriptures teach that faith, repentance, and water baptism are inseparably joined to procure pardon or salvation." (Blackford affirmed, Nevil denied). Proposition 2: "The Scriptures teach that salvation is by grace through faith, at the point of faith in Christ, without further acts of obedience." (Nevil affirmed, Blackford denied).
Steve Epley (Oneness Pentecostal Church); Owensboro, KY; June 9-10, 12, 1986; Holy Spirit baptism & miracles
Steve Epley (Oneness Pentecostal Church); _, KY; March 9-10, 12-13, 1987; godhead, baptismal formula; their 2nd debate
Travis Quertermous (Church of Christ) & Marion W. Ferrell (Church of Christ); Vanduser & Charleston, MO; August 8-9, 12-13, 1991; w/ Dan Richardson (Church of Christ). Proposition: "The sponsoring church method of evangelism, such as the One Nation Under God campaign sponsored by the Sycamore Church of Christ, Cookeville, Tennessee, is authorized by the New Testament." (Quertermous & Ferrell affirmed, Richardson & Blackford denied).

William Stanley Blackman [Church of Christ]
Birth: December 10, 1921 (Vidalia, GA)

Death: November 11, 1982 (_, ?GA)
Biographical sketch: *Preachers of Today, Volume Two* (Batsell Barrett Baxter & M. Norval Young, eds.). Nashville, TN: The Gospel Advocate Company, 1959, p. 40.
Biographical sketch: *Preachers of Today, Volume Three* (Batsell Barrett Baxter & M. Norval Young, eds.). Nashville, TN: The Gospel Advocate Company, 1964, pp. 34-35.
George D. Duplissy (Oneness Pentecostal Church); 1952; godhead, water baptism, Holy Spirit baptism, footwashing; 4 nights

Luther E. Blackmon [Church of Christ]
Birth: March 24, 1907 (_, _)
Death: July 5, 1977 (_, _)
C. Briggs (Baptist Church); _, TX; 1941

Arthur Coy Blackwell [Church of Christ]
Birth: April 26, 1922 (Warm Springs, AR)
Death: 1987 (_, ?AR_)
Biographical sketch: *Preachers of Today, Volume Two* (Batsell Barrett Baxter & M. Norval Young, eds.). Nashville, TN: The Gospel Advocate Company, 1959, p. 40.
_ (?); Klamath Falls, OR; before 1959; instrumental music in worship
_ (?); Rockford, IL; before 1959; salvation, Holy Spirit baptism, apostasy
Floyd Chappelear (Church of Christ); St. Louis, MO; 1968; orphan homes, sponsoring church
James Ivy (Baptist Church); Walnut Ridge, AR; 1971

Ralph Blair [Evangelical]
Birth: 19_ (_, _)
Death: _ (_, _)
Dan Billingsly (Church of Christ); Denton, TX; February 26, 1983; homosexuality. Book publication: *Blair/Billingsly Debate*.

Anthony Charles Lynton "Tony" Blair [Roman Catholic Church]
Birth: May 6, 1953 (Edinburgh, Scotland)
Death: _ (_, _)
Autobiography: *A Journey*. London: Hutchinson, 2010.
Christopher Hitchens (Atheist); Toronto, Canada; November 26, 2010. Topic: Is religion good for the world?

W. T. Blair [Baptist Church]
Birth: _ (_, _)
Death: _ (_, _)
Harold Sain (Church of Christ); written; November 1952- February 1953; newspaper (Cave City, KY)

William Wallace Blair [Reorganized Church of Jesus Christ of Latter Day Saints]
Birth: October 11, 1828 (Holly, Orleans County, New York)
Death: April 18, 1896 (_, _)
A. A. John (Seventh Day Adventist Church); Norway, LaSalle County, IL; August 9-_, 1879
_ Thurman (Church of Jesus Christ of Latter Day Saints) & _ Evans (Church of Jesus Christ of Latter Day Saints); Lehi, UT; January 29-30, 1881; w/ _ Anthony (Reorganized Church of Jesus Christ of Latter Day Saints)
_ Watson (?); c 1892. Book publication: *The Watson-Blair Debate*. 1892.

Given O. Blakely [Christian Church]
Birth: November 3, 1935 (_, _)
Death: _ (_, _)
Carroll Puckett (Church of Christ); instrumental music in worship
_ (Evolutionist); 1960; evolution
Guy N. Woods (Church of Christ); Marlow, OK; June 14-15, 1985; indwelling of the Holy Spirit. Book publication: *Indwelling of the Holy Spirit: A Debate between Guy N. Woods and Given O. Blakely*. Marlow, OK: G. N. Woods, 1985.
John Gibbs (?); 1988; instrumental music in worship
Alan Highers (Church of Christ); Neosha, MO; April 12-15, 1988; instrumental music in worship. Book publication: *The Highers-Blakely Debate*. Denton, TX: Valid Publications, Inc., 1988.

_ Blalock [Church of Christ]
Birth: 18_ (_, _)
Death: _ (_, _)
I. N. White (Reorganized Church of Jesus Christ of Latter Day Saints); Schell City, MO; December 27-_, 1886; 6 days

Jonathan Blanchard [Presbyterian Church]
Birth: January 19, 1811 (_, VT)
Death: May 14, 1892 (_, IL)
Biography: Kilby, Clyde S., *Minority of One: the Biography of Jonathan Blanchard*. Grand Rapids, MI: Eerdmans, 1959.
Biographical sketch: http://en.wikipedia.org/wiki/ Jonathan _

Blanchard_(abolitionist)
N. L. Rice (Presbyterian Church); Cincinnati, OH; October 1-2, 3, 6, 1845. Subject: Is slave-holding in itself sinful, and the relation between master and slave, a sinful relation? Book publication: *A Debate on Slavery*. Cincinnati, OH: Wm. H. Moore & Co., 1846.

_ Blankenship [Baptist Church]
Birth: 18_ (_, _)
Death: _ (_, _)
J. D. Tant (Church of Christ); Ben Hur, TX; November 1903

W. C. Blansett [Baptist Church]
Birth: _ (_, _)
Death: _ (_, _)
Jesse T. Lashlee (Church of Christ); Augusta, AR

_ Blanton [?]
Birth: _ (_, _)
Death: _ (_, _)
C. R. Nichol (Church of Christ); _, TX

Howard Alexander Blazer, Sr. [Church of Christ]
Birth: September 9, 1909 (Huntsville, AL)
Death: December 25, 1995 (_, ?AL)
Biographical sketch: *Preachers of Today, Volume Two* (Batsell Barrett Baxter & M. Norval Young, eds.). Nashville, TN: The Gospel Advocate Company, 1959, p. 41.
Biographical sketch: *Preachers of Today, Volume Three* (Batsell Barrett Baxter & M. Norval Young, eds.). Nashville, TN: The Gospel Advocate Company, 1964, p. 36.
Biographical sketch: *Preachers of Today, Volume Four* (Batsell Barrett Baxter & M. Norval Young, eds.). Nashville, TN: The Gospel Advocate Company, 1970, pp. 26-27.
_ (?); 1960
Carrol Sutton (Church of Christ); Athens, AL; July 25-26, 28-29, 1960; benevolent organizations; w/ Albert Hill, Jr. (Church of Christ)
Carrol Sutton (Church of Christ); Florence, AL; September 1960; benevolent organizations

T. H. Blenus [Church of Christ]
Birth: _ (_, _)
Death: _ (_, _)
W. E. Archibald (Presbyterian Church); 1878. Book publication: *A Debate on the Action of Baptism*. 1878.

C. H. Bliss [Seventh-day Adventist Church]
Birth: 18_ (_, _)
Death: _ (_, _)

Clark Braden (Christian Church); Lovington, IL; 1874
Clark Braden (Christian Church); St. Elmo, IL; 1899

Richard Bliss [Creationist]
Birth: 19_ (_, _)
Death: _ (_, _)

Ken Gjemere (Evolutionist), Virginia Currey (Evolutionist), Wilford Bailey (Evolutionist), _ Jagger (Evolutionist) & _ (Evolutionist); Dallas, TX; February 24, 1977; 300; broadcast on TV; w/ Harold Slusher (Creationist), Jody Dillow (Creationist), Tom Newberger (Creationist) & Haddon Robinson (Creationist)
_ (Evolutionist); Winnipeg, Manitoba, Canada; March 1985
_ (Evolutionist); Nipawier, Canada; March 1985

Jerry L. Blount [Church of Christ]
Birth: September 2, 1955 (_, _)
Death: _ (_, _)
Nelda Brock (?); written

Joe Hubert Blue [Church of Christ]
Birth: September 18, 1875 (Mt. Pleasant, Izard County, AR)
Death: September 1, 1954 (Batesville, AR)
Biographical sketch: *Preachers of Today* (Batsell Barrett Baxter & M. Norval Young, eds.). Nashville, TN: The Christian Press, 1952, pp. 40-41.
Biographical sketch: *Arkansas Angels* by Boyd E. Morgan. Paragould, AR: College Bookstore & Press, 1967 (Second Printing), pp. 79-92.
107 debates
Sam Ballard (Missionary Baptist Church); Wheeling, AR; March 3-6, 1903; general church propositions
W. Ezekiel "Zeke" Sherrill (Baptist Church); Urbanette, AR; February 1914; 4 days
Allen Hawkins (Baptist Church); Shaddy Chapel (near Hartville), MO; November 1-6, 1915; general church
Verne Sizemore (First Day Adventist Church); Northview, MO; November 13-15, 1917; punishment of wicked, state of the dead, establishment of kingdom
_ Wheatley (Baptist Church);
E. F. Thorpe (?); Grubbs, AR; March 13-18, 1922; establishment of kingdom; 6 sessions
Ben M. Bogard (Missionary Baptist Church); Clover Bend (near Alicia), AR; October 13-16, 1925; 4 days
_ (Baptist Church); Grubbs, AR
Sam Ballard (Baptist Church); Harmony, AR
Ben M. Bogard (Missionary Baptist Church); Convenience (near Sulphur Rock),

AR; October 25-27, 1927; 3 days; debate ended due to Blue's hoarseness with plans to re-schedule later

D. N. Jackson (Missionary Baptist Church); Spearsville, LA; 1934

_ Lassley (Baptist Church);

_ Baker (Church of Jesus Christ of Latter Day Saints)

J. Ervin Waters (Church of Christ); _, MO; 1943; drinking vessels, classes

William Thomas Boaz [Church of Christ]

Birth: January 7, 1875 (_, KY)
Death: March 31, 1957 (Toronto, Canada)
Obituary:
https://www.findagrave.com/memorial/50219622
More than 100 debates

H. K. Thomas (Baptist Church); Spring Creek, ?TN; April 11, 1899; necessity of baptism

L. Y. Brown (Baptist Church); Pilot Oak, KY; November 1899

T. F. Moore (Baptist Church); Cottage Grove, TN; December 12-14, 1899; baptism and salvation

G. T. Mayo (Primitive Baptist Church); ?Palmersville, TN; c October 1900

W. M. Rudolph (Missionary Baptist Church); Cuba, KY; December 4-_, 1900; Boaz's 6th debate

W. M. Rudolph (Missionary Baptist Church); Mayfield, KY; December 17-20, 1901. Proposition: "Baptism to a believing penitent is one of the conditions of pardon of past or alien sins." (Boaz affirmed, Rudolph denied).

C. K. Haines (Primitive Baptist Church); Bumpus Mills, TN; July 21-22, 1901; conditional or unconditional salvation

Claude H. Cayce (Primitive Baptist Church); Sedalia, KY; December 9-12, 1902. Proposition 1: "The church with which I stand identified is scriptural in origin, doctrine and practice." (Boaz affirmed, Cayce denied). Proposition 2: "The Church of Christ embraces all of the saved." (Boaz affirmed, Cayce denied).

L. Y. Brown (Baptist Church); Johnson's Grove (near Fulton), KY; March 3-6, 1903; Boaz's 9th debate

J. E. Skinner (Missionary Baptist Church); Murray, KY; March 14-17, 1903

J. E. Skinner (Missionary Baptist Church); Henry Co., TN; c December 1903; general church propositions

A. U. Nunnery (Missionary Baptist Church); _, ?TN; c December 1903

H. B. Taylor (Missionary Baptist Church); Murray, KY; December 22-25, 1903

H. B. Taylor (Missionary Baptist Church); Cottage Grove, TN; March 27-30, 1906. Proposition 1: "The Bible teaches that the true believer receives remission of sins before baptism." (Taylor affirmed, Boaz denied). Proposition 2: "The Bible teaches that the church of the New Testament was set up, or established on the first Pentecost after the resurrection of Christ." (Boaz affirmed, Taylor denied).

J. E. Skinner (Missionary Baptist Church); Tobaccoport (Stewart Co.), TN; November 1906; 4 days. Proposition 1: "Baptism as a condition of pardon to penitent believer." (Boaz affirmed, Skinner denied). Proposition 2: "The establishment of the church before Christ's death." (Skinner affirmed, Boaz denied).

_ Reid (Christian Church); Fulton, KY; c July 1907; instrumental music in worship

O. A. Utley (Baptist Church); Safford, TN; July 16-19, 1907; 500-1000. Proposition 1: "A true believer is saved before baptism." (Utley affirmed, Boaz denied). Proposition 2: "The New Testament Church was set up, organized, or established on the day of Pentecost." (Boaz affirmed, Utley denied).

J. E. Skinner (Baptist Church); Stewart Co., TN; November 5-8, 1907; 500-600; establishment of church, design of baptism

C. H. Cayce (Primitive Baptist Church); Perry Co., TN; December 10-14, 1907. Proposition 1: "The Bible teaches that all for whom Christ died will be saved in heaven." (Cayce affirmed, Boaz denied). Proposition 2: "Baptism as a condition to salvation." (Boaz affirmed, Cayce denied).

I. N. Penick (Baptist Church); Newbern, TN; c 1908

_ Horton (Seventh-day Adventist Church); Nashville, TN; c November 1908. Proposition: "The Sabbath of the decalogue is binding on Christians of the present day." (Horton affirmed, Boaz denied).

H. B. Taylor (Missionary Baptist Church); Hardin, KY; June 1-_, 1909. Proposition 1: "The Bible teaches that the penitent believer has salvation, or remission of sins, before baptism." (Taylor affirmed, Boaz denied). Proposition 2: "The establishment of the church on Pentecost." (Boaz affirmed, Taylor denied).

J. B. Hardy (Primitive Baptist Church); Barton's Creek, Dickson Co., TN; November 16-18, 1909; 3 days. The debate was closed when both men agreed that remission is received when a person is baptized.

O. A. Utley (Missionary Baptist Church); Hickman Co., __; December 16-20, 1909. Proposition 2: "A true believer is saved before water baptism." (Utley affirmed, Boaz denied).

J. B. Hardy (Primitive Baptist Church); Centerville, TN; c 1910

E. L. Maxwell (Seventh-day Adventist Church); Sheffield, AL; c 1911. Proposition: "The scriptures teach that the first day of the week is the Lord's day, and was observed as such by early disciples." (Boaz affirmed, Maxwell denied).

I. N. Penick (Baptist Church); Viola, KY; February 27-March 1, 1912; establishment of church, design of baptism

A. B. Gardner (Baptist Church); Ohio Co., KY; c May 1913; salvation, establishment of church

H. H. Wallace (Missionary Baptist Church); Duquain, IL; December 9-12, 1913; Boaz's 44th debate

J. A. Locklear (Ordinance Branch of the Holiness Church of Anderson, Indiana);

New Decatur, AL; January 31-February 5, 1916; general church propositions [*Gospel Advocate*, Vol. 58, No. 3 (January 20, 1916), 70], [*Gospel Advocate*, Vol. 58, No. 8 (February 24, 1916), 190-192]

W. R. Foulston (Seventh-day Adventist Church); written; 1945; Sabbath day. Publication: *A Discussion on the Sabbath Question*.

Steve Bobbitt [Church of Christ]
Birth: 19_ (_, _)
Death: _ (_, _)
Jeremy Morris (Church of Christ); written. Proposition 1: "The Scriptures teach that all of or most of the public preaching and teaching of a congregation is not to be done by a single man. It is the responsibility of all male members to publicly instruct the congregation." (Morris affirmed, Bobbitt denied). Proposition 2: "The Scriptures teach that all or most of the public preaching and teaching of a congregation may be restricted to a single individual." (Bobbitt affirmed, Morris denied). Web publication.

David Henry Bobo [Church of Christ]
Birth: October 4, 1910 (Birmingham, AL)
Death: 1985 (_, ?IN)
Biographical sketch: *Preachers of Today* (Batsell Barrett Baxter & M. Norval Young, eds.). Nashville, TN: The Christian Press, 1952, p. 41.
Biographical sketch: *Preachers of Today, Volume Two* (Batsell Barrett Baxter & M. Norval Young, eds.). Nashville, TN: The Gospel Advocate Company, 1959, p. 42.
Biographical sketch: *Preachers of Today, Volume Three* (Batsell Barrett Baxter & M. Norval Young, eds.). Nashville, TN: The Gospel Advocate Company, 1964, p. 36.
M. K. Lawson (Holiness Church); Cleveland, TN; 1937; godhead, Holy Spirit baptism

Darrell L. Bock [Evangelical]
Birth: December 12, 1953 (Calgary, Alberta, Canada)
Death: _ (_, _)
Robert N. Wilkin (Grace Evangelical Church)

Andreas Rudolf Bodenstein (Protestant Reformer)
Birth: 1480 (Carlstadt, Bavaria)
Death: December 24, 1541 (Basel, Switzerland)
Also known as von Carlstadt or Karlstadt
John Eck (Roman Catholic Church); Leipzig, Germany; June 27 – July 15, 1519; office of the pope, purgatory,

indulgences; w/ Martin Luther (Protestant Reformer). Publication: *The Leipzig Debate of 1519: Leaves from the Story of Luther's Life* by W. H. T. Dau, 1919. [Review: D'Aubigne, Merle, *History of the Reformation*, Book 5, Chapter 4]

_ Boem [?]
Birth: 19_ (_, _)
Death: _ (_, _)
Steve Epley (Oneness Pentecostal Church);Yahweh or Jesus

Benjamin Marcus Bogard [Missionary Baptist Church]
Birth: March 9, 1868 (Elizabethtown, Hardin Co., KY)
Death: May 29, 1951 (Little Rock, Pulaski Co., AR)
Biography: *Life and Works of Benjamin Marcus Bogard* by L. D. Foreman and Alta Payne. Little Rock, AR: Seminary Press, 1965. (3 volumes)
Biography*: The Father of Modern Landmarkism: The Life of Ben M. Bogard* by J. Kristian Pratt. Mercer University Press, 2013.

Turpin, Calvin C. "A Critique of Ben M. Bogard's Leadership." Unpublished S.T.D. thesis, Golden Gate Baptist Theological Seminary, 1967.
Participated in 237 debates; 193 by 1933.
John T. Hinds (Church of Christ); Elm Springs, AR; July 12-15, 1904; Bogard's first debate
Stanley J. Clark (Atheist)
Stanley J. Clark (Atheist)
Stanley J. Clark (Atheist)
Stanley J. Clark (Atheist)
Stanley J. Clark (Atheist)
Stanley J. Clark (Atheist)
Stanley J. Clark (Atheist)
Stanley J. Clark (Atheist)
Stanley J. Clark (Atheist)
Stanley J. Clark (Atheist)
Stanley J. Clark (Atheist)
Stanley J. Clark (Atheist)
Stanley J. Clark (Atheist)
Stanley J. Clark (Atheist)
J. C. Weaver (Methodist Church)
R. H. Pigue (Methodist Church)
?James A. Harding (Church of Christ)
W. A. Goodwin (Church of Christ); Jesup (near Little Rock), AR; August 16-19, 1905. Book publication.
E. M. Borden (Church of Christ); Bryant, AR; December 12-15, 1905; 4 days
E. M. Borden (Church of Christ); Mammouth Springs, AR; February 20-23,

1906; general church, salvation; 4 days
Bynum Black (Church of Christ); Plunkett, AR; August 14-17, 1906; general church; 4 days
R. S. Lyons (Church of Christ); October 9-12, 1906; general church
Joe S. Warlick (Church of Christ); near Bearden, AR; October 23-26, 1906; 4 days
R. W. Arrington (Church of Christ); near Bearden, AR; December 18-21, 1906; general church; 4 days
R. S. Lyons (Church of Christ); Fourche, AR; February 4-9, 1907
Bynum Black (Church of Christ); Clay, White County, AR; February 18-23, 1907; general church; 6 days
J. M. Brandon (Church of Christ); Ford's Well, MS; July 16-20, 1907; 5 days
John T. Hinds (Church of Christ); Grubbs, AR; September 8-12, 1907
Bynum Black (Church of Christ); near Williford, AR; September 24-29, 1907; 6 days
E. M. Borden (Church of Christ); Minturn, AR; November 19-22, 1907; 4 days
C. R. Nichol (Church of Christ); Millport, AL; April 1908; 1st of 11 debates between them
Joe S. Warlick (Church of Christ); Oak Grove, AR; July 1908; 6 days
James B. Hardy (Primitive Baptist Church); _, AR; ?July 1908; close communion
J. M. Brandon (Church of Christ); Ford's Well, MS; August 1-6, 1908; 6 days
Joe S. Warlick (Church of Christ); Holmes, AR; December 1-4, 1908; 4 days
?John R. Williams (Church of Christ); Roosevelt, AR; December 9-10, 1908
J. W. Chism (Church of Christ); Tenaha, TX; February 9-12, 1909; 4 days
W. F. Lemmons (Church of Christ); Bellemont, OK; February 16-19, 1909
Joe S. Warlick (Church of Christ); near Amory, MS; March 16-19, 1909; 4 days
George T. Searcy (Church of Christ); Lamar, AR; June 29 - July 2, 1909
E. M. Borden (Church of Christ); Balch, AR; July 26-29, 1909. Proposition 1: "The Scriptures teach that the Church of Christ was established on the first Pentecost after the resurrection of Christ." (Borden affirmed, Bogard denied). Proposition 2: "The Scriptures teach that the sinner is so depraved that in his conviction and conversion, the Holy Spirit must of necessity exercise a power or influence, distinct from and in addition to the written word." (Bogard affirmed, Borden denied). Proposition 3: "The Scriptures teach that a child of God or Saint, may so apostatize as to be lost in hell." (Borden affirmed, Bogard denied). Proposition 4: "The Scriptures teach that a sinner is saved by grace through faith, before baptism." (Bogard affirmed, Borden denied). Book publication: *Borden-Bogard Debate*.
E. M. Borden (Church of Christ); Roosevelt, AR; September 13-16, 1909; 4 days
J. H. Lawson (Church of Christ); Carpenter, OK; October 13-16, 1909
Charles Henry Kennedy (Church of Christ); Collinsville, TX; October 19-22, 1909
E. M. Borden (Church of Christ); Hickory Ridge, AR; October 26-29, 1909; 4

days
C. R. Nichol (Church of Christ); Shover Springs, AR; November 7-10, 1909
R. S. Lyons (Church of Christ); Donaldson, AR; December 7-10, 1909
N. B. Hardeman (Church of Christ); Obion, TN; December 23-26, 1909
John E. Dunn (Church of Christ); Corinth, MS; January 3-8, 1910; 6 days
Ulyses Grant Wilkerson (Church of Christ); Comanche, OK; February 12-15, 1910; 4 days
J. D. Tant (Church of Christ); Paragould, AR; May 31- June 3, 1910; 4 days
E. M. Borden (Church of Christ); Buford, AR; June 28-30, 1910; 3 days
E. M. Borden (Church of Christ); near Newport, AR; August 31 - September 3, 1910; 4 days
Joe W. Crumley (Church of Christ); Rosalie, TX; September 21-24, 1910
I. N. Penick (Regular Baptist); Johnson's Grove, Crockett County, TN; November 1-4, 1910. Book publication: *The Penick-Bogard Debate: Mission Methods*. Jackson, TN: n.p., 1910.
Joe S. Warlick (Church of Christ); Slater, TX; December 18-21, 1910; 4 days
Joe W. Crumley (Church of Christ); Stuart, OK; October 2-5, 1911
Foy E. Wallace, Sr. (Church of Christ); near Stratford, OK; October 10-13, 1911; church, faith only, baptism; 4 days
G. W. Wolf (Church of Christ); near Lockesburg, AR; November 20-25, 1911; 6 days
W. H. Sandy (Church of Christ); near Hamburg, AR; December 4-7, 1911
Bynum Black (Church of Christ); Newark, AR; December 12-15, 1911; general church; 4 days
Joe S. Warlick (Church of Christ); Fish, TX; December 27-30, 1911; 4 days
C. R. Nichol (Church of Christ); Chism, OK; January 2-5, 1912
W. G. Roberts (Church of Christ); near Woodside, MO; October 1-6, 1912
W. N. Warlick (Church of Christ); Maydelle, TX; October 15-18, 1912; 4 days
Joe W. Crumley (Church of Christ); near Maud, OK; October 22-25, 1912
E. M. Borden (Church of Christ); Enola, AR; November 12-15, 1912; 4 days
N. B. Hardeman (Church of Christ); Dyer, TN; December 6-9, 1912
Joe S. Warlick (Church of Christ); near Aspermouth, TX; January 7-9, 1913; 3 days
Joe S. Warlick (Church of Christ); near Center Point, AR; January 15-20, 1913; 6 days
E. M. Borden (Church of Christ); July 8-11, 1913; 4 days
Joe S. Warlick (Church of Christ); Clover, TX; July 21-24, 1913; 4 days
Bynum Black (Church of Christ); Reese, TX; July 29 - August 1, 1913; 4 days
H. F. Oliver (Church of Christ); near Center, TX; November 11-14, 1913
Joe S. Warlick (Church of Christ); Malone, TX; December 15-19, 1913; 5 days
Albert W. Young (Church of Christ); Leslie, TX; December 24-25, 1913; 2 days
C. R. Nichol (Church of Christ); Dodsonville, TX; January 27-30, 1914
_ Capers (Church of Christ); Briston, Ellis County, TX; March 30 - April 3, 1914; 5 days
J. W. Chism (Church of Christ); Morse, OK; October 6-12, 1914; 7 days

C. R. Nichol (Church of Christ); Haworth, OK; November 24-27_, 1914

J. W. Chism (Church of Christ); Locust Bayou, AR; December 1-6, 1914; 6 days

Joe S. Warlick (Church of Christ); written; 1914. Proposition 1: "The Scriptures teach that the sinner is so depraved that in his conviction and conversion the Holy Spirit exercises a power or influence, distinct from and in addition to the written word." (Bogard affirmed, Warlick denied). Proposition 2: "The Scriptures teach that baptism to the believing penitent, is for (in order to) the remission of past, alien sins." (Warlick affirmed, Bogard denied). Proposition 3: "The Scriptures teach that the sinner obtains remission of sins in answer to prayer before baptism." (Bogard affirmed, Warlick denied). Proposition 4: "The Scriptures teach that a saint or child of God may so apostatize as to be finally lost." (Warlick affirmed, Bogard denied). Periodical publication: *Gospel Guide*, January 20 – May 5, 1914. Book publication: *Bogard-Warlick Debate Involving Issues Between Baptists and Christians*. Dallas, TX: B. C. Warlick, 1915. This written debate was intended to reproduce as much as possible their oral debate at Malone, TX.

H. F. Oliver (Church of Christ); Tell, TX; April 27-30, 1916

Albion Eugene Findley (Church of Christ); Mexia, TX; July 25-28, 1916; 4 days

C. R. Nichol (Church of Christ); Scurry, TX; October 17-20, 1916

F. B. Srygley (Church of Christ); County Line (near Center Point), AR; December 12-15, 1916; establishment of church, baptism, apostasy

A. Leroy Elkins (Church of Christ); Gallatin, TX; December 26, 1916 - January 1, 1917; 7 days

Joe S. Warlick (Church of Christ); near Crowder, OK; January 30 - February 2, 1917; 4 days

Joe S. Warlick (Church of Christ); Row, OK; May 14-17, 1917; 4 days

I. B. Bradley (Church of Christ); Curtis, AL; January 2-5, 1918; 4 days

Will M. Thompson (Church of Christ); near Marysville (?Maysville), OK; December 25-28, 1918; 4 days; their first debate

W. G. Roberts (Church of Christ); St. John, KS; September 23-26, 1919

Joe S. Warlick (Church of Christ); near Foreman, AR; October 8-11, 1919; 3 days

R. V. Sarrels (Church of Christ); near Pearcy, AR; November 11-14, 1919

Joe S. Warlick (Church of Christ); Duncan, AZ; December 17-21, 1919; 5 days

Will M. Thompson (Church of Christ); near Shawnee, OK; December 30, 1919 - January 2, 1920; 4 days

George T. Searcy (Church of Christ); near Coal Hill, AR; September 21-24, 1920

H. F. Oliver (Church of Christ); Union Hill (near Rusk), TX; October 19-22, 1920

J. D. Tant (Church of Christ); Guin, AL; November 8-11, 1921; 4 days

Francis O. Howell (Church of Christ); near Chewalla, TN; November 15-18, 1921

C. R. Nichol (Church of Christ); Ambrose, TX; December 13-16, 1921

Charles C. Fuqua (Church of Christ); August 29 - September 1, 1922; 4 days
Joe S. Warlick (Church of Christ); near Ada, OK; September 5-8, 1922; 4 days
R. L. Whiteside (Church of Christ); Hutson, AR; October 24-27, 1922; work of Holy Spirit; 4 days
Frank Strickland (Church of Christ); Lorado, AR; November 28 - December 1, 1922
Joe S. Warlick (Church of Christ); near Paragould, AR; April 10-13, 1923; 4 days
C. H. Cayce (Primitive Baptist Church); Leedy, MS; July 1923; church identity
John Henry Hamilton (Church of Christ); Truman, AR; September 17-21, 1923
I. B. Bradley (Church of Christ); Hodges, AL; September 2-4, 1925; 3 days
Joe H. Blue (Church of Christ); Clover Bend (near Alicia), AR; October 13-16, 1925; 4 days
C. R. Nichol (Church of Christ); Hickory Ridge, AR; December 15-19, 1925
C. R. Nichol (Church of Christ); Tomberlin, AR; December 7-10, 1926
Joe S. Warlick (Church of Christ); Springdale, AR; December 14-17, 1926; 4 days
A. G. Freed (Church of Christ); Nashville, TN; January 11-22, 1927; church, baptism, apostasy; 12 days
J. D. Tant (Church of Christ); Texarkana, TX; September 27 - October 2, 1927; 6 days
Joe H. Blue (Church of Christ); Convenience (near Sulphur Rock), AR; October 25-27, 1927; 3 days
Will M. Thompson (Church of Christ); Oakland, OK; November 15-_, 1927
C. R. Nichol (Church of Christ); near Patmos, AR; November 21-24, 1927
A. G. Freed (Church of Christ); Little Rock, AR; January 3-9, 1928; church; 7 days
Joe S. Warlick (Church of Christ); Troy (near Stephens), AR; July 17-20, 1928; 4 days
Joe S. Warlick (Church of Christ); Acton, TN; August 18-21, 1928; 4 days
Joe S. Warlick (Church of Christ); Corinth, MS; 1928
Cecil B. Douthitt (Church of Christ); Mulberry, FL; December 12-15, 1928; 4 days
Joe S. Warlick (Church of Christ); Blevins, AR; 1929
J. L. Hines (Church of Christ); Hodges, AL; August 13-16, 1929; church
G. C. Brewer (Church of Christ); Humphrey, AR; November 19-22, 1929; 4 days
James L. Davis (Church of Christ); Somerset, KY; January 25-28, 1930; 4 days
G. C. Brewer (Church of Christ); Jonesboro, AR; June 15-19, 1931; 5 days
Will M. Thompson (Church of Christ); near Ada, OK; September 8-11, 1931; 4 days
James Edgar Laird (Church of Christ); Bloomer (near Charleston), AR; October 5-9, 1931
W. L. Oliphant (Church of Christ); Fort Smith, AR; January 7-10, 1932
G. C. Brewer (Church of Christ); McDougal, AR; January 12-15, 1932; 4 days

J. D. Tant (Church of Christ); Memphis, TN; May 24-27, 1932; 4 days
Will M. Thompson (Church of Christ); near Hazel, OK; June 27-30, 1933; 4 days
C. R. Nichol (Church of Christ); near Amory, MS; July 25-28, 1933
C. R. Nichol (Church of Christ); Dodsonville, TX
E. M. Borden (Church of Christ); Crossroads (near Bradford), AR; November 21-24, 1933; 4 days
Will M. Thompson (Church of Christ); Haskell, OK; February 5-9, 1934; 5 days; their 6th debate
Aimee Semple McPherson (Foursquare Gospel Church); North Little Rock, AR; May 22, 1934; 1 session; tent. Proposition: "Resolved that Miracles and Divine Healing, as taught and manifested in the word of God, ceased with the closing of the Apostolic Age." (Bogard affirmed, McPherson denied). Book publication: *Bogard-McPherson Debate*. Dallas, TX: Rock of Ages, n.d. Book publication: *Bogard-McPherson Debate*. Mablevale, AR: Foreman-Payne Publishers, Inc., n.d. Book publication: *Bogard-McPherson Debate*. Decatur, AL: Thrasher Publications, 2000.
Emmett G. Creacy (Church of Christ); Windsor, KY; July 7-10, 1936; 4 days
W. G. Roberts (Church of Christ); West Fork, MO; December 2-5, 1936
W. G. Roberts (Church of Christ); Canalou, MO; September 21-24, 1937
J. D. Tant (Church of Christ); near Greenwood, AR; November 30 - December 3, 1937; 4 days
J. D. Tant (Church of Christ); Lone Star, AR; January 1938; their last debate
N. B. Hardeman (Church of Christ); Little Rock, AR; April 19-22, 1938; 1000. Proposition 1: "The Bible teaches that in conviction and conversion the Holy Spirit exercises a power or influence in addition to the written or spoken word." (Bogard affirmed, Hardeman denied). Proposition 2: "The Bible teaches that baptism, as taught in the commission of our Lord, is for, in order to, the remission of sins, to the penitent believer." (Hardeman affirmed, Bogard denied). Proposition 3: "The church of the New Testament was set up and organized by Jesus Christ during his personal ministry on earth." (Bogard affirmed, Hardeman denied). Proposition 4: "The Bible teaches that it is possible for a child of God to apostatize so as to be finally lost." (Hardeman affirmed, Bogard denied). Book publication: *Hardeman-Bogard Debate*. Nashville, TN: Gospel Advocate Company, 1938.
Clyde Lee Embrey (Church of Christ); Texarkana, TX; December 28, 1937 - January 1, 1938; 5 days
Glen Earl Green (Church of Christ)
Sidney Claude Kinningham (Church of Christ); Arcadia (near Center), TX; July 30 - August 2, 1940; salvation, apostasy, church
W. Curtis Porter (Church of Christ); Hulbert, OK; October 29-November 2, 1940; apostasy; 8 sessions
Byron B. Conley (Church of Christ); Trenton (or Bell), FL; December 18-22, 1940; 5 days
John W. Hedge (Church of Christ); Sulphur Springs (near Mt. Enterprise), TX;

December 9-12, 1941; salvation, apostasy
Vaughn Crumley (Church of Christ)

Eugene S. Smith (Church of Christ); Dallas, TX; May 12-15, 1942; 2500. Proposition 1: "The Bible teaches that the church of the New Testament was set up or established, on the Day of Pentecost following the resurrection of Christ." (Smith affirmed, Bogard denied). Proposition 2: "The Bible teaches that in conviction and conversion, the Holy Spirit exercises a power or influence in addition to the written or spoken word." (Bogard affirmed, Smith denied). Proposition 3: "The Bible teaches that baptism, as taught in the commission of our Lord, is for, in order to obtain, the remission of sins to the penitent believer." (Smith affirmed, Bogard denied). Proposition 4: "The Bible teaches that it is impossible for a child of God to apostatize so as to be finally lost." (Bogard affirmed, Smith denied). Book publication: *Smith-Bogard Debate*. Dallas, TX: Gospel Broadcast, 1942.

W. Curtis Porter (Church of Christ); Damascus, AR; March 23-26, 1948; 8 sessions; Bogard's 237th and final debate. Proposition 1: "The church known as the Missionary Baptist Church is Scriptural in origin, doctrine, practice and name." (Bogard affirmed, Porter denied). Proposition 2: "The church known as the Church of Christ is Scriptural in origin, doctrine, practice and name." (Porter affirmed, Bogard denied). Book publication: *Porter-Bogard Debate*. Monette, AR: W. Curtis Porter, 1951.

Walter Nelson Bohannan [Church of Christ]
Birth: May 9, 1885 (Huntsville, AR)
Death: March 31, 1969 (Cherry Valley, CA)
Biographical sketch: *Preachers of Today* (Batsell Barrett Baxter & M. Norval Young, eds.). Nashville, TN: The Christian Press, 1952, p. 41.
Biographical sketch: *Preachers of Today, Volume Three* (Batsell Barrett Baxter & M. Norval Young, eds.). Nashville, TN: The Gospel Advocate Company, 1964, p. 37.
Obituary: https://www.findagrave.com/memorial/53975873/walter-n-bohannan
_ Logan (?); 1939; classes, drinking vessels
_ Lynn (?); 1944; kingdom, binding of Satan

Wyatt Jefferson Bohannan [Church of Christ]
Birth: September 20, 1887 (near Mants, AR)
Death: 19 (_, _)
Biographical sketch: *Gospel Preachers Who Blazed The Trail* by C. R. Nichol. Austin, TX: Firm Foundation Publishing House, n.d.

Oron T. Bolding [Church of Christ]
Birth: _ (_, _)
Death: _ (_, _)
_ Henshaw (Church of God); Maulden, MO; 1940

Henry Jefferson Boles [Church of Christ]
Birth: November 19, 1845 (Caldwell County, KY)
Death: September 6, 1923 (?McMinnville, TN)
Biographical sketch: *Biographical Sketches Of Gospel Preachers* by H. Leo Boles. Nashville, TN: Gospel Advocate, 1932, pp. 342-346
Public debates with Baptists, Methodists, Presbyterians, Mormons, and Holiness
_ (Baptist Church); c 1871; Boles later baptized this opponent

Henry Leo Boles [Church of Christ]
Birth: February 22, 1874 (Flynn's Creek, near Gainesboro, Jackson County, TN) Death: February 7, 1946 (Nashville, TN)
Son of Henry Jefferson Boles
Biographical sketch: *Gospel Advocate* (March 28, 1946)
Biography: *The Life and Preaching of H. Leo Boles* by William Slater Banowsky. Unpublished Master's Thesis (University of New Mexico, c 1958).
Biographical sketch: *The Trail Blazers: Heroes of the Faith* by J. Porter Wilhite. Oklahoma City, OK: Telegram Book Company, 1965, pp. 54-56.

Biography: "Henry Leo Boles: Distinguished Preacher, Teacher, Debater, Commentator" by Fanning Yater Tant. *They Being Dead Yet Speak* (Florida College Annual Lectures, 1981). Temple Terrace, FL: Florida College Bookstore, 1981, pp. 62-73.
Biography: *Life and Lessons of H. Leo Boles* by Arthur Kay Gardner and John Waddey (editors). Delight, AR: Gospel Light Publishing Company, 1987.
Biographical sketch: *In Memoriam* by Gussie Lambert. Shreveport, LA: Gussie Lambert, 1988, pp. 24-27.
_ (Methodist Church); _, TX; c 1902; denominationalism
O. W. Burnell (Seventh-day Adventist Church); Hickory Grove (Warren Co.), TN; late December 1906. Proposition 1: "The Lord had sanctified the seventh day (Saturday) as a special day of worship under the Christian dispensation." (Burnell affirmed, Boles denied). Proposition 2: "the Lord had sanctified the first day of the week (Sunday) as a special day of worship for Christians." (Boles affirmed, Burnell denied).
W. J. Watson (Missionary Baptist Church); Walter Hill, Rutherford County, TN; May 26-29, 1908. Proposition 1: "The kingdom, or church of God. to which H. Leo Boles belongs, was set up on the first Pentecost after the

resurrection of Christ." (Boles affirmed, Watson denied). Proposition 2: "The church of Christ with which I, W. J. Watson am identified, was set up during the personal ministry of Christ on earth." (Watson affirmed, Boles denied). Proposition 3: "The Scriptures teach that a sinner may pray for pardon of his sins and may expect the answer to his prayer after he has repented of his sins and believed on Christ before his baptism." (Watson affirmed, Boles denied). Proposition 4:"The Scriptures teach that baptism to a penitent believer, out of Christ, is unto the remission of sins." (Boles affirmed, Watson denied).

M. D. Clubb (Christian Church); written; 1926, instrumental music in worship. Book publication: *Discussion: Is Instrumental Music in Christian Worship Scriptural?* Nashville, TN: Gospel Advocate Co., 1927.

Robert H. Boll (Church of Christ); written; 1927; premillennialism. Book publication: *Unfulfilled Prophecy: A Discussion of Prophetic Themes*. Nashville, TN: Gospel Advocate Co., 1954. (Reprint of 1928 edition)

J. M. Hoffman (Seventh-day Adventist Church); Nashville, TN; 1944

W. H. Boles [Church of Christ]
Birth: 1850 (_, IL)
Death: 19_ (_, _)
Biography: *Our Living Evangelists of the Church of Christ* by Henry Clay Patterson. St. Louis, MO: Christian Publishing Company, 1894.

Matthew Stokes (Universalist Society); near Moscow, IL; 1874

W. P. Throgmorton (Baptist Church); Marion, IL; 1875; Holy Spirit, apostasy, church

John R. Daily (Primitive Baptist Church); Dahlgren, IL; 1909; 4 days; church identity

Henry Sparling (Church of Jesus Christ of Latter Day Saints); Springerton, IL: 1910; 6 days

Lyn Boliek [Atheist]
Birth: 19_ (_, _)
Death: _ (_, _)
James White (Reformed Baptist Church)

T. S. Bolin [Baptist Church]
Birth: 18_ (_, _)
Death: 19_ (_, _)
C. R. Nichol (Church of Christ); Smithville, MS

Foy E. Wallace, Sr. (Church of Christ); Savanna, OK; August 8-13, 1916; establishment of the church

J. D. Tant (Church of Christ); Madisonville, TX; 1932

J. D. Tant (Church of Christ); Combes, TX; 1938

Tilford Bolin [Stumblingstoner]
Birth: _ (_, _)
Death: _ (_, _)

C. R. Nichol (Church of Christ); Amory, MS; c 1930

Lee Boling [Christian Church]
Birth: _ (_, _)
Death: _ (_, _)
Hugo McCord (Church of Christ); Ladoga, IN; 1933; instrumental music in worship

Robert Henry Boll [Church of Christ]
Birth: June 7, 1875 (Badenweiler, Germany)
Death: April 13, 1956 (Louisville, KY)
Biography: "R. H. Boll: Premillennial Visionary" by Robert C. Welch. *They Being Dead Yet Speak* (Florida College Annual Lectures, 1981). Temple Terrace, FL: Florida College Bookstore, 1981, pp. 50-61.
Biographical sketch: *Faith and Facts Quarterly*, Volume 9, Number 2 (April 1981), 19.
H. Leo Boles (Church of Christ); written; 1927; premillennialism. Book publication: *Unfulfilled Prophecy: A Discussion of Prophetic Themes*. Nashville, TN: Gospel Advocate Co., 1954. (Reprint of 1928 edition)

Bernard Bolton [Church of Christ]
Birth: 19_ (_, _)
Death: _ (_, _)
Dudley Ross Spears (Church of Christ); written; 1972; women teachers. Periodical publication: *Torch* (starting May 1972).

James Bond [Evolutionist]
Birth: 19_ (_, _)
Death: _ (_, _)
Henry M. Morris (Creationist); Chicago, IL; March 30, 1976; 900

E. E. Bone [Baptist Church]
Birth: _ (_, _)
Death: _ (_, _)
Eugene Britnell (Church of Christ); Beedeville, AR; September 9-12, 1952; salvation, apostasy; Britnell's first debate

Richard Vanderhorst "Van" Bonneau [Church of Christ]
Birth: February 24, 1902 (_, TX)
Death: May 4, 1986 (_, ?TX)
Obituary: https://www.findagrave.com/memorial/82165198/richard-vanderhorst-bonneau
W. Wallace Layton (Church of Christ); 1938; classes
G. W. Graves (Church of Christ); Nashville, TN; 1943
Vernon L. Barr (Missionary Baptist Church); _, OK
Guy N. Woods (Church of Christ)
Guy N. Woods (Church of Christ)

Guy N. Woods (Church of Christ)
Guy N. Woods (Church of Christ)
Guy N. Woods (Church of Christ)
Guy N. Woods (Church of Christ)
W. Curtis Porter (Church of Christ); Houston, TX; October 30 - November 2, 1945; classes
Homer Putnam Reeves (Church of Christ); 1947
Louie L. Stout (Church of Christ); 1950
L. W. Hayhurst (Church of Christ) & Logan Buchanan (Church of Christ); Brownfield, TX; January 1950; classes; 4 nights; w/ Alva Johnson (Church of Christ). Proposition 1: "It is scriptural to teach the Bible by the Class Method of teaching as is practiced by the Church of Christ (Crescent Hill) in Brownsfield, Texas." (Hayhurst & Buchanan affirmed, Johnson & Bonneau denied). Proposition 2: "That the Churches of Christ 'Which oppose the teaching of the Bible in Classes' more than one class at one time using women teachers, are scriptural in such opposition." (Johnson & Bonneau affirmed, Hayhurst & Buchanan denied). Book publication: *A Debate on the Bible Class Question*. Brownfield, TX: J. R. Chisholm and Jimmy Wood, 1950.
Ward Hogland (Church of Christ); Savannah, GA; November 20-22, 1951; classes & women teachers
Lloyd Moyer (Church of Christ); Vallejo & Rodeo, CA; June 16-19, 1952
Lloyd Moyer (Church of Christ); Fresno, CA; February 16-19, 1953; classes & women teachers
A. C. Grider (Church of Christ); Liberty, KY; 1957; classes & women teachers
A. C. Grider (Church of Christ); Phil, KY; 1959; classes & women teachers
Joseph H. Cox (Church of Christ); Bethany, KY; 1959

David D. Bonner [Church of Christ]
Birth: 19_ (_, _)
Death: _ (_, _)
Dwaine E. Dunning (Christian Church); Scottsbluff, NE; November 5-8, 1969; instrumental music in worship
Dwaine E. Dunning (Christian Church); Delhart, TX; April 20-21, 23-24, 1970; instrumental music in worship
Ralph D. Gage (Church of Christ); Dumas, TX; February 28-29, March 2-3, 1972; classes & women teachers, benevolence
Paul O. Nichols (Church of Christ); Yakima, WA; May 14-15, 17-18, 1973; number of drinking vessels in the Lord's supper, classes
Paul O. Nichols (Church of Christ); Duncan, OK; October 15-16, 18-19, 1973; number of drinking vessels in the Lord's supper, classes
_ Johnson (Church of Christ); Joplin, MO; February 8-9, 11-12, 1982; drinking vessels, classes & women teachers
Paul O. Nichols (Church of Christ); Seattle, WA; February 14-15, 17-18, 1983; number of drinking vessels in the Lord's supper, second serving of the Lord's

supper

Joe Hisle (Church of Christ); Francis, OK; February 23-24, 26-27, 1987; drinking vessels in Lord's supper, classes

Keith Sharp (Church of Christ); written; 1993. Proposition: "Men are not 'able' to live above sin in a perfect, sinless life of perfect law keeping." (Bonner affirmed, Sharp denied). Periodical publication: *With All Boldness & Gospel Truths*. Book publication: *The Bonner-Sharp Debate*. Gordon, GA: Cavender Publications, n.d.

Raymond G. Bishop (Pentecostal Church)

Hoyt Chastain (Missionary Baptist Church); Pernell, OK; June 8-11, 1998; church; 4 sessions

Hoyt Chastain (Missionary Baptist Church); Lufkin, TX; October 5-6, 8-9, 1998; church; 4 sessions

Bobby L. Sparks (Missionary Baptist Church); Henderson, TX; May 17-18, 20-21, 1999; salvation at the point of faith, necessity of baptism

Jeff Asher (Church of Christ); Amarillo, TX; August 2-3, 5-6, 1999; deity & humanity of Jesus; 80-200; 4 sessions

Jeff Asher (Church of Christ); Lufkin, TX; August 23-24, 26-27, 1999; deity & humanity of Jesus; 150-250; 4 sessions

Morris Butler Book [Christian Church]

Birth: January 27, 1912 (Columbus, IN)
Death: April 1965 (Dade City, FL)
Obituary: https://www.findagrave.com/memorial/ 110797644/ morris-butler-book

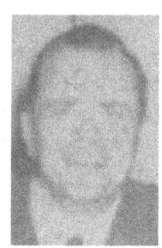

James P. Miller (Church of Christ); Orlando, FL; March 15-17, 1955; instrumental music in worship; 1000-1500. Book publication: *Book-Miller Debate*. Gainesville, FL: Phillips Publications, 1955.

_ Booker [Church of Jesus Christ of Latter Day Saints]

Birth: _ (_, _)
Death: _ (_, _)
Ira C. Moore (Church of Christ); Moundsville, WV; 9 consecutive evenings

J. B. Booth [African Methodist Episcopal Church]

Birth: 18_ (_, _)
Death: 19_ (_, _)
Alexander Cleveland Campbell (Church of Christ); Lillard's Chapel, Marshall Co., TN; March 15-17, ?1920; Proposition: "The church of Christ, with which I (Alexander Campbell) stand identified, is apostolic in origin, doctrine, and practice." (Campbell affirmed, Booth denied). Reference: *Gospel Advocate*, LXII; 16 (April 15, 1920), 389.

W. P. Bootman [Reorganized Church of Jesus Christ of Latter Day Saints]

Birth: 18_ (_, _)
Death: 19_ (_, _)

E. M. Borden (Church of Christ); Woodside, MT; 1917; general church propositions; 10 days

_ Borah [?]
Birth: _ (_, _)
Death: _ (_, _)
_ Butler (?). Book publication: *Borah-Butler Debate*.

Albert Borden [Pentecostal Church]
Birth: _ (_, _)
Death: _ (_, _)
Will M. Thompson (Church of Christ); Coalgate, OK; July 2-5, 1951
O. J. Russell (Church of Christ)
O. J. Russell (Church of Christ)

Elbert Montgomery ("E. M., Jr.") Borden [Church of Christ]
Birth: November 2, 1908 (Batesville, AR)
Death: July 5, 1984 (_, ?TX)
Biographical sketch: *Preachers of Today, Volume Two* (Batsell Barrett Baxter & M. Norval Young, eds.). Nashville, TN: The Gospel Advocate Company, 1959, p. 44.
Biographical sketch: *Preachers of Today, Volume Three* (Batsell Barrett Baxter & M. Norval Young, eds.). Nashville, TN: The Gospel Advocate Company, 1964, p. 39.
J. Ervin Waters (Church of Christ); Hanford, CA; drinking vessels, classes

Eli Monroe ("E. M., Sr.") Borden [Church of Christ]
Birth: January 30, 1874 (_, _)
Death: April 27, 1951 (_, _)
Biography: *Life, Incidents and Sermons of Eli Monroe Borden* by Eli Monroe Borden. Delight, AR: Gospel Light Publishing Company, 1948.
Joe S. Newman (Primitive Baptist Church); Marquez, TX; c 1894; w/J. J. Moye
_ Elder (Baptist Church); Bend, TX; c 1897
_ Elder (Baptist Church); Nix, TX; c 1897
N. R. Townsend (Baptist Church); c August 1902; design of baptism
Ben M. Bogard (Missionary Baptist Church); Bryant, AR; December 12-15, 1905; 4 days
Ben M. Bogard (Missionary Baptist Church); Mammouth Springs, AR; February 20-23, 1906; general church, salvation; 4 days
C. H. Cayce (Primitive Baptist Church); near Bennett (Ripley County), MO; October 2-5, 1906. Subject: "Which church is apostolic in origin, doctrine and practice?"
Ben M. Bogard (Missionary Baptist Church); Minturn, AR; November 19-22, 1907; 4 days

Joe Fairchilds (Primitive Baptist Church); Yocum, AR; February 1908; 5 nights

Ben M. Bogard (Missionary Baptist Church); Balch, AR; July 26-29, 1909. Proposition 1: "The Scriptures teach that the Church of Christ was established on the first Pentecost after the resurrection of Christ." (Borden affirmed, Bogard denied). Proposition 2: "The Scriptures teach that the sinner is so depraved that in his conviction and conversion, the Holy Spirit must of necessity exercise a power or influence, distinct from and in addition to the written word." (Bogard affirmed, Borden denied). Proposition 3: "The Scriptures teach that a child of God or Saint, may so apostatize as to be lost in hell." (Borden affirmed, Bogard denied). Proposition 4: "The Scriptures teach that a sinner is saved by grace through faith, before baptism." (Bogard affirmed, Borden denied). Book publication: *Borden-Bogard Debate*.

Ben M. Bogard (Missionary Baptist Church); Roosevelt, AR; September 13-16, 1909; 4 days

Ben M. Bogard (Missionary Baptist Church); Hickory Ridge, AR; October 26-29, 1909; 4 days

Ben M. Bogard (Missionary Baptist Church); Buford, AR; June 28-30, 1910; 3 days

Ben M. Bogard (Missionary Baptist Church); near Newport, AR; August 31 - September 3, 1910; 4 days

Ben M. Bogard (Missionary Baptist Church); Enola, AR; November 12-15, 1912; 4 days

_ Zilmer (Christadelphian); Marrietton, _; c March 1913; establishment of kingdom, nature of man, birth of the Spirit, punishment of wicked, resurrection

L. S. Ballard (Baptist Church); Salem, AR; 1913

Ben M. Bogard (Missionary Baptist Church); July 8-11, 1913; 4 days

L. S. Ballard (Baptist Church); Little Rock, AR; March 3-8, 1914; 6 sessions. Proposition 1: "The Scriptures teach that faith in Christ procures salvation without further acts of obedience." (Ballard affirmed, Borden denied). Proposition 2: "The Scriptures teach that water baptism is for (in order to) remission of past sins." (Borden affirmed, Ballard denied). Book publication: *The Ballard-Borden Debate*.

A. U. Nunnery (Baptist Church); between Wildersville and Parsons, TN; February 8-11, 1916. Proposition 1: "The Baptist Church is scriptural in origin, doctrine, and practice." (Nunnery affirmed, Borden denied). Proposition 2: "The Church of Christ is scriptural in origin, doctrine, and practice." (Borden affirmed, Nunnery denied). [*Gospel Advocate*, Vol. 58, No. 11 (March 16, 1916), 272]

W. P. Bootman (Reorganized Church of Jesus Christ of Latter Day Saints); Woodside, MT; 1917; general church propositions; 10 days

A. U. Nunnery (Baptist Church); between Wildersville and Parsons, TN; c March 1918; their second debate at same location on same subjects. Proposition 1: "The Baptist Church is scriptural in origin, doctrine, and practice." (Nunnery affirmed, Borden denied). Proposition 2: "The Church

of Christ is scriptural in origin, doctrine, and practice." (Borden affirmed, Nunnery denied).
C. F. Parker (Primitive Baptist Church); Galatia, IL; c September 1932
Ben M. Bogard (Missionary Baptist Church); Crossroads (near Bradford), AR; November 21-24, 1933; 4 days
_ (Holiness Church); Bakersfield, CA
A. S. Bradley (Materialist); Goldthwaite, TX; 7 days
A. H. Zilmer (Christadelphian); Morrilton, AR
_ Purtle (Methodist Church);
Richard H. Pigue (Methodist Church);
_ Beckham (Methodist Church);
_ ("Come-outer"); _ , AR
_ ("Come-outer"); _ , AR
_ ("Come-outer"); _ , AR
_ ("Come-outer"); _ , AR
_ ("Come-outer"); _ , AR
_ ("Come-outer"); Wheeling , AR
Frank Strickland (Church of Christ); Judsonia, AR; materialism
_ Townsend (Baptist Church); Black Rock, AR
_ Townsend (Baptist Church); Noland, AR
_ Townsend (Baptist Church)
_ Townsend (Baptist Church)
C. E. Hunt (Baptist Church); Porterville, CA; 1940
_ Johnson (Jehovah's Witness?); Porterville, CA; c 1941
J. Ervin Waters (Church of Christ); Hanford, CA; drinking vessels in Lord's supper; classes

Alfred Oran Border [Church of Christ]
Birth: March 22, 1901 (Edgewood, IL)
Death: October 1971 (_, ?AR)
_ Crawford (?); 1934; Sabbath

John Darrell Boren [Church of Christ]
Birth: July 9, 1898 (Wynnewood, OK)
Death: May 24, 1993 (Bedford, TX)
Biographical sketch: *Preachers of Today, Volume Two* (Batsell Barrett Baxter & M. Norval Young, eds.). Nashville, TN: The Gospel Advocate Company, 1959, p. 44.
Biographical sketch: *Preachers of Today, Volume Three* (Batsell Barrett Baxter & M. Norval Young, eds.). Nashville, TN: The Gospel Advocate Company, 1964, p. 39.
_ (Baptist Church); before 1959
_ (Holiness Church); before 1959
_ (Atheist); before 1959

Ira Matthew Boswell [Christian Church]
Birth: April 28, 1866 (Columbus, Lowndes Co., MS)
Death: January 18, 1950 (Louisville, Jefferson Co., KY)
Biographical sketch: *Lives of Mississippi Authors, 1817-1967* by James B. Lloyd (Ed.). Jackson, MS: University Press of Mississippi, 1981.
Biographical sketch: *Who Was Who in America. A companion biographical reference work to Who's Who in America. Volume 2, 1943-1950.* Chicago: A.N. Marquis Co., 1963.
Obituary: https://www.findagrave.com/memorial/37830244/ira-matthew-boswell

N. B. Hardeman (Church of Christ); Nashville, TN; May 31-June 5, 1923; 6 sessions; 6000. Proposition: "Instrumental music in church worship is scriptural." (Boswell affirmed, Hardeman denied). Book publication: *Boswell-Hardeman Discussion on Instrumental Music in the Worship.* Nashville, TN: Gospel Advocate Co., 1924. [*Gospel Advocate*, June 14, 1923]

Raymond Bosworth [Jehovah's Witnesses]
Birth: _ (_, _)
Death: _ (_, _)
B. H. Atkinson (Church of Christ); Sunbury, PA; 1947

Shmuel "Shmuley" Boteach [Jewish Rabbi]
Birth: November 19, 1966 (Los Angeles, CA)
Death: _ (_, _)
Biographical sketch: https://en.wikipedia.org/wiki/Shmuley_Boteach
Christopher Hitchens (Atheist); 2008
Douglas Jacoby (?); 2008
Shabir Ally (Muslim); 2008
Michael Brown: (Messianic Jew); 2008; Is belief in Jesus is compatible with Judaism?
Douglas Jacoby (?); 2009; Judaism & Christianity: Which is the Religion of Peace?

Arthur James Boucot [Evolutionist]
Birth: May 26, 1924 (Philadelphia, PA)
Death: April 10, 2017 (Denver, CO)
Biographical sketch: https://en.wikipedia.org/wiki/Arthur_James_Boucot
Duane T. Gish (Creationist); Eugene, OR; January 20, 1977

J. Bourne [?]
Birth: _ (_, _)
Death: _ (_, _)
J. L. Hines (Church of Christ); premillennialism. Periodical publication:

American Christian Review. 1951

J. M. Bovee [Church of Christ]
Birth: 18_ (_, _)
Death: _ (_, _)
J. W. Miller (?); Bay, Calhoun County, IL; 1897; instrumental music in worship

Malcom Bowen [Church of Christ]
Birth: April 3, 1911 (El Dorado, AR)
Death: January 3, 1976 (Lake City, AR)
Biographical sketch: *Preachers of Today, Volume Three* (Batsell Barrett Baxter & M. Norval Young, eds.). Nashville, TN: The Gospel Advocate Company, 1964, pp. 40-41.
Biographical sketch: *In Memoriam* by Gussie Lambert. Shreveport, LA: Gussie Lambert, 1988, pp. 27-28.
_ (Pentecostal Church); Cypert, AR; 1935
_ (Church of Christ); before 1965; classes

G. M. Bowers (Seventh-day Church of God)
Birth: 19_ (_, _)
Death: _ (_, _)
Cecil Willis (Church of Christ); Huntsville, TX; March 5-6, 8-9, 1979; Sabbath & Sunday

John Bowes [?]
Birth: _ (_, _)
Death: _ (_, _)
T. H. Milner (Church of Christ); Dundee, Scotland; March 29-31, 1859. Book publication: *A Discourse on Baptism and Other Papers.*

Walter Payton "Wat" Bowles [Church of Christ]
Birth: January 5, 1811 (Bourbon County, KY)
Death: March 19, 1863 (DeWitt County, IL)
James Barger (Methodist Episcopal Church); DeWitt County, IL; 1840's

George Phillip Bowser [Church of Christ]
Birth: February 17, 1874 (Maury County, TN)
Death: March 23, 1950 (Detroit, MI)
_ Terry (Baptist Church); Nashville, TN; c June 1925
Abe Young (Christian Church); Jarvis, TX; c 1932

Charles Box [Church of Christ]
Birth: 19_ (_, _)
Death: _ (_, _)
E. J. "Gene" Reynolds (Church of God); 1975
Frank Butler (Church of Christ); 1975. Proposition: "The Scriptures teach that in the work of benevolence, the church may, from its treasury relieve both saints and non-Christians." (Box affirmed, Butler denied). Book publication: *The Butler-Box Debate*. 1975.

William F. Boyakin [Baptist Church]
Birth: May 29, 1807 (_, NC)
Death: _ (_, _)
Heman C. Smith (Reorganized Church of Jesus Christ of Latter Day Saints); Blue Rapids, KS; June 4-_, 1877

P. P. Boyd [Reformed Presbyterian Church]
Birth: 18_ (_, _)
Death: _ (_, _)
Addison Pickerill (Church of Christ); Superior, NE; February 11-12, 1889. Proposition: "Immersion of the body in water is essential to scriptural baptism." (Pickerill affirmed, Boyd denied). Report: *Christian Leader*, Volume 3(8), February 19, 1889.

W. S. "Bill" Boyett [Church of Christ]
Birth: March 3, 1911 (San Saba County, TX)
Death: September 20, 1982 (Comanche, TX)
Biographical sketch: *Preachers of Today* (Batsell Barrett Baxter & M. Norval Young, eds.). Nashville, TN: The Christian Press, 1952, p. 45.
Biographical sketch: *Preachers of Today, Volume Two* (Batsell Barrett Baxter & M. Norval Young, eds.). Nashville, TN: The Gospel Advocate Company, 1959, pp. 46-47.
Biographical sketch: *Preachers of Today, Volume Three* (Batsell Barrett Baxter & M. Norval Young, eds.). Nashville, TN: The Gospel Advocate Company, 1964, p. 42.
Biographical sketch: *Preachers of Today, Volume Four* (Batsell Barrett Baxter & M. Norval Young, eds.). Nashville, TN: The Gospel Advocate Company, 1970, p. 29.
_ (Seventh-day Adventist Church); Lewiston, ID, 1942; 3 nights
_ (Seventh-day Adventist Church); Jerome, ID; 1942

Elvis Euen Bozarth [Church of Christ]
Birth: December 21, 1925 (_, _)
Death: August 20, 2010 (_, _)
William Mizell (?); Chicago, IL; December 1966
Windell R. Fikes (Church of Christ); Chicago, IL; 1967

Charles Clark Braden [Christian Church]

Birth: August 8, 1831 (Gustavus, Trumbull County, OH)
Death: March 6, 1915 (Shasta County, CA)
133 public debates, 26 in Illinois; 2 written debates; 18 debates with LDS

J. P. Den (Methodist Episcopal Church); Richview, IL; 1866; baptism
H. V. Spencer (?); Richview, IL; Bible revision
Jacob Ditzler (Methodist Episcopal Church); De Soto, IL; 1866; baptism
R. C. Dennis (Infidel); Duquoin, IL; 1868
G. W. Hughey (Methodist Episcopal Church); Vienna, Johnson County, IL; August 18-27, 1868; baptism, Holy Spirit, Methodist Episcopal Discipline, human creeds; 9 days. Proposition 1: "Pouring or sprinkling water on a proper person in the name of the Father, Son and Holy Spirit is the scriptural Christian baptism." (Hughey affirmed, Braden denied). Book publication: *Debate on the Action of Baptism, the Design of Baptism, the Subjects of Baptism, the Work of the Holy Spirit, the Discipline of the M. E. Church, and Human Creeds*. Cincinnati, OH: Franklin & Rice, 1870. [*American Christian Review* (December 5, 1871)]
B. F. Underwood (Atheist); Duquoin, IL; 1870; Christianity and materialism
Samuel Binns (Cumberland Presbyterian Church); Casey, IL; 1870; baptism
B. F. Underwood (Atheist); Time, IL; 1871; Christianity and materialism
B. F. Underwood (Atheist); Bushnell, IL; 1871; Christianity and materialism
Sam Binnus (Universalist Society); Reynoldsburg, OH; 1871
B. F. Underwood (Atheist); Washington, IL; 1872; Christianity and materialism
John Hughes (Universalist Society); LaFayette, IL; 1872
C. R. Sanborn (Free Congregationalist); Bloomington, IL; 1873; infidelity
C. H. Bliss (Seventh-day Adventist Church); Lovington, IL; 1874
B. F. Underwood (Atheist); Jacksonville, IL; summer 1876
John Hughes (Universalist Society); Lewistown, IL; 1877
W. F. Jamison (?); Salem, IL; 1878; Christianity and materialism
B. F. Underwood (Atheist)
B. F. Underwood (Atheist)
B. F. Underwood (Atheist)
B. F. Underwood (Atheist)
E. L. Kelley (Reorganized Church of Jesus Christ of Latter Day Saints); Wilber, NE; November 7-_, 1883
E. L. Kelley (Reorganized Church of Jesus Christ of Latter Day Saints); Kirkland, OH; February 12 - March 8, 1884. Book publication: *Public Discussion of the Issues Between the Reorganized Church of Jesus Christ of Latter Day Saints and the Church of Christ (Disciples)*. St. Louis, MO: Clark Braden, 1884.
J. W. Gillen (Reorganized Church of Jesus Christ of Latter Day Saints);

Stewartsville, MO; December 1884
E. L. Kelley (Reorganized Church of Jesus Christ of Latter Day Saints); Bellair, IL; 1889
B. F. Underwood (Atheist); 1889; their 11th debate
E. L. Kelley (Reorganized Church of Jesus Christ of Latter Day Saints); Bellair, IL; March 6-13, 1890; Book of Mormon, Scriptures
John Williams (First-day Adventist Church); Chicago, IL; 1894
A. J. Fishback (Spiritualist); Sturgis, MI
Thomas Williams (Christadelphian); 1896; 7 nights. Book publication: Chicago, IL: Advocate Printing Co., 1897.
I. N. White (Reorganized Church of Jesus Christ of Latter Day Saints); Orchardville, IL; 1898
Joe S. Warlick (Church of Christ); Dallas, TX; ?April, 1898; instrumental music in worship; 4 sessions
I. N. White (Reorganized Church of Jesus Christ of Latter Day Saints); Alma, IL; 1899; Mormonism
C. H. Bliss (Seventh-day Adventist Church); St. Elmo, IL; 1899
Joe S. Warlick (Church of Christ); written; instrumental music in worship
_ Hicks (Baptist Church); Nebo, IL; 1901; church
W. G. Roberts (Church of Christ); Belmont, IL; November 1902
A. P. Roberts (?); Olney, IL; 1903
D. B. Turney (Protestant Methodist Church); Wayne City, IL; 1903; baptism
Charles Watts (Materialist)
Moses Hull (Spiritist)

Dave Bradford [Church of Christ]
Birth: 19_ (_, _)
Death: _ (_, _)
Harry Cobb, Jr. (Church of Christ); Birmingham, AL; April 19-20, 26-27, 1968; classes
Jim Clements (Church of Christ); Hixson, TN; May 17-18, 20-21, 1976; church treasury

_ Bradford [?]
Birth: _ (_, _)
Death: _ (_, _)
Billy Norris (Church of Christ); 1939; instrumental music in worship

Charles Bradlaugh [Atheist]
Birth: September 26, 1833 (Hoxton, London, England)
Death: January 30, 1891 (_, _)
Sometimes used the designation "Iconoclast"
Biography: *The Biography of Charles Bradlaugh* by Adolphe S. Headingley.
Biography: *Charles Bradlaugh* by John M. Robertson. London: Watts & Co., 1920.

Biography: *Charles Bradlaugh: A Record of His Life and Work by his daughter* by Hypatia Bradlaugh Bonner. London, T. Fisher Unwin, 1908.
Biography: Bonner, Hypatia Bradlaugh. *Charles Bradlaugh: A Record of His Life and Work by his daughter*. London: T. Fisher Unwin, 1908.
Brewin Grant (?). Book publication: *A Full Report of the Discussion between B.G. and 'Iconoclast'*. 1858.
T. D. Matthias (Baptist Church); Halifax, _; October 31-November 4, 1859. Proposition 1: "The history of Jesus Christ as narrated in the four gospels, incredible." (Bradlaugh affirmed, Matthias denied). Proposition 2: "The doctrine of Jesus Christ not calculated to benefit humanity." (Bradlaugh affirmed, Matthias denied). Book publication: *The Only Authorized and Verbatim Report of the Five Nights' Discussion, at Halifax; between the Rev. T. D. Matthias, Baptist Minister; and Iconoclast*. London: Farrah, Wilks, & Dunbar, 1860.
_ Brindley (?). Book publication: *Discussion Between 'Iconoclast' and Dr. Brindley*. c. 1860.
Joseph Baylee (?); June 1860; 3 nights. Book publication: *God, Man, and the Bible. Three Nights' Discussion between the Rev. Joseph Baylee ... and Charles Bradlaugh ... June, 1860 ...*
_ Mackie (?); 1861. Book publication: *A Full Report of the Discussion between Mr. Mackie ... and Iconoclast (Mr. Bradlaugh) ... 1861, on the question, What does the Bible teach about God?* 1861.
J. H. Rutherford (?). Book publication: *Are the Doctrines and precepts of Christianity, as taught in the New Testament calculated to benefit humanity? Report of the debate ... between "Iconoclast" and J.H. Rutherford*. 1861.
W. Hutchins (?); 1861. Book publication: *Christianity and Secularism; Report of a Public Discussion Between Mr. W. Hutchins and Mr. C. Bradlaugh ... 1861 ...* 1861.
T. Lawson (?). Book publication: *A discussion on the Question, Has Man a Soul? between the Rev. T. Lawson ... and Iconoclast ...* 1861.
Woodville Woodman (?). Book publication: *The Existence of God: A Discussion between Rev. Woodville Woodman, and "Iconoclast"*. 1861.
Woodville Woodman (?). Book publication: *Is the Bible a Divine Revelation? A Discussion between Rev. W. Woodman and Iconoclast ...* 1861.
W. Barker (?) Book publication: *Modern Atheism and the Bible: Report of the Discussion between the Rev. W. Barker ... and Iconoclast ...* 1862.
John Watts (Secularist). Book publication: *Half-hours with Freethinkers*. 1864.
Thomas Cooper (Believer); London, England; February 1, 3, 1864; 2 sessions. Book publication: *Two Nights' Public Discussion between Thomas Cooper and Charles Bradlaugh, on the Being of a God as the Maker and Moral Governor of the Universe*. London: Austin and Co., 1864. Book publication: *Two Nights' Public Discussion between Thomas Cooper and Mr. C. Bradlaugh, on the Being of a God as the Maker and Moral Governor of the Universe*. London: C. Watts, 1874.

W. Gillespie (Theist). Book publication: *Atheism Or Theism? Debate between Iconoclast ... and W. Gillespie* c 1869.

G. J. Holyoake (?); 2 nights. Book publication: *Secularism, Skepticism, and Atheism. Verbatim Report of the proceedings of a two-nights' public debate between Messrs. G. J. Holyoake and C. Bradlaugh.* 1870.

David King (Church of Christ). Book publication: *Christianity v. Secularism. Report of a ... discussion between D. King ... and C. B...* Subject: "What can Secularism do for Man that Christianity cannot?" 1870.

David King (Church of Christ); Bury, Lancashire, England; September 27, 1870. Book publication: *What Is Christianity? Report of a Public Discussion.*

Alexander J. Harrison (Methodist New Connexion); 1870; 5000. Book publication: *Secularism. Report of a public discussion between the Rev. Alexander J. Harrison ... and Mr. Charles Bradlaugh ... 1870.*

A. Robertson (?). Book publication: *The Existence of God. Verbatim report of ... debate between Messrs, A. Robertson and C.B.* 1870.

Alexander J. Harrison (Methodist New Connexion); Newcastle-upon-Tyne, England; September 13-14, 1870; 2 nights. Proposition 1: "That secularism, distinctively considered, is not a system of truth, and therefore, cannot justify its existence to the reason." (Harrison affirmed, Bradlaugh denied). Proposition 2: "That secularism, distinctively considered, is not a system of morality, and therefore, is unworthy of trust as a guide." (Harrison affirmed, Bradlaugh denied). Book publication: *Report of a Public Discussion between the Rev. Alexander J. Harrison, (Minister of the Methodist New Connexion,) and Mr. Charles Bradlaugh, (President of the National Secular Society,) Held in the New Town Hall, Newcastle-upon-Tyne, on the Evenings of Sept. 13 & 14, 1870.* London: Austin & Co., 1870. Book publication: *Verbatim report of the two nights' discussion between the Rev. A.J. Harrison and C. Bradlaugh.* 1909.

Brewin Grant (?); 1875. Book publication: *Discussion on Atheism. Report of a public discussion between the Rev. Brewin Grant ... and C. Bradlaugh ... 1875 ...* 1875.

William Simpson (?). Book publication: *Disestablishment and Disendowment of the English Church. ... Report ... of the debate between ... C. Bradlaugh and W. Simpson, ...* 1876.

Walter R. Browne (?); 2 nights. Book publication: *Can Miracles be proved possible? Verbatim report of the two nights' public debate between ... Bradlaugh and W. R. Brown, ...* 1876.

Brewin Grant (?); Finsbury, London, England; June 22, 29, July 6, 13, 20, 27, 1875. Subject: "Is atheism or is Christianity the true Secular Gospel, as tending to the improvement and happiness of mankind in this life by human efforts and material means?" Book publication: *Grant-Bradlaugh Debate.* London, England: Anti-Liberation Society, 1890.

Robert Roberts (?Christadelphian); Leicester & Birmingham, England; June 13-15, 20-22, 1876. Proposition: "That the Scriptures are the reliable and authentic record of Divine revelation." (Roberts affirmed, Bradlaugh denied). Book publication: *A Six Nights' Discussion Between Mr. Charles Bradlaugh, of London, (Editor of the National Reformer,) and Mr. Robert Roberts, of Birmingham, (Editor of The Christadelphian, and Author of Twelve Lectures)*. London: F. Pitman, 1876.

John Lightfoot (?); written; 1876. Book publication: *Eternal Torment. A Written debate between the Rev. John Lightfoot ... and Charles Bradlaugh ... 1876.* 1888.

R. A. Armstrong (?); 2 nights. Book publication: *Is it Reasonable to Worship God? Verbatim report of two nights' debate at Nottingham between the Rev. R. A. Armstrong and Charles Bradlaugh.* 1878.

James M. McCann (?); London, England; December 7, 14, 21, 1881; 3 nights. Book publication: *Secularism: Unphilosophical, immoral, and anti-social. Verbatim Report of a Three Nights' Debate between the Rev. Dr. McCann and Charles Bradlaugh.* London: Freethought Publishing Company, 1881.

H. M. Hyndman (?); April 17, 1884. Book publication: *Will Socialism Benefit the English People? Verbatim Report of a Debate between H. M. Hyndman and C. Bradlaugh Held at St. James' Hall on April 17th, 1884.* London: Freethought Publishing Company, 1884.

Ernest Belfort Bax (?); written. Book publication: *Will Socialism Benefit the English People? A Written debate between E. Belfort Bax and Charles Bradlaugh.* 1887.

Annie Besant (?); written. Book publication: *Socialism; for and against: written debate with Mrs. Besant.* 1887.

Marsden Gibson (?); 2 nights. Book publication: "Has Humanity Gained from Unbelief?" 1889.

H. M. Hyndman (?). Book publication: *Eight Hours Movement. Verbatim report of a debate between H. M. Hyndman and C. Bradlaugh.* 1890.

W. C. Magee (?). Book publication: *Christianity in Relation to Freethought, Skepticism, and Faith. Three Discourses by the Bishop of Peterborough, with special replies by Charles Bradlaugh.* 1892.

W. M. Westerby (?). Subject: "Has, or is, Man a Soul?" Book publication: *Debate between Rev. W. M. Westerby and Charles Bradlaugh.* 1909.

A. S. Bradley [Materialist]

Birth: 18_ (_, _)
Death: 19_ (_, _)

C. R. Nichol (Church of Christ); Rule, TX; April 20-22, 1906; 6 sessions. Proposition 1: "The Scriptures teach that the kingdom of Christ was established on the first Pentecost after the resurrection of Christ." (Nichol affirmed, Bradley denied). Proposition 2: "The Scriptures teach that man is wholly mortal and unconscious from death till the resurrection." (Bradley affirmed, Nichol denied). Book publication: *The Nichol-Bradley Debate*. Clifton, TX: Nichol Publishing Co., 1907.

George W. Austin (Church of Christ); 1910

E. M. Borden (Church of Christ); Goldthwaite, TX; 7 days

Samuel A. Ribble (Church of Christ); 1914

I. B. Bradley [Church of Christ]
Birth: June 26, 1868 (_, _)
Death: January 24, 1952 (_, _)
48 debates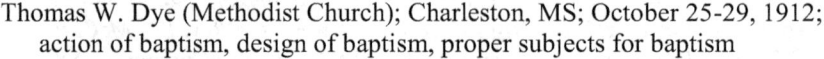
_ (Baptist Church); Lancaster, TN; c 1906
C. H. Cayce (Primitive Baptist Church); Bon Aqua, TN; July 5-
_, 1910; 4 days; general church propositions
W. A. Gaugh (Missionary Baptist Church); Belmont, MS;
September 10-13, 1910; establishment of church, conditions
of pardon
Thomas W. Dye (Methodist Church); Charleston, MS; October 25-29, 1912;
action of baptism, design of baptism, proper subjects for baptism
D. W. Pauley (Seventh-day Adventist Church) & John A. Cargile (Seventh-day
Adventist Church); Delina, TN; May 6-_, 1913; punishment of wicked,
unconscious dead
I. N. Penick (Baptist Church); Burt, TN; July 1-4, 1913. Proposition 1: "The
scriptures teach that a believer has remission of sins before and without
baptism in water." (Penick affirmed, Bradley denied). Proposition 2:
"Baptism is for the remission of sins." (Bradley affirmed, Penick denied).
A. N. Hollis (Missionary Baptist Church); Greenwood, TN; c December 1913; 4
days; baptism, apostasy
Samuel Ford (Holiness Church); Taft, TN; January 8-9, 1914. Proposition 1:
"What all men and women who are truly converted, or sins pardoned, are at
that time sanctified." Bradley affirmed, Ford denied). Proposition 2: "That
men and women are sanctified subsequent to regeneration, or conversion, or
sins pardoned, and that all saved people, or Christians, live lives of sinless
perfection." (Ford affirmed, Bradley denied).
_ Massey (Missionary Baptist Church); Rock Bridge (Sumner Co.), TN;
February 24-27, 1914. Proposition 1: "The scriptures teach that the alien
sinner must pray for and expect pardon in answer to his prayer before water
baptism." (Massey affirmed, Bradley denied). Proposition 2: "The scriptures
teach that water baptism as a condition of pardon to the penitent believer is
for the remission of past or alien sins." (Bradley affirmed, Massey denied).
H. B. Taylor (Missionary Baptist Church); Auburn, TN; July 7-11, 1914
John R. Daily (Primitive Baptist Church); Red Spring (near Stewart). MS; c
December 1914; 6 days. Proposition 1: "The scriptures teach the doctrine of
unconditional and personal election." (Daily affirmed, Bradley denied).
Proposition 2: "Baptism is for remission of sins." (Bradley affirmed, Daily
denied). Proposition 3: "The scriptures teach that the regeneration of sinners
is entirely the work of the Spirit of God, independent of human means or
instrumentalities." (Daily affirmed, Bradley denied).
J. E. Skinner (Missionary Baptist Church); Jordan Springs (Montgomery Co.),
TN; February 16-20, 1915. Proposition 1: "The scriptures teach close or

restricted communion as generally taught and practiced by the Missionary Baptist Church." (Skinner affirmed, Bradley denied). Baptism, Holy Spirit, and apostasy were also discussed.

Don Q. Smith (Missionary Baptist Church); Glasgow, KY; November 2-5, 1915; 4 days

H. D. Rice (Missionary Baptist Church); Lowes, KY; July 6-9, 1917

_ (?); _, AL; September 4-7, 1917

Ben M. Bogard (Missionary Baptist Church); Curtis, AL; January 2-5, 1918; 4 days

C. H. Cayce (Primitive Baptist Church); near Burns, TN; September 23-27, 1918; tent debate

A. U. Nunnery (Baptist Church); Pleasant Grove (near Wildersville), TN; c November 1919; 5 days

A. B. Cargile (Seventh-day Adventist Church); Grant, AL; c July 1923; establishment of kingdom, punishment of wicked, consciousness of dead

W. D. Hargrove (Missionary Baptist Church); near Dover, TN; March 11-14, 1924

C. H. Cayce (Primitive Baptist Church); Woodville, AL; August 4-7, 1924

Ben M. Bogard (Missionary Baptist Church); Hodges, AL; September 2-4, 1925; 3 days

R. L. Jackson (Adventist Church); Carroll Co., MS; October 26-29, 1925; state of the dead, punishment of the wicked

W. D. Hargrove (Missionary Baptist Church); Poplar Springs, Stewart Co., TN; November 30-December 4, 1925

_ Daughtery (Baptist Church); Sylvania, TN; c March 1934

J. R. Bradley [Church of Christ]
Birth: 18_ (_, _)
Death: 19_ (_, _)
_ Haysmer (Seventh-day Adventist Church); Taft, Lincoln Co., TN; c May 1906

Van A. Bradley [Church of Christ]
Birth: 18_ (_, _)
Death: 19_ (_, _)
G. S. Raburn (Baptist Church); Burnsville, MS; 1932

_ Bradley [Sabbatarian]
Birth: _ (_, _)
Death: _ (_, _)
Frederick William Fenton (Church of Christ); 1922; Sabbath, Lord's day

Frank Bradshaw [Church of Jesus Christ of Latter Day Saints]
Birth: 19_ (_, _)
Death: _ (_, _)
Patrick Madrid (Roman Catholic Church). Subjects: (1) Who holds the keys, prophet or pope? (2) Was the Book of Mormon inspired by God?

James C. Brady [Baptist Church]
Birth: 19_ (_, _)
Death: _ (_, _)
Ray Hawk (Church of Christ); written; c 1978; apostasy. Book publication: "Brady-Hawk Debate on Apostasy," *The Beacon*, 1978.

Edward O. Bragwell, Sr. [Church of Christ]
Birth: May 28, 1936 (_, _)
Death: _ (_, _)
Frederick Beversdorf (Lutheran Church); Hanceville, AL; 1960
Paul V. Dobson (Church of Christ); written. Proposition: It is scriptural for a church of Christ to send a donation to another church of Christ only when the receiving church is an object of charity." (Bragwell affirmed, Dobson denied). Book publication: *Bragwell-Dobson Debate*. No publication data.
Don Huddleston (Church of Christ); Grenada, MS; November 19-20, 1970; sponsoring church, fellowship halls; 225
B. C. Bailey (Baptist Church); Gardendale, AL; May 22-23, 25-26, 1972; baptism; 4 sessions

Edward O. "Eddie" Bragwell, Jr. [Church of Christ]
Birth: November 2, 1956 (_, _)
Death: December 21, 2012 (?Russellville, AL)
Obituary: http://www.legacy.com/obituaries/timesdaily/obituary.aspx?pid=161895556
Roger Jackson (Church of Christ); Anniston, AL; January 14-15, 17-18, 1985. Proposition 1: "It is in harmony with the scriptures for churches of Christ to contribute from their treasuries to benevolent institutions structured like Childhaven so that the needs of orphaned children might be adequately met." (Jackson affirmed, Bragwell denied). Proposition 2: "The Scriptures teach that the local church, in its work of benevolence, may only provide the needs of the saints." (Bragwell affirmed, Jackson denied).

Milton P. Brahman [?]
Birth: _ (_, _)
Death: 18_ (_, _)
Thomas Whittemore (Universalist Society); Danvers, MA; November 6, 1833; limited punishment after death. Book publication: *The Danvers Discussion: A Report Of the Discussion at Danvers, Mass. On November 6, 1833*. Boston, MA: B. B. Mussey, and Marsh, Capen & Lyon, 1833.

J. M. Brandon [Church of Christ]
Birth: 18_ (_, _)
Death: 19_ (_, _)

Ben M. Bogard (Missionary Baptist Church); Ford's Well, Yolabusha Co., MS; July 16-20, 1907; 5 days

Ben M. Bogard (Missionary Baptist Church); Ford's Well, Yolabusha Co., MS; August 11-15, 1908; 6 days

Ralph Francis Brashears [Church of Christ]
Birth: November 8, 1908 (Wynnewood, OK)
Death: December 29, 1996 (Pauls Valley, OK)
Biographical sketch: *Preachers of Today, Volume Two* (Batsell Barrett Baxter & M. Norval Young, eds.). Nashville, TN: The Gospel Advocate Company, 1959, p. 48.
Obituary: https://www.findagrave.com/memorial/102904259/ralph-francis-brashears
_ Sandoval (?)
_ (?); Tayug, Pangasinan; 1950; deity of Christ

Herman Flake Braswell [True Light Church]
Birth: June 23, 1926 (Union Co, NC)
Death: December 17, 2017 (Union, NC)
Obituary: https://www.dignitymemorial.com/obituaries/monroe-nc/herman-braswell-7683661
Patrick T. Donahue (Church of Christ); Lucknow, SC; March 28, 1996; baptism; 1 session; 100
Patrick T. Donahue (Church of Christ); Unionville, NC; April 5, 1997; baptism; 1 session; 100
Patrick T. Donahue (Church of Christ); Lucknow, SC; August 29, 1998; limited atonement; 100
Eddie K. Garrett II (Church of Christ); Monroe, NC; January 1, 1999; For whom did Christ die?

Steve Bratteng [Atheist]
Birth: _ (_, _)
Death: _ (_, _)
Bill Jackson (Church of Christ); written; 1988; existence of God, humanism. Book publication: *Jackson-Bratteng Debate*. No publication data.

Bayard Holmes Brattstrom [Evolutionist]
Birth: July 3, 1929 (Chicago, IL)
Death: _ (_, _)
Biographical sketch: https://prabook.com/web/bayard_holmes.brattstrom/243005
Biographical sketch: http://www.fullerton.edu/emeriti/_resources/pdfs/Brattstrom-news.pdf

Duane T. Gish (Creationist) & Henry M. Morris (Creationist); Santa Ana, CA; November 17, 1975; 2800; w/ William Presch (Evolutionist)

Felix Abubo Bravo [Church of Christ]
Birth: January 30, 1937 (Cabanatuan City, Philippines)
Death: _ (_, _)
_ (Roman Catholic); by 1964; prayer

John Breckinridge [Presbyterian Church]
Birth: 1797 (_, _)
Death: 1841 (_, _)
John Hughes (Roman Catholic Church); Philadelphia, PA; 1836. Proposition 1: "Is the Roman Catholic religion, in any or in all its principles or doctrines, opposed to civil or religious liberty?" (Breckinridge affirmed, Hughes denied). Proposition 2: "Is the Presbyterian religion, in any or in all its principles or doctrines, opposed to civil or religious liberty?" (Hughes affirmed, Breckinridge denied). Book publication: *Discussion of the Question, Is the Roman Catholic Religion, in any or in all its Principles or Doctrines, Inimical to Civil or Religious Liberty? And of the Question, Is the Presbyterian Religion, in any or in all its Principles or Doctrines, Inimical to Civil or Religious Liberty?* Philadelphia, PA: Carey, Lea, and Blanchard, 1836.

Robert Jefferson Breckinridge [Presbyterian Church]
Birth: March 8, 1800 (Cabell's Dale, KY)
Death: December 27, 1871 (Danville, KY)
Biographical sketch: https://en.wikipedia.org/wiki/Robert_Jefferson_Breckinridge
George Thompson (?); Glasgow, Scotland; June 13-17, 1836.
  Book publication: *Discussion on American Slavery*. Boston, MA: Isaac Knapp, 1836.

Ernie Brennaman [Atheist]
Birth: 19_ (_, _)
Death: _ (_, _)
David Smitherman (Church of Christ)); Corpus Christi, TX: November 28-29, December 1-2, 1994; existence of God; 4 sessions; 100; first debate for each

S. Brennan [?]
Birth: _ (_, _)
Death: _ (_, _)

Thomas Wesley Brents [Church of Christ]
Birth: February 10, 1823 (Lincoln County, TN)
Death: June 27, 1905 (Lewisburg, TN)
Biographical Sketches of Gospel Preachers by H. Leo Boles. Nashville, TN: Gospel Advocate, 1932.
Correspondence for Debate between T. W. Brents and J. B.

Moody. Nashville, TN: Lipscomb & Sewell, 1887.
Timothy Frogge (Presbyterian Church)
J. B. Moody (Baptist Church); before 1889
Jacob Ditzler (Methodist Church); Flat Creek, Bedford County, _; 1873
Jacob Ditzler (Methodist Church); Fayetteville, _; November 1873
Jacob Ditzler (Methodist Church); Franklin, _
Jacob Ditzler (Methodist Church);
Jacob Ditzler (Methodist Church);
Jacob Ditzler (Methodist Church);
Jacob Ditzler (Methodist Church); their 7th and last debate
E. D. Herod (Primitive Baptist Church); Franklin, KY; March 29 - April 1, 1887; conditional salvation, unconditional salvation; 4 sessions. Book publication: *A Theological Debate: Between T. W. Brents and E. D. Herod*. Cincinnati, OH: Guide Printing & Publishing Co., 1887.

Gordon Brewer [Church of Christ]
Birth: 19_ (_, _)
Death: _ (_, _)
Larry R. Hafley (Church of Christ); Plano, IL; March 7, 1971
Larry R. Hafley (Church of Christ); Joliet, IL; 1971
James Fox (Church of Christ); Peoria, IL; April 18, 1971; church benevolence

Grover Cleveland Brewer [Church of Christ]
Birth: December 25, 1884 (Pulaski, Giles County, TN)
Death: June 9, 1956 (Searcy, AR)
Autobiography: *A Story of Toil and Tears, of Love and Laughter, Being the Autobiography of G. C. Brewer* by G. C. Brewer. Murfreesboro, TN: DeHoff Publications, 1957.
Biographical sketch: *The Trail Blazers: Heroes of the Faith* by J. Porter Wilhite. Oklahoma City, OK: Telegram Book Company, 1965, pp. 65-67.

Biography: "G. C. Brewer: Perennial Protagonist" by Ron Halbrook. *They Being Dead Yet Speak* (Florida College Annual Lectures, 1981). Temple Terrace, FL: Florida College Bookstore, 1981, pp. 198-219.
Biographical sketch: *Preachers of Today* (Batsell Barrett Baxter & M. Norval Young, eds.). Nashville, TN: The Christian Press, 1952, p. 48.
Biographical sketch: *In Memoriam* by Gussie Lambert. Shreveport, LA: Gussie Lambert, 1988, pp. 34-35.
Debated 35 Baptists and 15 Seventh-day Adventists
L. H. "Bud" Baker (Missionary Baptist Church); Liberty Hill (near Oakman), AL; November 5-8, 1906; establishment of church, order of faith & repentance, justification by faith before baptism, possibility of apostasy; Brewer's first debate.
L. R. Robinson (Universalist Society); Chattanooga, TN; December 1-4, 1913. Proposition 1: "The Bible (and reason) teaches that those who die in their sins will suffer endless punishment." (Brewer affirmed, Robinson denied).

Proposition 2: "The Bible and reason teach the final salvation of all mankind." (Robinson affirmed, Brewer denied).

W. H. Branson (Seventh-day Adventist Church); Ooltewah, TN; October 28-30, 1913; Sabbath day

Stewart J. Spence (Russellite); written; c 1914. Proposition 1: "The immortality of the soul." (Brewer affirmed, Spence denied). Proposition 2: "Man passes from death state to life state at conversion." (Spence affirmed, Brewer denied). Book publication: *The Immortality of the Soul*. Cincinnati, OH: F. L. Rowe, 1916.

T. W. Fields (Seventh-day Adventist Church) & _ McCutcheon (Seventh-day Adventist Church); Parker (near Clebern), TX; June 1922.

J. J. Walker (Christian Church); Columbia, TN; March 4-7, 1924. Proposition: "Instrumental music in church worship is scriptural." (Walker affirmed, Brewer denied).

Ben Barr Lindsey (Infidel); Memphis, TN; April 2, 1928; companionate marriages; Lindsey's 24th debate. Book publication: *Debate between Judge Ben Lindsey and G. C. Brewer on "Companionate Marriage"*. Cincinnati, OH: The Christian Leader Corporation, c 1928.

Ben M. Bogard (Missionary Baptist Church); Humphrey, AR; November 19-22, 1929; 4 days; establishment of kingdom, baptism, depravity, apostasy

Ben M. Bogard (Missionary Baptist Church); Jonesboro, AR; June 15-19, 1931; 5 days

D. N. Jackson (Missionary Baptist Church); Texarkana, _; c 1931

Ben M. Bogard (Missionary Baptist Church); McDougal, AR; January 12-15, 1932; 4 days

J. C. Coleman (Communist); Los Angeles, CA; February 28-29, 1936. Proposition: "Resolved that Communism or Sovietism, as it today reigns in Russia, contemplates world revolution, and, as a means to that end, seeks to destroy the Christian religion." (Brewer affirmed, Coleman denied).

W. Carl Ketcherside (Church of Christ); St. Louis, MO; December 16-19, 1946; colleges; 4 sessions; 600. Proposition 1: "The organization of schools, such as David Lipscomb College, Nashville, Tennessee for the purpose of teaching the Bible and other subjects in connection, is in harmony with God's word, and, therefore, scriptural." (Brewer affirmed, Ketcherside denied). Proposition 2: "The organization of schools, such as David Lipscomb College, Nashville, Tennessee for the purpose of teaching the Bible and other subjects in connection, violates God's word, and is, therefore, sinful." (Ketcherside affirmed, Brewer denied).

W. Carl Ketcherside (Church of Christ); Henderson, TN; January 7, 1947; colleges; 2 sessions

C. J. Weaver (Church of God) & Napoleon J. Jones (Church of God); Valdosta, GA; March 18-21, 1947

W. O. Davis (Evolutionist); Memphis, TN; c 1948; evolution

J. D. Holder (Primitive Baptist Church); Fulton, MS; December 27-30, 1949; 4 days; unconditional or conditional salvation

D. N. Jackson (Missionary Baptist Church); Fulton, MS; May 9-12, 1950; baptism, apostasy

J. W. Brewer [Baptist Church]
Birth: _ (_, _)
Death: _ (_, _)
J. H. Lawson (Church of Christ); Pottsboro, TX; October 28 - November _, 1917
J. Porter Wilhite (Church of Christ); New Waverly, TX; 1919
J. F. Reese (Church of Christ); Billstown, AR; 1928

Steve Brewer [Church of Christ]
Birth: 19_ (_, _)
Death: _ (_, _)
David Lehman (Baptist Church); West Lafayette, IN; March 22, 1993; necessity of baptism; 1 session

Carvil Bricker [?Oneness Pentecostal Church]
Birth: _ (_, _)
Death: _ (_, _)
Joseph H. Cox (Church of Christ); Indianapolis, IN; 1941
J. T. Marlin (Church of Christ); Anderson & Alexandria, IN; 1941; godhead

Matthew Bridges [Roman Catholic Church]
Birth:
Death:
Joseph Baylee (?); 1856; Protestantism versus Catholicism. Book publication:

W. A. Bridges [Presbyterian Church]
Birth: _ (_, _)
Death: _ (_, _)
James A. Harding (Church of Christ); Lynnville, TN; October 1887
James A. Harding (Church of Christ); 1888

A. Q. Bridwell [Church of God]
Birth: _ (_, _)
Death: _ (_, _)
John L. Causey (Missionary Baptist Church); Yazoo City, MS; 1978; the true church. Book publication: *Causey-Bridwell Debate*. King's Press.

Robert Briffault [?]
Birth: 1876 (_, _)
Death: 1948 (_, _)
Bronislaw Malinowski (?). Book publication: *Marriage, past and present: A debate between Robert Briffault and Bronislaw Malinowski*. Edited with an introduction by M. F. Ashley Montagu. Boston: P. Sargent, c 1956.

C. Briggs [Baptist Church]
Birth: _ (_, _)

Death: _ (_, _)
Luther Blackmon (Church of Christ); _, TX; 1941

Edmund Clarke Briggs [Reorganized Church of Jesus Christ of Latter Day Saints]
Birth: February 20, 1835 (Wheeler, Steben County, NY)
Death: July 4, 1913 (_, _)
_ Johnson (Church of Christ); Hamburg, IA; January 1884

Jason W. Briggs [Reorganized Church of Jesus Christ of Latter Day Saints]
Birth: June 25, 1821 (Pompey, Onondaga County, New York)
Death: January 11, 1899 (Harris, Colorado)
William O. Owen (?); Birmingham, England; July 18-_, 1863; revelation, Book of Mormon; w/ Charles Derry (Reorganized Church of Jesus Christ of Latter Day Saints)
_ Fisk (Church of Christ); Buffalo Prairie, _; 1866

R. W. Briggs [Reorganized Church of Jesus Christ of Latter Day Saints]
Birth: _ (_, _)
Death: _ (_, _)
_ Elzea (Adventist Church); Sandwich, IL; June 1864

Charles Bright [Freethinker]
Birth: 18__ (_, _)
Death: _ (_, _)
M. Wood Green (Church of Christ); Dunedin, New Zealand; January 21-25, 1879; divine origin of Christianity. Book publication.

Tom L. Bright [Church of Christ]
Birth: November 5, 1939 (_, _)
Death: _ (_, _)
Bob L. Ross (Baptist Church); Spring, TX; January 16-17, 19-20, 1995; instrumental music in worship
Robert Johnson (Oneness Pentecostal); Chelsey, OK; miracles
Patrick T. Donahue (Church of Christ); Oak Mountain & Montevallo, AL; June 25-26, 28-29, 2001; indwelling of Holy Spirit; 100. Web publication: http://www.oabs.org/Archives/Debates/bright-donahue.htm

Hulon Briley [Church of Christ]
Birth: _ (_, _)
Death: _ (_, _)

_ (Baptist Church); 1944

_ Brindley [?]
Birth: _ (_, _)
Death: _ (_, _)
Charles Bradlaugh (Atheist). Book publication: *Discussion Between 'Iconoclast' and Dr. Brindley*. c. 1860.

John Benton Briney [Christian Church]
Birth: February 1, 1839 (Botland, Nelson County, KY)
Death: July 20, 1927 (Rural Retreat, VA)
Biographical sketch: *Twentieth Century Sermons and Addresses, being a Series of Practical and Doctrinal Discourses by Some of our Representative Men and Women* (Louis C. Wilson, ed.). Cincinnati, OH: Standard Publishing Company, 1902, pp. 209-210.

The Form of Baptism: An Argument Designed to Prove Conclusively that Immersion Is the Only Baptism Authorized By the Bible by J. B. Briney. St. Louis, MO: Christian Publishing Co., 1892.
Approximately 30 debates by 1904
_ Miller (?); 1870
T. W. Caskey (Church of Christ);
J. W. Fitch (Methodist Church); Kirksville, KY
J. W. McGarvey (Church of Christ);
J. B. Moody (Baptist Church); before 1889
W. P. Throgmorton (Baptist Church); Dixon Springs, IL; 1897
W. W. Otey (Church of Christ); Louisville, KY; September 14-18, 1908; instrumental music in worship, missionary societies; 400. Book publication: *Otey-Briney Debate*. Cincinnati, OH: F. L. Rowe, Publisher, n.d.
F. B. Srygley (Church of Christ); Oklahoma City, OK; May 1927

John H. Brinn [Church of Christ]
Birth: September 16, 1918 (Murray, KY)
Death: _ (_, _)
F. R. Bingham (Baptist Church); Bandana, KY; 1940

Ollie Eugene Britnell [Church of Christ]
Birth: September 28, 1924 (Russellville, AL)
Death: June 4, 2013 (Huntsville, AL)
Biographical sketch: *Preachers of Today* (Batsell Barrett Baxter & M. Norval Young, eds.). Nashville, TN: The Christian Press, 1952, p. 49.
Biographical sketch: *Preachers of Today, Volume Two* (Batsell Barrett Baxter & M. Norval Young, eds.). Nashville, TN:

The Gospel Advocate Company, 1959, p. 51.

Biographical sketch: *The Restoration Heritage in America: A Biblical Appeal for Today* (Florida College Annual Lectures, 1976). Marion, IN: Cogdill Foundation, 1976, page 199.

Biographical sketch: *They Being Dead Yet Speak* (Florida College Annual Lectures, 1981). Temple Terrace, FL: Florida College Bookstore, 1981, page 156.

Obituary: http://quadcitiesdaily.com/?p=97306

E. E. Bone (Baptist Church); Beedeville, AR; September 9-12, 1952; salvation, apostasy; Britnell's first debate

W. Ezekiel "Zeke" Sherrill (Baptist Church); Batesville, AR; October 26-29, 1954; salvation, apostasy; Britnell's 2nd debate, Sherrill's 207th debate

Ray Nichols (Baptist Church); Mountain View, AR; May 23-28, 1955; baptism, frequency of Lord's supper, establishment of church

Frank E. Durham (Baptist Church); Trumann, AR; October 9-12, 1956; church

Frank E. Durham (Baptist Church); Trumann, AR; February 5-8, 1957; church

?Jerry Jenkins (Church of Christ); institutionalism

John Simpson (Church of Christ); written; church benevolence. Book publication: *The Simpson-Britnell Debate on the Care of Orphaned Children and Benevolence*. Judsonia, AR: John Simpson, 1962.

Paul S. Knight (Church of Christ); Little Rock, AR; January 17-18, 1962; located preachers

Ralph Staten (Freewill Baptist Church); Tuckerman, AR; December 6-10, 1965; baptism, establishment of church

Boyd E. Morgan (Church of Christ); Pocahontas, AR; September 9-10, 12-13, 1968; church benevolence, cooperation

_ Foster (Church of Christ); 1977; benevolence

Guy N. Woods (Church of Christ); Suffolk, VA; May 16-17, 1977; church benevolence. Book publication: *Britnell-Woods Debate*. Fairmount, IN: Guardian of Truth Foundation, 1981. Review: "Britnell-Woods Debate" by Marshall E. Patton. *Truth's Appeal*, 11(24), June 15, 1977, p. 2.

_ Kidwell (Church of Christ); 1977; benevolence

Jesse R. Alexander (Missionary Baptist Church); Camden, AR; April 4-8, 1983; baptism

Rolf L. Miller (Church of Christ); written; smoking. Book publication: *Britnell-Miller Debate on Smoking*. Little Rock, AR: Eugene Britnell, n.d.

Thomas H. Broadfoot [?]
Birth: _ (_, _)
Death: _ (_, _)
R. L. Colley (Church of Christ); _, TX; 1932

A. T. Brock [?]
Birth: _ (_, _)
Death: _ (_, _)
E. H. Miller (Church of Christ)

Darrell Brock [?]
  Birth: 19_ (_, _)
  Death: _ (_, _)
  Bart Ehrman (Agnostic)

Nelta K. Brock [Church of Christ]
  Birth: c 1956 (_, _)
  Death: July 28, 2017 (_, _)
  Obituary: https://www.legacy.com/obituaries/kansascity/obituary.aspx?n=nelta-k-brock&pid=186234521&fhid=6338
  Dennis Francis (Church of Christ); written. Proposition 1: "The New Testament teaches that a Christian is not to take the life of another human being, even in war." (Brock affirmed, Francis denied). Proposition 2; "The New Testament teaches that a Christian must obey the call to war by his government, which results in killing other people." (Francis affirmed, Brock denied). Web publication.

William Paul Brock [Church of Christ]
  Birth: November 17, 1918 (LaFayette, GA)
  Death: May 10, 1993 (Volusia County, FL)
  Biographical sketch: *Preachers of Today, Volume Two* (Batsell Barrett Baxter & M. Norval Young, eds.). Nashville, TN: The Gospel Advocate Company, 1959, p. 51.
  Obituary: https://www.findagrave.com/memorial/46348947/william-paul-brock
  Willie Waddell (?) & A. T. Brock (?)
  Don McWhorter (Church of Christ); Rossville, GA; October 25-29, 1965; cooperation, benevolence
  Jim A. Clements (Church of Christ); Rossville, GA; February 27- March _, 1967. Proposition: "The Scriptures teach that churches may from their treasuries support colleges, such as David Lipscomb College." (Clements affirmed, Brock denied).
  Jim A. Clements (Church of Christ); Hixon, TN; 1971
  Richard W. Forsythe (Oneness Pentecostal Church); Brandon, MS; November 3-4, 6-7, 19_. Proposition 1: "The Scriptures teach that the Baptism of the Holy Ghost is for all New Testament Christian Believers, and will continue until the end of the New Testament Church age." (Forsythe affirmed, Brock denied). Proposition 2: "The Scriptures teach that special miraculous gifts of the Holy Spirit were given only to confirm the oral word of God, and were to cease when the word of God was completely revealed." (Brock affirmed, Forsythe denied).

_ Brockway [Methodist Church]
  Birth: _ (_, _)

Death: _ (_, _)
Henry R. Pritchard (Church of Christ); Westport, IN; 1860

Jessie Broesh [?]
Birth: _ (_, _)
Death: _ (_, _)
E. H. Miller (Church of Christ)

T. S. Brogdon [?]
Birth: _ (_, _)
Death: _ (_, _)
?Tice Elkins (Church of Christ); 1920; salvation
?Tice Elkins (Church of Christ); 1921; salvation
J. D. Tant (Church of Christ); Fort Worth, TX; 1929

Darrell L. Broking [Church of Christ]
Birth: August 11, 1961 (Douglas, AZ)
Death: _ (_, _)
Al Maxey (Church of Christ); written; divorce and remarriage. Internet publication:
Thomas N. Thrasher (Church of Christ) & Patrick T. Donahue (Church of Christ); Galax, VA; May 30-June 1, 2002; recipients of church benevolence, church social meals; 4 sessions; 20-50
Gerry Parker (Church of Christ); written. Proposition 1: "The Bible teaches that when a Matthew 19:6 marriage ends in divorce, the person put away for fornication may marry another with the Lord's approval." (Parker affirmed. Broking denied). Proposition 2; "The Bible teaches that when Matthew 19:6 marriage ends in divorce, the only party with scriptural authority to marry another is one innocent of fornication, who put away a spouse guilty of fornication." (Broking affirmed, Parker denied). Web publication.

H. C. Bronson [Reorganized Church of Jesus Christ of Latter Day Saints]
Birth: _ (_, _)
Death: _ (_, _)
_ Pressen (?); Wilber, NE; June 25-29, 1888; water baptism
_ Williamson (Church of Christ); Nebraska City, NE; November 12-17, 1888; church

John A. Brooks [Christian Church]
Birth: 18_ (_, _)
Death: _ (_, _)
J. W. Fitch (Methodist Church); September 13-18, 1869; baptism Christian Church, Methodist Church. Book publication: *A Debate on the Beginning of Messiah's Reign, the Abrogation of the Mosaic Law, and First Proclamation of the Gospel*. Cincinnati, OH: R. W. Carroll, 1870.

Ray Brooks [Church of Christ]

Birth: 19_ (_, _)
Death: _ (_, _)
Mark Ward (Church of Christ); written. Proposition 1: "The Scriptures authorize a given local church to come together to break bread, tarry, and eat together the Lord's Supper in only one assembly on the same first day of the week." (Ward affirmed, Brooks denied). Proposition 2:
Ethan Longhenry (Church of Christ); written. Proposition 1: "The Scriptures teach that Christians ought only use their voice when praising God in song." (Longhenry affirmed, Brooks denied). Proposition 2:
Randy Dodson (Church of Christ); written. Proposition 1: "The silence of the scriptures restricts the New Testament church in its work, worship, and service." (Dodson affirmed, Brooks denied). Proposition 2: "The silence of the scriptures constitutes liberty for the New Testament church in its work, worship, and service." (Brooks affirmed, Dodson denied). Web publication.

R. L. Brooks [Universalist Society]
Birth: 18_ (_, _)
Death: 19_ (_, _)
J. D. Tant (Church of Christ); Jonah, TX; March 11-_, 1919

Theodore Brooks [Church of Christ]
Birth: 18_ (_, _)
Death: _ (_, _)
R. N. Davies (Methodist Episcopal Church); Mechanicsburg, IL; c 1870

Thomas Sylva Brooks [Methodist Episcopal Church]
Birth: May 1, 1813 (Campbell County, KY)
Death: August 9, 1890 (Henryville, IN)
Henry R. Pritchard (Church of Christ); Cloverdale, IN; 1866; 9 days
James M. Mathes (Church of Christ); Bedford, IN; January 28-February 3, 1868; 6 days. Book publication: *Debate on Baptism and Kindred Subjects*. Cincinnati, OH: H. S. Bosworth, 1868.

_ Brooks [Universalist Society]
Birth: _ (_, _)
Death: _ (_, _)
Foy E. Wallace, Jr. (Church of Christ); October 1917; endless punishment

_ Brooks [Church of Christ]
Birth: _ (_, _)
Death: _ (_, _)
Reginald Woodrow Beaver (Church of Christ); 1955; classes & women teachers

_ Brooks [Pentecostal]
Birth: _ (_, _)
Death: _ (_, _)
Bennie Lee Fudge (Church of Christ); 1940

Z. Brooks [Church of Christ]
  Birth: 18_ (_, _)
  Death: _ (_, _)
  J. A. Currie, Jr. (Church of Jesus Christ of Latter Day Saints); Stockdale, TX; July 1889; Brooks was formerly a Latter Day Saint

J. W. Brookshire [Church of Christ]
  Birth: _ (_, _)
  Death: _ (_, _)
  Floyd I. Stanley (Church of Christ); Morton, TX; January 15-18, 1957; institutionalism

_ Brost [Church of God]
  Birth: _ (_, _)
  Death: _ (_, _)
  J. C. Bailey (Church of Christ); Estevan, Saskatchewan, Canada; c 1950; spiritual gifts

Uriah Marion Browder [Church of Christ]
  Birth: 1846 (Jamestown, OH)
  Death: 1907 (Dayton, OH)
  T. W. Woodroe (Universalist); McPherson, KS; May 17-24 1881; endless punishment
  F. Smith (Methodist Episcopal Church); Smithfield, IL; 1886; faith only, baptism
  W. P. Throgmorton (Baptist Church); before 1895
  W. P. Throgmorton (Baptist Church); before 1895; their second debate

Bert Brown [Church of Christ]
  Birth: January 10, 1922 (Bandy, KY)
  Death: _ (_, _)
  Biographical sketch: *Preachers of Today, Volume Two* (Batsell Barrett Baxter & M. Norval Young, eds.). Nashville, TN: The Gospel Advocate Company, 1959, pp. 52-53.
  Biographical sketch: *Preachers of Today, Volume Three* (Batsell Barrett Baxter & M. Norval Young, eds.). Nashville, TN: The Gospel Advocate Company, 1964, p. 49.
  _ (Baptist Church); before 1964
  _ (Methodist Church); before 1964
  _ (Church of the Nazarene); before 1964
  _ (Seventh-day Adventist); before 1964
  _ (Holiness Church); before 1964

Charles Lee Brown [Church of Christ]
  Birth: October 10, 1930 (Henderson County, TN)
  Death: _ (_, _)

Biographical sketch: *Preachers of Today, Volume Two* (Batsell Barrett Baxter & M. Norval Young, eds.). Nashville, TN: The Gospel Advocate Company, 1959, p. 53.

J. W. Holcomb (Church of Christ); Lockport, KY; September 27, 1969; Bible classes; 2 sessions

C. C. Brown [Church of Christ]
Birth: _ (_, _)
Death: _ (_, _)
?B. F. Hawthorn (Pentecostal); 1933

C. C. Brown [Baptist Church]
Birth: _ (_, _)
Death: _ (_, _)
J. J. Porter (Baptist Church); Sumter, SC; 1903; baptism. Book publication: *Sumter Discussion*. Post Printing & Publishing Co., 1903.

David Brown [Church of Christ]
Birth: 19_ (_, _)
Death: _ (_, _)
Mark Davis (Church of Christ); Huntsville, AL; November 12, 1990; 1 session. Proposition: "The scriptures teach that only those who are Christians are under the internal law of Christ's covenant." (Davis affirmed, Brown denied).

David Brown [Church of Christ]
Birth: 19_ (_, _)
Death: _ (_, _)
Bob L. Ross (Baptist Church); Houston, TX; January 27-28, 30-31, 1992

David A. Brown [Oneness Pentecostal Church]
Birth: 19_ (_, _)
Death: _ (_, _)
Patrick T. Donahue (Church of Christ); Huntsville, AL; November 6, 1989; baptismal formula; 100
Patrick T. Donahue (Church of Christ); Huntsville, AL; March 11, 1991; tongues; 50

Eddy Brown [Baptist Church]
Birth: 19_ (_, _)
Death: _ (_, _)
David Watts (Church of Christ); Louisville, KY; September 12-13, 1985; baptism; radio debate

G. C. Brown [Universalist Society]
Birth: 18_ (_, _)
Death: _ (_, _)
J. M. Norwood (Church of Christ); Barney, AR; 1898; resurrection, universal

salvation; 5 sessions

H. M. Brown [Lutheran Church]
Birth: 18_ (_, _)
Death: _ (_, _)
M. C. Kurfees (Church of Christ); Davie County, NC; 1893

Henry C. Brown [Church of Christ]
Birth: _ (_, _)
Death: _ (_, _)
Dana Halstead (Church of Christ); Stanley, LA; February 15-16, 1962; benevolence

James Brown [Reorganized Church of Jesus Christ of Latter Day Saints]
Birth: _ (_, _)
Death: _ (_, _)
_ Doolittle (Church of Christ); ?Graysville, OH; 1875

James J. Brown [Christian Church]
Birth: _ (_, _)
Death: _ (_, _)
James Walter Nichols (Church of Christ); Ottumwa, IA; February 1950; instrumental music in worship; 6 nights
James Walter Nichols (Church of Christ); Cedar Rapids, IA; March 1950; instrumental music in worship; 6 nights
Floyd Decker (Church of Christ); Ferriday, LA; March 18-22, 1952; 6 nights
Gussie Lambert (Church of Christ); 1952; instrumental music in worship
Guy N. Woods (Church of Christ); Chadron, NE; December 15-20, 1953; instrumental music in worship

J. L. Brown [Missionary Baptist Church]
Birth: _ (_, _)
Death: _ (_, _)
Andy T. Ritchie (Church of Christ); Bayou Academy, Independence County, AR; December 28-31, 1904; church succession, general church question

J. Newton Brown [?]
Birth: _ (_, _)
Death: _ (_, _)
William Taylor (?); 6 propositions. Book publication: *The Obligation of the Sabbath: A Discussion.* 1853.

L. H. Brown [Missionary Baptist Church]
Birth: _ (_, _)
Death: _ (_, _)
Harold V. Trimble (Church of Christ); Bemis, TN; October 13-19, 1947; 1st debate for both men
G. E. Woods (Church of Christ); 1947; church

G. E. Woods (Church of Christ); 1948; baptism, apostasy
James R. Cope (Church of Christ); Huntingdon, TN; September 6-11, 1948; establishment of church, baptism, apostasy. Related publication: *Debate Notes on Baptist Doctrine* by James R. Cope. Tampa, FL: Florida Christian College, 1954.
?G. E. Woods (Church of Christ); 1949; baptism, apostasy
W. Curtis Porter (Church of Christ); Juno, TN; October 1953; baptism
B. B. James (Church of Christ); before 1957
Logan Buchanan (Church of Christ); before 1957
Alan Highers (Church of Christ); Poplar Springs, TN; July 16-19, 1957

L. L. Brown [Baptist Church]
Birth: _ (_, _)
Death: _ (_, _)
H. C. McCaghren (Church of Christ); _, TX; September 1-4, 1952
Marvine Kelley, Jr. (Church of Christ); 1953
Marvine Kelley, Jr. (Church of Christ); 1953

Lowell Dean Brown [Church of Christ]
Birth: September 28, 1934 (Fort Worth, TX)
Death: _ (_, _)
Biographical sketch: *Preachers of Today, Volume Four* (Batsell Barrett Baxter & M. Norval Young, eds.). Nashville, TN: The Gospel Advocate Company, 1970, p. 35.
Edgar J. Dye (Church of Christ); Bay, AR; December 2-5, 1958; orphan homes, Herald of Truth

Marion Brown [Baptist Church]
Birth: _ (_, _)
Death: _ (_, _)
Harmon Gregg (Church of Christ); Edgar County, IL; 1864

Michael Brown [?]
Birth: 19_ (_, _)
Death: _ (_, _)
Bart Ehrman (Agnostic)

Ralph E. Brown [Church of Jesus Christ of Latter Day Saints]
Birth: _ (_, _)
Death: _ (_, _)
Wendle Don Scott (Church of Christ); McAllen, TX; April 1961; 2 sessions; conducted in Spanish

R. Bruce Brown [?Church of Christ]
Birth: 18_ (_, _)
Death: 19_ (_, _)
_ (Church of Jesus Christ of Latter-day Saints); before 1910

_ (Church of Jesus Christ of Latter-day Saints); before 1910
_ (Church of Jesus Christ of Latter-day Saints); before 1910
_ (Church of Jesus Christ of Latter-day Saints); before 1910

Tanya Brown [Oneness Pentecostal Church]
Birth: 19_ (_, _)
Death: _ (_, _)
Patrick T. Donahue (Church of Christ); Dyersburg, TN; August 22-24, 2002; miraculous gifts, women preachers; 4 sessions; 50-150; w/ Richard W. Forsythe (Oneness Pentecostal Church)

Thomas Joseph Brown [Roman Catholic Church]
Birth: May 2, 1796 (Bath, Somerset, England)
Death: April 12, 1880 (Lower Bullingham, Herefordshire, England)
Obituary: https://www.findagrave.com/memorial/152680233/thomas-joseph-brown
Edward Tottenham (Protestant) & John Lyons (Protestant); Stratton-on-the-Fosse, near Bath, England; February 25-27, March 5-7, 1834.; "The Rule of Faith" & "The Sacrifice of the Mass"; w/ T. M. MacDonnell (Roman Catholic Church) & Francis Edgeworth (Roman Catholic Church). Book publication: *The Authenticated Report of the Discussion which took place in the chapel of the Roman Catholic College of Downside, near Bath, on the 25th, 26th, and 27th of February, and the 5th, 6th, and 7th of March, 1834.* London: J. G. and F. Rivington, 1836.

W. J. Brown [Church of Christ]
Birth: 18_ (_, _)
Death: 19_ (_, _)
_ Shuler (Seventh-day Adventist Church); Bowling Green, FL; January 17-22, 1914; Sabbath day, first day of week

Walter T. "Walt" Brown, Jr. [Creationist]
Birth: 19_ (_, _)
Death: _ (_, _)
Biographical sketch: http://creationwiki.org/Walt_Brown
Larry Knight (Evolutionist); Chicago, IL; September 1983; 500
Charles Dyer (Evolutionist); November 1983
Langdon Gilkey (Evolutionist); Albion College, MI; January 1984
Craig Nelson (Evolutionist); Indianapolis, IN; May 1984

William H. Brown [Church of Christ]
Birth: _ (_, _)
Death: _ (_, _)
_ (?); Shelbyville, IL
_ Davis (Universalist Society); Clinton, IL; c 1857

William M. Brown [Church of Christ]

Birth: c November 1813 (_, _)
Death: November 22, 1863 (_, IL)
John B. Luccock (Methodist Episcopal Church); Washington, IL; 1853; 9 days. Report: *The Christian Sentinel*, 2:4 (December 1853) page 160. Report: *The Christian Sentinel*, 2:6 (February 1854), page 189.

W. P. Brown [Whitmerite]
Birth: _ (_, _)
Death: _ (_, _)
A. J. Moore (Reorganized Church of Jesus Christ of Latter Day Saints); near Oenaville, TX; December 1888

_ Brown [?]
Birth: _ (_, _)
Death: _ (_, _)
T. W. Caskey (Church of Christ)

_ Brown [?]
Birth: _ (_, _)
Death: _ (_, _)
Harold V. Trimble (Church of Christ)

_ Brown [?]
Birth: _ (_, _)
Death: _ (_, _)
_ Taylor (?)

_ Brown [Seventh-day Adventist]
Birth: _ (_, _)
Death: _ (_, _)
Charles Edward Crouch (Church of Christ); Mitchellville, TN; 1947

_ Brown [Church of Christ]
Birth: _ (_, _)
Death: _ (_, _)
Don Ross Patton (Church of Christ); Panama City, FL; May 1964; classes

Walter R. Browne [?]
Birth: _ (_, _)
Death: _ (_, _)
Charles Bradlaugh (Atheist); 2 nights. Book publication: *Can Miracles be proved possible? Verbatim report of the two nights' public debate between ... Bradlaugh and W. R. Brown, ...* 1876.

Don Earl Browning [Church of Christ]
Birth: April 1, 1937 (Snyder, TX)
Death: _ (_, _)
Biographical sketch: *Preachers of Today, Volume Three* (Batsell Barrett Baxter & M. Norval Young, eds.).

Nashville, TN: The Gospel Advocate Company, 1964, p. 52.
Biographical sketch: *Preachers of Today, Volume Four* (Batsell Barrett Baxter & M. Norval Young, eds.). Nashville, TN: The Gospel Advocate Company, 1970, p. 37.
_ (Church of Jesus Christ of Latter Day Saints); _, ?UT; before 1964
_ (Church of Jesus Christ of Latter Day Saints); _, ?UT; before 1964

Leroy Brownlow [Church of Christ]
Birth: April 30, 1914 (Whitesboro, Cooke County, TX)
Death: November 8, 2002 (Fort Worth, TX)
Biographical sketch: *Preachers of Today* (Batsell Barrett Baxter & M. Norval Young, eds.). Nashville, TN: The Christian Press, 1952, p. 52.
Biographical sketch: *Preachers of Today, Volume Two* (Batsell Barrett Baxter & M. Norval Young, eds.). Nashville, TN: The Gospel Advocate Company, 1959, p. 55.
Biographical sketch: *Preachers of Today, Volume Three* (Batsell Barrett Baxter & M. Norval Young, eds.). Nashville, TN: The Gospel Advocate Company, 1964, p. 52.
Lawrence M. DeFalco (Roman Catholic Church); written; 1951-1953. Book publication: *A Discussion between A Preacher and A Priest* by Leroy Brownlow. Fort Worth, TX: Leroy Brownlow Publications, 1953.

William Gannaway Brownlow [Methodist Church]
Birth: August 29, 1805 (Wythe County, VA)
Death: April 29, 1877 (Knoxville, TN)
Biographical sketch: https://en.wikipedia.org/wiki/William_G._Brownlow
Obituary: https://www.findagrave.com/memorial/6842094/william-gannaway-brownlow
Abram Pryne (?); Philadelphia, PA; September 1858; perpetuation of American slavery. Book publication: *Ought American slavery to be perpetuated?* Philadelphia, PA: J. B. Lippincott & Co., 1858.

J. A. Brubeck [Christian Church]
Birth: _ (_, _)
Death: _ (_, _)
V. H. Sellers (Church of Christ); Urbana, IL; March 1942; instrumental music in worship; 4 sessions

F. W. Brumley [?]
Birth: _ (_, _)
Death: _ (_, _)
E. H. Miller (Church of Christ)

William M. Brumley [Baptist Church]

Birth: 18_ (_, _)
Death: 19_ (_, _)
William Cicero Ramsey (Church of Christ); Stop, KY; September 5, 1919; apostasy

William T. Bruner [Baptist Church]
Birth: ?1903 (_, _)
Death: ?1971 (_, _)
Franklin T. Puckett (Church of Christ); Louisville, KY; March 1966
Clinton D. Hamilton (Church of Christ); Louisville, KY; May 23-28, 1966; 6 sessions. Proposition 1: "The Scriptures teach that since the fall of man, every child (Jesus alone excepted) has been born in original sin and total depravity. This sinful nature is innate (native or inborn) and yet it is not hereditary; each individual is conceived in his own personal sin and guilt, and is, therefore, absolutely responsible for it." (Bruner affirmed, Hamilton denied). Proposition 2: "The Scriptures teach that baptism in the name of Christ to a penitent believer is for (in order to) the remission of his past, or alien, sins, and is, therefore, essential to his salvation from alien sins." (Hamilton affirmed, Bruner denied). Proposition 3: "The Scriptures teach that every one who has been truly born again will persevere unto everlasting salvation, for he cannot so sin as to be finally lost." (Bruner affirmed, Hamilton denied).
_ Lyons (Church of Christ); Gratz, KY; 1968

Fabian Alegre Bruno [Church of Christ]
Birth: January 20, 1918 (Nampicuan, Nueva Emija, Philippines)
Death: _ (_, _)
Biographical sketch: *Preachers of Today, Volume Three* (Batsell Barrett Baxter & M. Norval Young, eds.). Nashville, TN: The Gospel Advocate Company, 1964, p. 53.
_ (Seventh-day Adventist Church); before 1964
_ (Church of God); before 1964
_ (Pentecostal Church); before 1964
_ (Pentecostal Church); before 1964
_ (Jehovah's Witnesses); before 1964
_ (Pilgrims Holiness Church); before 1964
_ (Spiritista); before 1964
_ (Manatista); before 1964
_ (Manatista); before 1964
_ (Manatista); before 1964

Giordano Bruno [?]
Birth: _ (_, _)
Death: _ (_, _)

G. J. Holyoake (Secularist). Book publication: 1889.

Choice Leach Bryant [Church of Christ]
Birth: May 10, 1910 (Throckmorton, TX)
Death: November 4, 2000 (Mesquite, TX)
Biographical sketch: *Preachers of Today* (Batsell Barrett Baxter & M. Norval Young, eds.). Nashville, TN: The Christian Press, 1952, p. 53.
Biographical sketch: *Preachers of Today, Volume Two* (Batsell Barrett Baxter & M. Norval Young, eds.). Nashville, TN: The Gospel Advocate Company, 1959, p. 56.
Obituary: https://www.findagrave.com/memorial/12962034/choice-leach-bryant
Clyde Goff (Church of Christ); Irving, TX; June 21-22, 24-25, 1982

Clarence Bryant [Church of Christ]
Birth: _ (_, _)
Death: _ (_, _)
?_ Crane (Adventist Church); Brownwood, TX; 1940

Henry Clyde Bryant [Church of Christ]
Birth: November 19, 1885 (_, TN)
Death: _ (_, _)
Biographical sketch: *Preachers of Today* (Batsell Barrett Baxter & M. Norval Young, eds.). Nashville, TN: The Christian Press, 1952, p. 54.
_ Burnett (Christadelphian)
_ Dillard (Baptist Church); 1918
_ Green (Russellite)

George Bryson [?]
Birth: 19_ (_, _)
Death: _ (_, _)
James White (Reformed Baptist Church). Subject: Who controls salvation?

James Robert "Bob" Buchanon [Church of Christ]
Birth: March 30, 1947 (Bowling Green, KY)
Death: _ (_, _)
Ronny Wade (Church of Christ); Bowling Green, KY; March 22-23, 2001; drinking vessels in the Lord's supper; 2 sessions; 250-300

Charles Aden Buchanan [Church of Christ]
Birth: January 31, 1888 (Paris, Henry County, TN)
Death: 19_ (_, _)
Biographical sketch: *Gospel Preachers Who Blazed The Trail* by C. R. Nichol. Austin, TX: Firm Foundation Publishing House, n.d.
Biographical sketch: *Preachers of Today* (Batsell Barrett Baxter

& M. Norval Young, eds.). Nashville, TN: The Christian Press, 1952, p. 55.
Biographical sketch: *Preachers of Today, Volume Two* (Batsell Barrett Baxter & M. Norval Young, eds.). Nashville, TN: The Gospel Advocate Company, 1959, p. 57.
Biographical sketch: *Preachers of Today, Volume Three* (Batsell Barrett Baxter & M. Norval Young, eds.). Nashville, TN: The Gospel Advocate Company, 1964, p. 55.
_ (Adventist Church); by 1964; 2 days

Robert Logan Buchanan, Sr. [Church of Christ]
Birth: February 22, 1913 (Frederick, OK)
Death: _ (_, _)
Biographical sketch: *Preachers of Today* (Batsell Barrett Baxter & M. Norval Young, eds.). Nashville, TN: The Christian Press, 1952, p. 55.
Biographical sketch: *Preachers of Today, Volume Four* (Batsell Barrett Baxter & M. Norval Young, eds.). Nashville, TN: The Gospel Advocate Company, 1970, p. 39.

18 debates by 1952
_ Martin (Methodist Church); 1932
_ (Methodist Church); Maysville, TX; 1933
_ Ballard (Baptist Church); 1935; baptism, apostasy
M. L. Welch (Primitive Baptist Church); 1938
J. Cullis Smith (Baptist Church); Denver, CO; 1943
Norman Gipson (Church of Christ); Breckenridge, TX; 1943; classes & women teachers
J. Ervin Waters (Church of Christ); Dallas, TX; 1949; classes
_ (Holiness); before 1970
Alva Johnson (Church of Christ) & Van Bonneau (Church of Christ);; Brownfield, TX; January 1950; 4 nights; w/ L. W. Hayhurst (Church of Christ). Proposition 1: "It is scriptural to teach the Bible by the Class Method of teaching as is practiced by the Church of Christ (Crescent Hill) in Brownsfield, Texas." (Hayhurst & Buchanan affirmed, Johnson & Bonneau denied). Proposition 2: "That the Churches of Christ 'Which oppose the teaching of the Bible in Classes' more than one class at one time using women teachers, are scriptural in such opposition." (Johnson & Bonneau affirmed, Hayhurst & Buchanan denied). Book publication: *A Debate on the Bible Class Question*. Brownfield, TX: J. R. Chisholm and Jimmy Wood, 1950.
Vernon L. Barr (Missionary Baptist Church); Healdton, OK; 1938; w/ Kermit Upshaw (Church of Christ)
Vernon L. Barr (Missionary Baptist Church); Marietta, OK

Hiram Buck [Methodist Episcopal Church]
Birth: March 1, 1819 (Steuben County, NY)
Death: August 21, 1892 (_, _)

George Campbell (Church of Christ); Shelbyville, IL; 1848

William Calmes Buck [Missionary Baptist Church]
Birth: August 23, 1790 (_, VA)
Death: May 18, 1872 (Waco, TX)
Richard M. Newport (Primitive Baptist Church); 1839; missionary operations and kindred institutions

Yusuf Buckas [Muslim]
Birth: 19_ (_, _)
Death: _ (_, _)
John Gilchrist (?). Topic: Is the Bible the Unadulterated Word of God?
Walt Stroker (?); w/ Gary Miller (?). Topic: The Qur'an or the Bible which is Authentic?

William Frank Buckley, Jr. [Roman Catholic Church]
Birth: November 24, 1925 (New York, NY)
Death: February 27, 2008 (Stamford, CT)
Biography: Judis, John B. (1990). *William F. Buckley, Jr.: Patron Saint of the Conservatives*. New York: Touchstone.
Biography: Winchell, Mark Royden. (1984). *William F. Buckley, Jr*. New York: MacMillan.
Biography: Miller, David. (1990). *Chairman Bill: A Biography of William F. Buckley, Jr*. New York: _.
Biography: Meehan, William F., III. (1990). *William F. Buckley Jr: A Bibliography*. New York: _.
Barry Lynne (Evolutionist), Eugenie Scott (Evolutionist), Michael Ruse (Evolutionist) & Kenneth Miller (Evolutionist); PBS TV *Firing Line*; December 19, 1997; w/ Philip Johnson (Creationist), Michael Behe (Anti-Darwinist) & David Berlinski (Anti-Darwinist). Proposition: "Resolved: Evolution should acknowledge creation."

Edward Milton "Ed" Buckner [Atheist]
Birth: March 8, 1946 (Fitzgerald, GA)
Death: _ (_. _)
Jay Lucas (Believer); Washington Court House, OH; March 12, 2010; 1 session. Topic: Moral foundations: "Which makes more sense, Christianity or Atheism?"
Daniel K. Williams (Church of Christ); Carrollton, GA; February 12, 2013; 300. Topic: Christian origins in the light of history.

Neal D. Buffaloe [Church of Christ]
Birth: November 15, 1924 (Leachville, AR)
Death: July 27, 2012 (_, _)
Obituary: http://www.legacy.com/obituaries/thecabin/

obituary.aspx?pid=158846173
Keith Sharp (Church of Christ); Conway, AR; February 27-28, 1978; creation & evolution

J. F. Buffington [Church of Christ]
Birth: _ (_, _)
Death: _ (_, _)
M. W. Matthews (Baptist Church); Ovett, MS; 1932

_ Bull [?]
Birth: 18_ (_, _)
Death: _ (_, _)
Glaud Rodger (Reorganized Church of Jesus Christ of Latter Day Saints); ?Lambton, Australia; c August 1875

Chester Bullard [Church of Christ]
Birth: March 12, 1809 (Framingham, MA)
Death: February 27, 1893 (?Snowville, VA)
Biographical sketch: http://www.mun.ca/rels/restmov/texts/cbullard/BULLAR2.HTM
Autobiography: http://www.mun.ca/rels/restmov/texts/cbullard/BULLARD.HTM
M. Ellison (Baptist Church); 1857. Proposition: "The Body Now called Baptists, has departed from the faith and practice of the New Testament, so far as to forfeit her title to be considered a truly Christian church." (Bullard affirmed, Ellison denied). Book publication: *Is the Baptist Church truly Christian? A Discussion.* _: William H. Clemmitt Printer, _.

Greg Bullard [Metropolitan Community Church]
Birth: 19_ (_, _)
Death: _ (_, _)
Patrick T. Donahue (Church of Christ); Birmingham, AL; April 3, 1995; 1 session; homosexuality and the Bible; 150
Patrick T. Donahue (Church of Christ); Nashville, TN; March 27, 29, 2001; homosexuality, women preachers; 200-300; 2 sessions
Patrick T. Donahue (Church of Christ); Madison, TN; May 26, 2012; 1 session; 100. Subject: Does The Bible Condemn Loving Committed (Married) Same Sex Relationships?

J. M. Bullard [Primitive Baptist Church]
Birth: _ (_, _)
Death: _ (_, _)
O. C. Lambert (Church of Christ); Tupelo, MS; August 30-September 2, 1949

W. S. Bullard [?]
Birth: _ (_, _)
Death: _ (_, _)
J. T. Showalter (Church of Christ); w/ J. R. Miller (?)

Alvin Carter Bullington [Church of Christ]
Birth: July 19, 1924 (Cleveland, Bradley Co., TN)
Death: April 12, 2007 (_, _)
Biographical sketch: *Preachers of Today, Volume Two* (Batsell Barrett Baxter & M. Norval Young, eds.). Nashville, TN: The Gospel Advocate Company, 1959, p. 58.
_ Cox (?); 1958; baptism

Jim Bullington [Church of Christ]
Birth: 19_ (_, _)
Death: _ (_, _)
Early Lovell (Church of Christ); Athens & Oliver, AL; 1977; 4 sessions; institutionalism

_ Bullman [?Baptist Church]
Birth: _ (_, _)
Death: _ (_, _)
Luther B. Jones (Church of Christ); apostasy

Larry A. Bunch [Church of Christ]
Birth: November 4, 1939 (_, _)
Death: _ (_, _)
A. J. Zenthoefer (Church of Christ); written; ?1999; an elder must have a plurality of submissive children
John Clark (Church of Christ); written; March 2000. Proposition 1: "It is scriptural for a congregation to teach the Bible in systematically arranged classes." (Bunch affirmed, Clark denied). Proposition 2:
Jason E. Stringer (Church of Christ); written. Proposition 1: "It is sinful for the Christian to celebrate the holiday known as Christmas, even if they attach no religious significance to it." (Stringer affirmed, Bunch denied). Proposition 2: "The Christian may celebrate December 25th as a national holiday." (Bunch affirmed, Stringer denied). Web publication.
Jason E. Stringer (Church of Christ); written; March 21 - April 14, 2001. Proposition 1: "The only scriptural cause for divorce in the New Testament is the departure of an unbelieving spouse, and neither party may scripturally remarry." (Stringer affirmed, Bunch denied). Proposition 2: "The New Testament teaches that the only cause for divorce and remarriage is when sexual immorality is involved and only the innocent party has a right to remarry." (Bunch affirmed, Stringer denied). Web publication.
Nelta Brock (Church of Christ); written; August-September 2001; church

treasury

Bob Strom (?); written. Proposition 1: "The scriptures teach that God gave miraculous gifts of the Holy Spirit to certain ones in New Testament times. God is still giving miraculous gifts to people today." (Strom affirmed, Bunch denied). Proposition 2:

A. J. Zenthoefer (Church of Christ); written. Proposition 1: "The Bible teaches (in 1st Timothy chapter 3 and verse 4, when teaching of the requirements to be possessed in considering a man for the elder's position) that he must have children, meaning a plurality, living in his respective home, submissive to the said candidate's rule, direction, and control." (Zenthoefer affirmed, Bunch denied). Proposition 2:

D. P. Bunn [Universalist Society]
Birth: _ (_, _)
Death: _ (_, _)
_ Lewis (Methodist Church); _, IL; c 1845
Andrew J. Kane (Church of Christ); Mt. Pulaski, IL; c 1858.
Benjamin Franklin (Church of Christ); Decatur, IL; 1860
J. W. McGarvey (Church of Christ); Georgetown, MO; November 20-26, 1860

A. A. Bunner [Church of Christ]
Birth: 18_ (_, _)
Death: _ (_, _)
_ (Russellite); c 1900
Ben E. Rich (Church of Jesus Christ of Latter Day Saints); Fairmont, WV; March 4-8, 1912. Proposition: "John the Baptist and Jesus Christ were the last Prophets sent by God and that the Bible as given to us by Christ and the Apostles in Palestine is sufficient to guide men and women to salvation from sin." (Bunner affirmed, Rich denied). Book publication: *The Bunner-Rich Debate*. Chicago, IL: Henry C. Etten & Co., 1912.

Robert H. "Bob" Bunting [Church of Christ]
Birth: 1927 (Detroit, MI)
Death: March 18, 2006 (Murfreesboro, TN)
Biographical sketch: *Great Bible Doctrines* (Florida College Annual Lectures, 1975). Marion, IN: Cogdill Foundation, 1975, page 191.
J. D. Marion (Christian Church); written; instrumental music in worship. Book publication: *Both Sides of the Music Question Discussed*. Athens, AL: The C.E.I. Store, 1957.

I. H. Burgess [?]
Birth: _ (_, _)
Death: _ (_, _)
George B. Curtis (Church of Christ); Springdale, AR; 1941
George B. Curtis (Church of Christ); Eureka Springs, AR; 1941

Otis Asa Burgess [Church of Christ]
   Birth: August 26, 1829 (Thompson, Windham County, CT)
   Death: 1882 (Chicago, IL)
   John B. Luccock (Methodist Episcopal Church); Cruger, IL; c 1858; Burgess' 1st public debate, Luccock's 32nd
   B. F. Underwood (Atheist); Fairbury, IL; c 1859; materialism & Christianity
   Grigg M. Thompson (Primitive Baptist Church); North Salem (Hendricks County), IN; September 25-October 3, 1867; total depravity, election, church polity, free moral agency, water baptism, final apostasy. Book publication: *A Debate on Total Depravity, Election, Church Polity, Free Moral Agency, Water Baptism, and Final Apostasy.* Indianapolis, IN: Levi Pennington, 1868.
   W. W. Curry (Universalist Society); Indianapolis, IN; November 20, 1867. Proposition 1: "The kingdom of Jesus Christ has been established on earth, and men must accept the conditions of initiations in this life in order to be finally saved." (Burgess affirmed, Curry denied). Proposition 2: "The mediatorial kingdom of Jesus Christ is not limited to earth, and all men will be finally reconciled and saved, whether they believe and obey the gospel in this life or not." (Curry affirmed, Burgess denied).
   Charles H. Burrows (Infidel); Atlanta, IL; 1868; the Bible & Christianity
   Jacob Ditzler (Methodist Episcopal Church); May 19-_, 1873; 12 days. Proposition 1: "Immersion is the action practiced by the Apostles for baptism." (Burgess affirmed, Ditzler denied). Proposition 2: "Sprinkling or pouring water on a proper person by a proper administrator is Christian baptism." (Ditzler affirmed, Burgess denied). Proposition 3: "Baptism, with its scriptural connections, is for the remission of sins." (Burgess affirmed, Ditzler denied). Proposition 4: "Infants are proper subjects for Christian baptism." (Ditzler affirmed, Burgess denied). Proposition 5: "The doctrines and practices of the Disciples are in accordance with the Word of God." (Burgess affirmed, Ditzler denied). Proposition 6: "The doctrines and practices of the M. E. Church, South are in accordance with the Word of God." (Ditzler affirmed, Burgess denied).
   B. F. Underwood (Atheist); Aylmer, Ontario, Canada; June 29-July 2, 1875; materialism & Christianity. Proposition 1: "The Christian religion, as set forth in the New Testament, is true in fact, and of divine origin." (Burgess afirmed, Underwood denied). Book publication: *The Burgess-Underwood Debate.* New York: D. M. Bennett, 1876. Web publication: http://books.google.com/books?id=ryPH8nIOGt4C&dq=bf+underwood&printsec=frontcover&source=web&ots=aDhYxQprqe&sig=ycoSFGbZcfVkNt4ytlcYe1FeHOk#PPP7,M1

Max Burgin [Church of Christ]
   Birth: 19_ (_, _)
   Death: _ (_, _)

_ (Church of Christ); _, Australia; AD 70 doctrine
Donnie V. Rader (Church of Christ); written; 1997; divorce & remarriage. Periodical publication: *Guardian of Truth*, XLI : 8 (April 17, 1997), 18-27.
John Cripps (Church of Christ); written; 1999-2000; marriage, divorce & remarriage
Doug Cyrus (Church of Christ); written. Proposition 1: "The Bible teaches that there is a distinction in single people, who are divorced, that avoids adultery in a further marriage." (Burgin affirmed, Cyrus denied). Proposition 2: "The Bible teaches that divorced adulterers may not marry." (Cyrus affirmed, Burgin denied). Web publication.
Ethan Longhenry (Church of Christ); written. Proposition 1: "The New Testament extends the privilege of remarriage to a person put away for having committed adultery." (Burgin affirmed, Longhenry denied). Proposition 2: "The New Testament does not extend the privilege of remarriage to a person put away for having committed adultery." (Longhenry affirmed, Burgin denied). Web publication.

Roy Wayne Burkett [Bible Baptist Church]
Birth: August 1, 1955 (_, _)
Death: _ (_, _)

Larry Ray Hafley (Church of Christ); St. Louis, MO; January 11-12, 14-15, 1971.
Larry Ray Hafley (Church of Christ); Dittmer, MO; 1971.
Thomas N. Thrasher (Church of Christ); St. Louis, MO; August 3, 1996; apostasy; 2 sessions
Patrick T. Donahue (Church of Christ); Eureka, MO; August 1-2, 1996; baptism; 2 sessions; 75
Thomas N. Thrasher (Church of Christ); Cullman, AL; July 17-18, 1997; apostasy; 2 sessions
Patrick T. Donahue (Church of Christ); Cullman, AL; July 19, 1997; baptism; 2 sessions; 100
Patrick T. Donahue (Church of Christ); Hazlewood, MO; July 16-17, 1998; divorce & remarriage; 2 sessions
Thomas N. Thrasher (Church of Christ); Hazlewood, MO; July 18, 1998; hereditary depravity; 2 sessions
Eddie K. Garrett II (Church of Christ); Osprey, FL; June 10-12, 1999; apostasy, salvation; 4 sessions
Patrick T. Donahue (Church of Christ); High Ridge, MO; June 3, 2000; salvation; 1 session; their 4th debate
Thomas N. Thrasher (Church of Christ); High Ridge, MO; June 3, 2000; apostasy; 1 session; their 4th debate
John Carroll (Oneness Pentecostal); _, 2000; baptism, apostasy

Robert Burks [Church of Christ]
Birth: 19_ (_, _)
Death: _ (_, _)

Steve Wallace (Church of Christ); February 8, 1992; benevolence, sponsoring church; first debate for both men

Charles C. Burleigh [?]
Birth: _ (_, _)
Death: _ (_, _)
Frederick Plummer (Church of Christ); _, ?PA; c 1851; 6 sessions. Proposition: "Ought capital punishment to be abolished?" (Plummer affirmed, Burleigh denied). Book publication: *A Defence of Capital Punishment*." Philadelphia, PA: Christian General Book Association, 1851.

J. D. Burleson [Church of Christ]
Birth: December 27, 1856 (_, MS)
Death: 19_ (_, _)
Biographical sketch: *Gospel Preachers Who Blazed The Trail* by C. R. Nichol. Austin, TX: Firm Foundation Publishing House, n.d.
Several debates by 1911

O. W. Burnell [Seventh-day Adventist Church]
Birth: 18_ (_, _)
Death: _ (_, _)
H. Leo Boles (Church of Christ); Hickory Grove, Warren County, TN; December 26-29, 1906. Proposition 1: "The Scriptures teach that God has ordained and sanctified Saturday, or the Seventh Day of the week as a special day for worship for Christians under the Christian Dispensation." (Burnell affirmed, Boles denied). Proposition 2: "The Scriptures teach that God has ordained and sanctified the First Day of the week as a special day of worship for Christians under the Christian Dispensation." (Boles affirmed, Burnell denied).

David Staats Burnet [Disciples of Christ]
Birth: July 6, 1808 (Dayton, OH)
Death: July 8, 1867 (Baltimore, MD)
Biography: *The Story of D. S. Burnet: Undeserved Obscurity* by Noel L. Keith. St. Louis, MO: The Bethany Press, 1954. [1st edition]

R. S. Burnett [Christadelphian]
Birth: _ (_, _)
Death: _ (_, _)
W. L. Totty (Church of Christ); Chattanooga, TN; 1940

Thomas Raines Burnett [Church of Christ]
Birth: January 23, 1842 (_, TN)
Death: June 26, 1916 (Dallas, TX)
Biographical sketch: *Faith and Facts Quarterly*, Volume 23, Number 2 (April

1995), 21.
Biographical Sketches of Gospel Preachers by H. Leo Boles. Nashville, TN: Gospel Advocate, 1932.
About 30 debates; 13 with Methodists by 1911
_ (Methodist Church)
_ (Methodist Church)
_ (Methodist Church)
J. C. Weaver (Methodist Church); sprinkling, infant baptism; operation of the Holy Spirit. Book publication: *Burnett-Weaver Debate, Volume One, Action and Subjects of Baptism*. Austin, TX: Firm Foundation Publishing House, n.d. Book publication: *Burnett-Weaver Debate, Volume Two, Influence of the Holy Spirit*. Austin, TX: Firm Foundation Publishing House, n.d.
_ (Methodist Church)
_ (Methodist Church)
_ (Methodist Church)
_ (Methodist Church)
_ (Methodist Church)
_ (Methodist Church)
_ (Methodist Church)
_ (Methodist Church)
_ (Presbyterian Church)
D. B. Ray (Baptist Church); written, Missionary Baptist Church. Periodical publication: *American Baptist Flag* and *Christian Messenger*. Book publication: *Ray-Burnett Debate: A Discussion of the Doctrines and Practices of the Missionary Baptist Church*. Cincinnati, OH: Standard Publishing Co., 1884.
_ (Baptist Church)
_ (Baptist Church)
_ (Baptist Church)
_ (Baptist Church)
T. S. Dalton (Primitive Baptist Church); Alexander, Erath County, TX; January 18-21, 1886. Proposition 1: "The Scriptures teach that the heirs of salvation and eternal life were by the God of heaven unconditionally elected or chosen thereunto, independent of the performance of conditions by man." (Dalton affirmed, Burnett denied). Proposition 2: "The Scriptures teach that in conversion, or regeneration, the Holy Spirit acts directly, or immediately, on the sinner's heart, and in many cases independent of the written or preached word of truth." (Dalton affirmed, Burnett denied). Book publication: *Debate on Salvation: Is It Conditional or Unconditional?* Nashville, TN: Gospel Advocate Publishing Company, 1897.
_ (Adventist Church)
_ (Adventist Church)
_ (Adventist Church)

_ (Adventist Church)
_ (Adventist Church)
_ (Adventist Church)
_ (Adventist Church)
James R. Wilmeth (Church of Christ); Corinth, AR
James R. Wilmeth (Church of Christ); written/ Proposition: "A belief that baptism is for the remission of sins is essential to its validity." (Wilmeth affirmed, Burnett denied). Periodical publication: "Debate on Valid Baptism," *Firm Foundation*. Book publication: *Debate on Valid Baptism*. No publication data (c 1894).
Austin McGary (Church of Christ); written. Proposition: "A belief that baptism is for the remission of sins is essential to its validity." (McGary affirmed, Burnett denied). Book publication: *Valid Baptism*. Nashville, TN: Gospel Advocate, 1899.
Austin McGary (Church of Christ) & John W. Denton (Church of Christ); written; the Holy Spirit. Book publication: *The Holy Spirit*. Dallas, TX: The Samuel Jones Printing Company, 1905.

_ Burnett [Christadelphian]
Birth: _ (_, _)
Death: _ (_, _)
Henry Clyde Bryant (Church of Christ)

A. Burns [Church of Christ]
Birth: 18_ (_, _)
Death: _ (_, _)
_ Reynolds (Sabbatarian); North Lancaster, Erie County, NY; March 5-11, 1872; 7 days. Proposition 1: "The Sabbath of the fourth commandment is now binding." (Reynolds affirmed, Burns denied). Proposition 2: "Jesus Christ has a kingdom now, and his Church is that kingdom." (Burns affirmed, Reynolds denied). Proposition 3: "Man dies soul and body together and is unconscious until the resurrection." (Reynolds affirmed, Burns denied).
_ Dimmick (Sabbatarian); Pleasant Grove, MN; winter 1877; Sabbatarianism. Book publication: Central Book Concern, 1877.

Robert L. Burns [Church of Christ]
Birth: _ (_, _)
Death: _ (_, _)
Lee M. Rogers (?); Ft. Worth, TX; 1960

_ Burns [Church of Jesus Christ of Latter Day Saints]
Birth: _ (_, _)
Death: _ (_, _)
Gussie Lambert (Church of Christ); 1949; Book of Mormon, baptism for the dead

William Henry Burr [?]
Birth: 1819 (_, _)
Death: 1908 (_, _)
C. A. Walworth (?); c 1873. Book publication: *The Doctrine of Hell, ventilated in a Discussion between the Rev. C. A. Walworth and Mr. Henry Burr, Esq.* New York, 1873.

Charles H. Burrows [Atheist]
Birth: 1823 (_, _)
Death: March 28, 1875 (_, _)
O. A. Burgess (Church of Christ); Atlanta, IL; 1868; the Bible & Christianity
Owen Davis (Baptist Church); Atlanta, IL; January 16-18, 1868
_ Orvis (Congregationalist); _, IL; 1868

John C. Burruss [Universalist Society]
Birth: _ (_, _)
Death: _ (_, _)
C. F. R. Shehane (?); Americus, GA; March 1850. Related publication: *Universalism Examined and Condemned* by John C. Burruss. Related publication: *Letters to Rev. Lovick Pierce, D. D., of the Georgia Conference*. Notasulga, AL. 1853.
William Hicks (Methodist Church); c 1859. Subject: Do the Scriptures Teach the Endless Punishment of any portion of the human race? Book publication: *A Discussion between Rev. William Hicks, Methodist, and Rev. John C. Burruss, Universalist, on an important point in Christian Theology*. 1859.
Lovick Pierce (Methodist Church); c 1859. Subject: Is Christ the Supreme God? Book publication: *Discussion of the Doctrine of the Trinity, between Rev. Lovick Pierce, D. D., of the Georgia Methodist Conference, and Rev. John C. Burruss, Editor of the Universalist Herald.* Notasulga, AL. 1859.
J. R. Graves (Baptist Church); written; c 1878. Proposition: "The Scriptures teach that a part of the human family will be finally lost." (Graves affirmed, Burruss denied). Periodical publication: *The Baptist & Universalist Herald*. Book publication: *A Discussion on the Doctrine of Endless Punishment*. Atlanta, GA: J. O. Perkins & Co., 1880.

Will Burson [Church of the Firstborn]
Birth: _ (_, _)
Death: _ (_, _)
Wayne Jackson (Church of Christ); Delta, CO; 1960

Glenn R. Burt [Church of Christ]
Birth: 19_ (_, _)
Death: _ (_, _)
Don Newcomer (Berean Christadelphian); Deer Park, TX; June 12-13, 15-16, 1972
Don Newcomer (Berean Christadelphian); Deer Park, TX; January 29-30, February 1-2, 1973; nature of man & eternal punishment

Ernest Finley (Church of Christ); written; 1974; human organizations teaching the Bible. Periodical publication: "Finley-Burt Discussion," *The Bible Standard*, beginning March 29, 1974

Marvin A. Hicks (Oneness Pentecostal Church); Baytown, TX; January 3-4, 6-7, 1977

Ron Howes (Church of Christ); written; 1983; religious collectivities. Periodical publication: *Gospel Anchor* (December 1983 - February 1984).

_ (Christadelphian); Hamilton, Ontario, Canada

Ezra Winston Burton [Church of Christ]
Birth: June 15, 1924 (Paragould, AR)
Death: September 19, 2012 (_, _)
Biographical sketch: *Preachers of Today* (Batsell Barrett Baxter & M. Norval Young, eds.). Nashville, TN: The Christian Press, 1952, p. 58.
Biographical sketch: *Preachers of Today, Volume Two* (Batsell Barrett Baxter & M. Norval Young, eds.). Nashville, TN: The Gospel Advocate Company, 1959, p. 61.
Biographical sketch: *Preachers of Today, Volume Four* (Batsell Barrett Baxter & M. Norval Young, eds.). Nashville, TN: The Gospel Advocate Company, 1970, p. 42.
Billy Sunday Myers (Pentecostal Church of God); 1949; water baptism
Thomas Evans (?); before 1959; church
W. W. McMicken (Church of God (Seventh Day)); 1951; Sabbath, eternal punishment

Joseph F. Burton [?Materialist]
Birth: 18_ (_, _)
Death: _ (_, _)
Fred Mogg (?Reorganized Church of Jesus Christ of Latter Day Saints); _, Australia; ?March 1886; "Is there a spirit in man which is a conscious and intelligent entity, and may exist apart from and independent of the body?"

Keith Burton [Seventh-day Adventist Church]
Birth: August 1, 1963 (London, England)
Death: _ (_, _)
Patrick T. Donahue (Church of Christ); Huntsville & Madison, AL; May 2-3, 2002; is the Sabbath binding today; 260; w/ James Doggette (Seventh Day Adventist Church)

Thomas Haden Burton [Church of Christ]
Birth: September 11, 1881 (Lynchburg, TN)
Death: December 25, 1961 (?Nashville, TN)
Biographical sketch: *Preachers of Today* (Batsell Barrett Baxter & M. Norval Young, eds.). Nashville, TN: The Christian Press, 1952, p. 58.
_ (Baptist Church); ?Hartsville, TN; 1918

W. L. Odum (Missionary Baptist Church); Johnson City, TN; February 24-25, 1944

_ Busbee [Oneness Pentecostal Church]
Birth: _ (_, _)
Death: _ (_, _)
Otis L. Winborn (Church of Christ); 1950; godhead, miracles, healing, baptism, instrumental music in worship
Eugene A. Pitts (Church of Christ); 1952; miracles, instrumental music in worship, godhead, tongues

Daryl Gene Busby [Church of Christ]
Birth: December 2, 1931 (Forrest City, AR)
Death: _ (_, _)
Biographical sketch: *Preachers of Today, Volume Three* (Batsell Barrett Baxter & M. Norval Young, eds.). Nashville, TN: The Gospel Advocate Company, 1964, pp. 58-59.
Jim Fagerskog (?Christian Church); Canton, IL; 1957; instrumental music in worship

_ Busby [?]
Birth: _ (_, _)
Death: _ (_, _)
Gus Nichols (Church of Christ)

_ Bush [Baptist Church]
Birth: _ (_, _)
Death: _ (_, _)
Bert Hamm (Church of Christ); Nelson Chapel, OK; 1925

Warren Buss [Church of Jesus Christ of Latter Day Saints]
Birth: _ (_, _)
Death: _ (_, _)
Wendell Wiser (Church of Christ); Williamsport, PA; 1960; Book of Mormon, establishment of church

Leonard Clayton Bussard [Church of Christ]
Birth: May 24, 1916 (Clever, MO)
Death: _ (_, _)
Biographical sketch: *Preachers of Today, Volume Two* (Batsell Barrett Baxter & M. Norval Young, eds.). Nashville, TN: The Gospel Advocate Company, 1959, p. 62.
Biographical sketch: *Preachers of Today, Volume Three* (Batsell Barrett Baxter & M. Norval Young, eds.). Nashville, TN: The Gospel Advocate Company, 1964, p. 59.
_ (Church of Jesus Christ of Latter Day Saints); before 1959
_ (Seventh-day Adventist Church); before 1959

_ Bussjaeger [Evolutionist]
   Birth: 19_ (_, _)
   Death: _ (_, _)
   Duane T. Gish (Creationist) & Harold Slusher (Creationist); radio debate; April 14, 1977; w/ _ Potts (Evolutionist)

B. Butchers [Methodist Church]
   Birth: 18_ (_, _)
   Death: _ (_, _)
   J. J. Haley (Church of Christ); Melbourne, Australia; April 24-28, 1882; subjects, purpose, and action of baptism. Book publication: *Are Infants Scriptural Subjects For Christian Baptism? Is Baptism for the Remission of Sins? Is Baptism by Pouring, Sprinkling or Immersion? A Debate.* Joplin, MO: College Press, ?1981.

Elmer Butler [Church of Christ]
   Birth: _ (_, _)
   Death: _ (_, _)
   Eddie K. Garrett (Primitive Baptist Church); Ava, MO; July 1958; general church

Frank Butler [Church of Christ]
   Birth: 19_ (_, _)
   Death: _ (_, _)
   Charles Box (Church of Christ); 1975. Proposition: "The Scriptures teach that in the work of benevolence, the church may, from its treasury relieve both saints and non-Christians." (Box affirmed, Butler denied). Book publication: *The Butler-Box Debate.* 1975.

James A. Butler [?Christian Church]
   Birth: _ (_, _)
   Death: _ (_, _)
   "The Trials of James A. Butler in Alabama" by Earl Kimbrough. *Faith and Facts Quarterly, 11*(3) (July 1983), pp. 192-206.
   W. P. Harrison (Methodist Church); Smithville, _; 6 days

J. W. Butler [Church of Christ]
   Birth: 18_ (_, _)
   Death: _ (_, _)
   _ Smith (Methodist Episcopal Church); Abingdon, IL; 1868
   Lemuel Potter (Primitive Baptist Church); Graves County, KY; 1877; eternal salvation

Michael R. Butler [?]
   Birth: 19_ (_, _)
   Death: _ (_, _)
   Michael Martin (Atheist)

Perry Eugene Butler [Church of Christ]

Birth: March 13, 1908 (Savannah, GA)
Death: _ (_, _)
Biographical sketch: *Preachers of Today* (Batsell Barrett Baxter & M. Norval Young, eds.). Nashville, TN: The Christian Press, 1952, p. 59.
Biographical sketch: *Preachers of Today, Volume Three* (Batsell Barrett Baxter & M. Norval Young, eds.). Nashville, TN: The Gospel Advocate Company, 1964, p. 59.
_ (Russellite); 1943; kingdom
_ (Holiness Church); 1948; healing, godhead
_ (Adventist Church); 1949; Sabbath

Thomas Gerald Butler [Church of Christ]

Birth: July 8, 1903 (Cairo, GA)
Death: July 30, 1996 (Lakeland, FL)
Biographical sketch: *Preachers of Today* (Batsell Barrett Baxter & M. Norval Young, eds.). Nashville, TN: The Christian Press, 1952, p. 60.
Biographical sketch: *Preachers of Today, Volume Three* (Batsell Barrett Baxter & M. Norval Young, eds.). Nashville, TN: The Gospel Advocate Company, 1964, p. 60.
Biographical sketch: *Preachers of Today, Volume Four* (Batsell Barrett Baxter & M. Norval Young, eds.). Nashville, TN: The Gospel Advocate Company, 1970, p. 43.
Obituary: https://www.findagrave.com/memorial/24508175/thomas-gerald-butler
Five debates by 1964
W. F. Connell (Missionary Baptist Church); Auburndale, FL; c October 1948; debate stopped after first night
Vernon L. Barr (Missionary Baptist Church); Lakeland, FL; May 30 - June 2, 1949; apostasy, baptism
_ Smith (?); 1949; church
Vernon L. Barr (Missionary Baptist Church); 1950; church

W. J. Butler [Church of Christ]
Birth: 18_ (_, _)
Death: 19_ (_, _)
R. J. Smothers (Socialist); Pfafftown, NC; August 23-26, 1915; Proposition 1: "Socialism, scientific and philosophic, as advocated by its founders, leading exponents, and propaganda literature, is detrimental to the Christian religion and marriage and is, therefore, subversive of morals and good order in society." (Butler affirmed, Smothers denied). Proposition 2: "Socialism is the best remedy for the evils of society." (Smothers affirmed, Butler denied).
D. L. Watson (?); Avant (near Georgiana), AL; October 31-November 3, 1915. Proposition 1: "Baptism in water, in the name of the Father, Son and Holy

Spirit, is in force now; also that the Lord's Supper as instituted by Jesus Christ and spoken of in I Corinthians 11 is to be kept at the present time." (Butler affirmed, Watson denied). Proposition 2: "Holy Spirit baptism is the only baptism required throughout the Christian dispensation, and it is the baptism mentioned in Ephesians 4:5." (Watson affirmed, Butler denied).

William Lucius Butler [Church of Christ]
Birth: 1848 (_, _)
Death: 1910 (_, _)
J. B. Hardy (Primitive Baptist Church); Tilden, Webster Co., KY; July 15-19, 1903; unconditional predestination, baptism for remission of sins, operation of the Spirit, apostasy

_ Butler [?]
Birth: _ (_, _)
Death: _ (_, _)
_ Borah (?). Book publication: *Borah-Butler Debate*.

Kyle Butt [Church of Christ]
Birth: 19_ (_, _)
Death: _ (_, _)
Dan Barker (Atheist); Columbia, SC; February 12, 2009; existence of God; 550. Book publication:
Blair Scott (Atheist); Florence, AL; September 29, 2011. Proposition: "God does not exist." (Scott affirmed, Butt denied).
Bart Ehrman (Agnostic); Florence, AL; April 4, 2014. Proposition: "The pain and suffering in the world indicate that the Christian God does not exist." (Ehrman affirmed, Butt denied).

Dean Paul Butterfield [Church of Christ]
Birth: January 2, 1905 (Buffalo, MO)
Death: November 24, 1970 (Golden City, MO)
Biographical sketch: *Preachers of Today, Volume Two* (Batsell Barrett Baxter & M. Norval Young, eds.). Nashville, TN: The Gospel Advocate Company, 1959, p. 63.
Biographical sketch: *Preachers of Today, Volume Three* (Batsell Barrett Baxter & M. Norval Young, eds.). Nashville, TN: The Gospel Advocate Company, 1964, p. 60.
Biographical sketch: *In Memoriam* by Gussie Lambert. Shreveport, LA: Gussie Lambert, 1988, pp. 43-45.
1 debate by 1964

Todd Buttermore [Church of Christ]
Birth: 19_ (_, _)
Death: _ (_, _)
Roger Jackson (Church of Christ); ?written; 1985. Proposition 1; "The

Scriptures teach that a mate who has been put away for fornication may not, with God's approval, remarry another person." (Jackson affirmed, Buttermore denied). Proposition 2: "The Scriptures teach that a mate who has been put away for fornication may, with God's approval, remarry another person." (Buttermore affirmed, Jackson denied). Book publication: *Jackson-Buttermore Debate*. 1986.

Mark C. Buzbee [Church of Christ]
Birth: November 6, 1962 (Pensacola, FL)
Death: _ (_, _)
Billy Duncan (Church of Christ); Huntsville, AL; October 8, 1990. Proposition: "The scriptures teach that it is a sin for a person to divorce his/her spouse for any reason other than fornication, even if he/she does not remarry." (Buzbee affirmed, Duncan denied).

R. A. Bynum [?]
Birth: _ (_, _)
Death: _ (_, _)
J. L. Hines (Church of Christ); written (?); c 1946

Wendell Lee Byrd [Church of Christ]
Birth: _ (_, _)
Death: _ (_, _)
Roy E. Davis (Baptist Church or Pentecostal Church); before 1951

_ Byrd [?]
Birth: _ (_, _)
Death: _ (_, _)
_ Jenkins (?)

THRASHER PUBLICATIONS
1705 Sandra Street S.W.
Decatur, AL 35601-5457
Email: thomas.thrasher@att.net

Bogard—McPherson Debate on miraculous healing
Ben M. Bogard (Baptist) and Aimee Semple McPherson (Foursquare)

Calhoun—Kurfees Discussion on instrumental music in the worship
H. L. Calhoun (Christian) and M. C. Kurfees (Christian)

Dating the Book of Revelation: Arguments for the Late Date.
Thomas N. Thrasher (Christian)

Donahue-Thrasher Exchange on eternal life as a present possession
Patrick T. Donahue (Christian) and Thomas N. Thrasher (Christian)

Falls—Franklin Debate on Holy Spirit Baptism & Gifts of the Spirit
Drew E. Falls (Christian) and Ben J. Franklin (Charismatic)

Falls—Speakman Debate on Miracles
Drew E. Falls (Christian) and Lummie Speakman (Pentecostal)

Falls—Storment Debate on the coverings of 1 Corinthians 11
Drew E. Falls (Christian) and Keith Storment (Christian)

Falls—Welch Debate on the coverings of 1 Corinthians 11
Drew E. Falls (Christian) and D. L. Welch (Pentecostal)

Garrett-Thrasher Debate on the Great Commission
Eddie K. Garrett (Primitive Baptist) and Thomas N. Thrasher (Christian)

Madrigal—Mayo Debate on the necessity of water baptism
Dan Mayo (Baptist) and John R. Madrigal (Christian)

McCay—Porter Debate on the communion cup
G. Earl McCay (Christian) and Rue Porter (Christian)

Must We Keep the Sabbath Today?
Carrol R. Sutton (Christian)

O'Neal—Hicks Debate on church-sponsored recreational activities
Thomas G. O'Neal (Christian) and Olan Hicks (Christian)

Porter—Dugger Debate on the Sabbath and the Lord's Day
W. Curtis Porter (Christian) and A. N. Dugger (Church of God–7th Day)

Rejecting Naturalistic Theories of Origins: Scientific and Scriptural Arguments. Thomas N. Thrasher (Christian)

Scambler—Langley Debate on the truth of Christianity
  T. H. Scambler (Christian) and J. S. Langley (Rationalist)
Sutton—Woods Debate on Congregational Benevolence
  Carrol Ray Sutton (Christian) and Guy N. Woods (Christian)
Tant—Frost Debate on instrumental music and societies
  J. D. Tant (Christian) and W. G. Frost (Christian)
Tant—Harding Debate on rebaptism
  J. D. Tant (Christian) and James A. Harding (Christian)
Tant—Smith Debate on Alexander Campbell's baptism
  J. D. Tant (Christian) and C. A. Smith (Baptist)
The Encyclopedia of Religious Debates, Volume 1 (A-B)
  Thomas N. Thrasher (Christian)
The Encyclopedia of Religious Debates, Volume 2 (C-G)
  Thomas N. Thrasher (Christian)
The Encyclopedia of Religious Debates, Volume 3 (H-L)
  Thomas N. Thrasher (Christian)
The Encyclopedia of Religious Debates, Volume 4 (M-Q)
  Thomas N. Thrasher (Christian)
The Encyclopedia of Religious Debates, Volume 5 (R-V)
  Thomas N. Thrasher (Christian)
The Encyclopedia of Religious Debates, Volume 6 (W-Z)
  Thomas N. Thrasher (Christian)
Thrasher—Barr Debate on the identity of the New Testament church
  Vernon L. Barr (Baptist) and Thomas N. Thrasher (Christian)
Thrasher—Coleman Debate on the Lord's Supper
  Pat S. Coleman (Pentecostal) and Thomas N. Thrasher (Christian)
Thrasher—Davis Debate: Will Everyone Be Eternally Saved?
  Myles Davis (Universalist) and Thomas N. Thrasher (Christian)
Thrasher—Forsythe Debate on the church of Christ
  Richard W. Forsythe (Pentecostal) and Thomas N. Thrasher (Christian)
Thrasher—Garrett Debate on unconditional salvation and apostasy
  Eddie K. Garrett (Primitive Baptist) and Thomas N. Thrasher (Christian)
Thrasher—Green Debate on the Christian and civil government
  Ken Green (Christian) and Thomas N. Thrasher (Christian)
Thrasher—Martignoni Debate: Was Peter the First Pope?
  John Martignoni (Roman Catholic) and Thomas N. Thrasher (Christian)
Thrasher—Maxey Debate on eternal punishment
  Al Maxey (Christian) and Thomas N. Thrasher (Christian)

Thrasher—Mayo Debate on the impossibility of apostasy
  Dan Mayo (Baptist) and Thomas N. Thrasher (Christian)
Thrasher—Miller Debate on Bible classes and women teachers
  E. H. Miller (Christian) and Thomas N. Thrasher (Christian)
Thrasher—Owens Debate on everlasting punishment for the wicked
  Lester Owens (Seventh Day Adventist) and Thomas N. Thrasher (Christian)
Thrasher—Waters Debate on divorce and remarriage
  Robert Waters (Christian) and Thomas N. Thrasher (Christian)
Thrasher—Welch Debate on the formula of words used in baptism
  D. L. Welch (Pentecostal) and Thomas N. Thrasher (Christian)
Thrasher—White Debate on Creation versus Evolution
  David L. White (Evolutionist) and Thomas N. Thrasher (Creationist)
Warnock—Williams Discussion on weddings and funerals in the meetinghouse
  Weldon E. Warnock (Christian) and Ralph D. Williams (Christian)

CPSIA information can be obtained
at www.ICGtesting.com
Printed in the USA
LVHW011048060621
689470LV00013B/578